Subject Knowledge

Falmer Press Teachers' Library

Series Editor: Professor Ivor F Goodson, Warner Graduate School, University of Rochester, USA and Applied Research in Education, University of East Anglia, Norwich, UK

Subject Knowledge:
Readings for the Study of School Subjects

Ivor F. Goodson
with Christopher J. Anstead
and J. Marshall Mangan

 The Falmer Press

(A member of the Taylor & Francis Group)
London • Washington, D.C.

UK   Falmer Press, 1 Gunpowder Square, London, EC4A 3DE
USA   Falmer Press, Taylor & Francis Inc., 1900 Frost Road, Suite 101,
       Bristol, PA 19007

First published in 1998

**A catalogue record for this book is available from the British
Library**

**Library of Congress Cataloging-in-Publication Data are available on
request**

ISBN 0 7507 0726 7 cased
ISBN 0 7507 0727 5 paper

Jacket design by Caroline Archer

Typeset in 10/12pt Times by

Graphicraft Typesetters Ltd., Hong Kong.

*Printed in Great Britain by Biddles Ltd., Guildford and King's Lynn on
paper which has a specified pH value on final paper manufacture of not
less than 7.5 and is therefore 'acid free'.*

Contents

Preface

Subject Knowledge is a collection of readings that acts as a companion volume to the guidebook *Studying School Subjects*. In that book we have provided an introduction to the wide range of writers and sources dealing with school subjects.

This collection provides a more personal viewpoint. I have been inquiring into and writing about school subjects as social constructions for over two decades. Hopefully, then, this collection manages to cover many of the genres available for *Studying School Subjects*.

In general, subject knowledge most resembles an uneasy compromise as a result of the varied motives and intentions which underpin its definition. On the one hand, the pedagogic needs of pupils play a hand in its definition; but so also do the demands of external 'constituencies' such as corporate interests and the universities; subject knowledge also has to accommodate the specific material interests of professional groups as they pursue status, esteem and power. Subject knowledge then, is located at the intersection of professional and pedagogic needs and the general patterning and prioritizing of political and economic life.

Subject knowledge sits at the centre of the activities of schooling. Hence any government or reform movement seriously interested in transforming patterns of access, equity and performance in school would be astonishingly short-sighted if they failed to re-examine subject knowledge in the general quest for improvement.

Centre for Applied Research in Education
University of East Anglia

June 1997

Acknowledgments

'Becoming a school subject' appeared in the *British Journal of Sociology of Education*, summer 1981.

'On explaining curriculum change' appeared in *The Curriculum Journal*, **4**, 3, 1993, pp. 403–20.

'Subject status and curriculum change' appeared in *Paedagogica Historica*, **XXIX**, 2, 1993, pp. 459–81.

'Subject cultures and the introduction of classroom computers' appeared in the *British Educational Research Journal*, **21**, 5, 1995.

'Computer studies as symbolic and ideological action' appeared in *The Curriculum Journal*, **3**, 3, 1993, pp. 261–76.

'On curriculum form' appeared in *Sociology of Education*, **65**, 1, January 1992, pp. 66–75.

'Nations at risk' and 'National curriculum' appeared in the *Handbook of the American Politics of Education Association*, 1991, pp. 219–32 and the *Journal of Education Policy*.

With C. Anstead, 'Structure and mediation: Glimpses of everyday life at the London Technical and Commercial High School, 1920–40', appeared in the *American Journal of Education*, **102**, 1, 1993, pp. 55–79. See Chapter 7.

1 Introduction: Studying Subject Knowledge

My interest in studying subject knowledge first surfaced in the early 1970s. In Britain at this time there was a wave of change in secondary schooling from a previously selective 'tripartite' system towards a fully comprehensive system where all types and abilities of children were grouped under the roof of one school. This transformation in the organization of secondary schooling led to an interesting series of curriculum debates both within schools and outside schools about the form that the comprehensive school curriculum should take. In addition to comprehensive reorganization, the regime of school examinations was fairly liberal at the time and a good deal of work was done to define 'mode 3' examinations. These examinations were set up and partially conducted by the teachers themselves in association with examination boards (the Associated Examining Board was a pioneer in developing this mode).

My own teaching began in a comprehensive school in 1970. Significantly, I had trained under Basil Bernstein, Michael Young and Brian Davis at the Institute of Education in 1969/70 and hence had already begun to think around issues of knowledge and control. When the opportunity to develop new school curriculum courses, which aimed at the comprehensive clientele, arose I became involved. A series of new mode 3 examinations were developed in new subject areas such as environmental studies, urban studies and community studies. These new subject areas seemed to offer the chance of better patterns of motivation and involvement for the children of working people than had been on offer from the more 'traditional subjects'. Certainly the levels of interest and engagement that these syllabuses facilitated seemed to imply that here were new approaches to learning which may well improve on or at the very least complement the traditional subjects of the secondary school curriculum.

In becoming so systematically involved in the production of courses on environmental studies and urban studies, I began to reflect on the genesis and genealogy of school subjects generally. Quite by chance, an advertisement in the *Times Educational Supplement* alerted me to the possibility of studying the question 'whatever happened to environmental studies?' There was a research project funded by the Leverhulme Foundation which had begun at the University of Sussex in 1974 and I was offered the chance to work as a research fellow on the project for two years beginning in 1975. Alongside the project work, I began a PhD which looked at the battle over environmental studies and ruminated about 'subject traditions implanted in school budgets and resources, nurtured by advisors over several decades, located in special school buildings and rooms, living in its teachers. This subject tradition would seem to act as a kind of curriculum investment: an investment offering the chances of continuity, evolution and of holding a gap in which innovations might be conceived, defined and grow.' At the time, I produced a position paper which stands as a reasonable statement of the research project I was tentatively trying to define at the time, so it is carried here in its original form. The paper was written in 1976 at the beginning of my doctoral studies.

Relevant Traditions

School knowledge has long been a subject of study for historians; a significant body of research has been completed, notably by specialist scholars in the field of 'history of education'. Much of the work concentrates on the educational aspects of *particular* historical periods, a focus that is probable where the historical tradition pursues understanding of 'the uniqueness of each individual event' (Burston, 1996, p. 31). However, this rigid periodization of educational history poses severe problems since links with contemporary education often remain undeveloped, or a kind of continuity thesis is assumed to operate.

Geoffrey Barraclough (1967) has drawn up a similar indictment of modern European history, where

> Historians of the recent past have assumed for the most part that, if they explained the factors leading to the disintegration of the old world, they were automatically providing an explanation of how the new world emerged. (p. 9)

Barraclough explains this partly by

> the tendency of historical writing today to emphasize the element of continuity in history. For most historians contemporary history does not constitute a separate period with distinctive characteristics of its own; they regard it rather as the most recent phase of a continuous process. (*ibid*, p. 11)

Whilst historians of education have often failed to link insights into the past with our knowledge of contemporary education, many sociological studies have inverted this problem. Blumer (1969) has drawn attention to the problem when studying large-scale organizations and argues a need 'to recognize that joint action is temporarily linked to previous joint action'. He warns that 'one shuts a major door to understanding any form or instance of joint action if one ignores this connection'. This 'historical linkage' is important because

> The designations and interpretations through which people form and maintain their organised relations are always in degree of carry-over from their past. To ignore this carry-over sets a genuine risk for the scholar. (p. 60)

Paradoxically, since Blumer wrote this in 1969 some developments in sociology have tended to move in the opposite direction, thereby involving the 'genuine risks' of which he warns. Interactionist studies have focused on the perspectives and definitions emerging through interaction and have stressed situation rather than background and history. In this work the backcloth to action is often presented as a somewhat monolithic 'structural' or 'cultural' legacy which constrains, in rather disconnected manner, the actors' potentialities. But in overreacting to more deterministic models, interactionists may be in danger of failing to present any clear connection with historical process. Of course, 'any process of interaction is never fully determined by social, structural or cultural forces' and 'social structures and cultures emerge out of and are sustained and changed by social interaction' (Hammersley and Woods, 1976, p. 3). But the danger of such stress on personal potential — 'actors always possess some degree of autonomy' (*ibid*) — is that historical linkages will remain undeveloped or, at any rate, underdeveloped.

In studying school knowledge the dangers of such an approach have been clearly evidenced in the past decade. Classroom practice, a crucial and often neglected area, can, by interactionist overreaction, be presented as the essential context wherein patterns of knowledge transmission are defined. One unfortunate side-effect of this focus is that when attempts to reform classroom practice fail, the teacher, who is the immediate and visible agency of that failure, may be presented as exclusively culpable. In seeking to explain attempts at reform in school knowledge, we need a strategy that is curative of the classroom myopia exhibited in such accounts.

Another major development in sociological studies, the sociology of knowledge, has laid claim to one such curative strategy. Knowledge is seen as evolving in response to the promotional and presentational agency of particular subject groups who act to defend and expand their 'interests'. Similarly, knowledge patterns are viewed as reflecting the status hierarchies of each society through the activities of the dominant groups. Very often, however, in spite of appeals from M.F.D. Young (1977) such work has not presented the evolutionary, historical process at work (pp. 250–62). Studies have developed horizontally, working out from theories of social structure and social order to evidence of their application. Such an approach inevitably obscures, rather than clarifies, those historical situations in which 'gaps, discrepancies and ambiguities are created within which individuals can manoeuvre' (Walker and Goodson, 1977, p. 223). As Herbert Butterfield (1951) once wrote, theories of causality are 'by no means sufficient in themselves to explain the next stage of the story, the next turn of events' (p. 94), and Barraclough (1967) has noted that 'at every great turning point of the past we are confronted by the fortuitous and the unforeseen' (p. 11).

The historical elements of recent interactionism and the sociology of knowledge may partly be a reflection of the historical period in which these 'new directions' have developed. A review of the documents and statements of the curriculum reform movement inaugurated in the 1960s reveals a widespread belief that there could be a more or less complete break with past traditions. At a time when traditions were thought to be on the point of being overthrown it was perhaps unsurprising that so many studies paid scant attention to the evolution and establishment of those traditions. In the event, radical change did not occur. We left in the position of needing to reexamine the emergence and survival of that which is seen as 'traditional'.

Towards a History of School Knowledge

Historical study seeks to understand how thought and action has evolved in past social circumstances. Following this evolution through time to the present day affords insights into how those circumstances we experience as contemporary 'reality' have been negotiated, constructed and reconstructed over time. Short-span interactive study on 'static' theoretical work, whilst of inestimable value in other ways, approaches the understanding of cultural and structural factors in a manner which is methodologically (and often in aspiration) distinct. The historical studies in this collection have a common intention: in following the evolution of thought and action through historical time, they seek to understand that which constitutes the contemporary reality we experience as 'school knowledge'.

The human process by which men make their own history does not, as Marx noted, take place in circumstances of their own choosing. However since both men and circumstances do vary over time, so too do the potentialities for negotiating reality. The human process takes place at different levels and, though in a sense falsely dichotomous, there are two basic levels that are amenable to historical study:

(i)   The individual life-history. The process of negotiation and change is continuous throughout a person's life and occurs 'both in episodic encounters and in longer-lasting socialisation processes over the life history'. (Blumer, 1976, p. 3)

(ii) The group or collective level: professions, subjects or disciplines, for instance, evolve as social movements over time.

Bucher and Strauss (1961) have developed the notion of professions:

> as loose amalgamations of segments pursuing different objectives in different manners and more or less delicately held together under a common name at a particular period of history. (pp. 325–34)

Layton (1972) has discerned three stages that school subjects go through: firstly, justify their presence on grounds of pupil relevance, taught by non-specialists who bring 'the missionary enthusiasm of pioneers to their task' to the final stage where 'the selection of subject matter is determined in large measure by the judgment and practices of the specialist scholars who lead enquiries in the field'. This last stage, where the teachers of the subject 'constitute a profession with established rules and values' (p. 11) leads to the situation Norwood described as long ago as 1943:

> Subjects have tended to become preserves belonging to specialist teachers; barriers have been erected between them, and teachers have felt unqualified or not free to trespass upon the dominions of other teachers. (Board of Education, 1943)

Similarly, Kuhn (1970) has developed an evolutionary, indeed revolutionary, model of 'paradigm' change in scientific disciplines. In a sense his work complements that of Ben-David and Collins (1966) who have scrutinized the social factors in the foundation of psychology. They note that whilst 'the ideas necessary for the creation of a new discipline are usually available over a relatively long period of time' and in 'several places', growth occurs only when people become interested in the idea 'not only as an intellectual content but also as a potential means of establishing a new intellectual identity and particularly a new occupational role' (pp. 451–66).

So far studies of the history of contemporary knowledge, let alone school knowledge, have tended to resemble the pre-paradigmatic stages of disciplines. The studies have been conducted in several places at different times and have often been undertaken by non-specialists who have brought the 'enthusiasm of pioneers' to their work. (This collection of papers may mark the transition to a new stage for an increasing number of educational researchers are undertaking historical work.) Macdonald and Walker (1976) have recently argued that in school curricula 'by extending our sense of history we can develop a different way of viewing the species' (p. 86). Mary Waring's work on Nuffield science was developed from a similar perspective:

> If we are to understand events, whether of thought or of action, knowledge of the background is essential. Knowledge of events is merely the raw material of history: to be an intelligible reconstruction of the past, events must be related to other events, and to the assumptions and practices of the milieu. Hence they must be made the subject of inquiry, their origins as products of particular social and historical circumstance, the manner in which individuals and groups have acted must be identified, and explanations for their actions sought. (Waring, 1975, p. 12)

The justifications for historical studies of the evolution of school knowledge can be found at the level of thought and action.

Firstly, such work will improve *our* knowledge of school knowledge. Historical studies can elucidate the changing human process behind the definition and promotion of school subjects. Employing this strategy shifts the emphasis from questions of the intrinsic and philosophic value of subjects, from their existence as objective realities, to the motives and activities immanent and inherent in their construction and maintenance. Further, historical scrutiny offers insights into the existence of patterns and recurring constraints: why, for instance, certain 'traditions' in school knowledge survive and others disappear. Whilst historical studies do not as their major intention seek to prove particular theories, nonetheless they may use and contribute to theory.

Secondly, at the level of school practice historical studies can aid analysis. Such studies might even aid in explaining the emergence and maintenance of

5

anti-research traditions among teachers. Partly, teachers' antipathy derives from the point Shipman (1974) makes about the curriculum project he was involved with:

> The end-product of the project was determined in the field, in contact with the school, not on the drawing board . . . in the end it was what worked that survived. (p. 2)

But the autonomy of the teacher, his capacity for active reinterpretation should not be overestimated for major constraints do exist. Hence, Shipman's judgment in a sense missed the point: only what is prepared on the drawing board goes into the school and therefore *has a chance* to be interpreted and to survive. Exploring the editing process which takes place on the drawing board of history with respect to school knowledge is more than static historicism. By understanding this process we can define a range of constraints that are immanent in the teachers' work. Historical studies should be a prerequisite to attempts to change classroom practice. Linking the teacher to the history of her/his working milieu could further the potential for actively creating new history.

Studying Subject Knowledge

A good deal of this research programme for developing a social history of school knowledge owed a debt to the work of critical theorists and sociologists of knowledge from the 1960s onwards.

At that time, a new impetus to scholarship on school subjects had come from sociologists and specifically from sociologists of knowledge. Writing in 1968, Frank Musgrove exhorted educational researchers to 'examine subjects both within the school and the nation at large as social systems sustained by communication networks, material endowments, and ideologies' (p. 101). In the communication networks, Esland (1971) later argued that research should focus in part, on the subject perspective of the teacher.

> The knowledge which a teacher thinks 'fills up' his subject is held in common with members of a supporting community who collectively approach its paradigms and utility criteria, as they are legitimated in training courses and 'official' statements. It would seem that teachers, because of the dispersed nature of their epistemic communities, experience the conceptual precariousness which comes from the lack of significant others who can confirm plausibility. They are, therefore, heavily dependent on journals, and, to a lesser extent, conferences, for their reality confirmation. (p. 79)

Esland and Dale (1973), later developed this focus on teachers within subject communities:

> Teachers, as spokesmen for subject communities are involved in an elaborate organization of knowledge. The community has a history, and, through it, a body

of respected knowledge. It has rules for recognizing 'unwelcome' or 'spurious' matter, and ways of avoiding cognitive contamination. It will have a philosophy and a set of authorities, all of which give strong legitimation to the activities which are acceptable to the community. Some members are accredited with the power to make 'official statements' — for instance, editors of journals, presidents, chief examiners and inspectors. These are important as 'significant others' who provide models to new or wavering members of appropriate belief and conduct. (pp. 70–1)

In particular Esland (1971) was concerned that scholarships were developed which illuminated the role of professional groups in the social construction of school subjects. These groups can be seen as mediators of the 'social forces' to which Foster Watson had alluded:

> The subject associations of the teaching profession may be theoretically represented as segments and social movements involved in the negotiation of new alliances and rationales, as collectively held reality constructions became transformed. Thus, applied to the professional identities of teachers within a school, it would be possible to reveal the conceptual regularities and changes which are generated through membership of particular subject communities, as they were manifested in textbooks, syllabi, journals, conference reports, etc. (p. 107)

In the light of the importance of historical perspectives Esland added that 'subjects can be shown to have "careers" which are dependent on the social-structural and social-psychological correlates of membership of epistemic communities' (*ibid*).

The relationship between what counts as education and issues of power and control had been elucidated in 1961 by Raymond Williams in *The Long Revolution*:

> It is not only that the way in which education is organized can be seen to express consciously and unconsciously, the wider organization of a culture and a society so that what has been thought of as a single distribution is in fact an actual shaping to particular social ends. It is also that the content of education which is subject to great historical agnation, again expresses, again both consciously and unconsciously, certain basic elements in the culture. What is thought of as 'an education' being in fact a particular set of emphases and omissions. (p. 146)

One might add to Williams notion of 'the content of education'. It has been noted elsewhere that 'the battle over the *content* of the curriculum while often more visible, is in many senses less important than the control over the underlying *forms*' (See Chapter 10).

Michael F.D. Young (1971) sought to follow up the relationship between school knowledge and social control and to do so in a manner which focused on content and form. He argued, following Bernstein, that:

> Those in positions of power will attempt to define what is to be taken as knowledge, how accessible to different groups any knowledge is, and what are the accepted relationships between different knowledge areas, and between those who have access to them and make them available. (p. 52)

His concern with the form of high status school subjects focused on the 'organizing principles' which he discerned as underlying the academic curriculum:

> These are literacy, or an emphasis on written as opposed to oral presentation, individualism (or avoidance of group work or cooperativeness) which focused on how academic work is assessed and is a characteristic of both the 'process' of learning and the way the 'product' is presented; abstractness of the knowledge and its structuring and compartmentalizing independently of the knowledge of the learner; finally and linked to the former is what I have called the unrelatedness of academic curricula, which refers to the extent to which they are 'at odds' with daily life and experience. (*ibid*, p. 38)

This emphasis on the form of school knowledge should not exclude concerns like that of Williams with the social construction of particular contents. The crucial point to grasp is that it is the interrelated force of form and content which should be at the centre of our study of school subjects. The study of subject, form and content should moreover be placed in an historical perspective.

In fact, Young later came to acknowledge the somewhat static determinism of his earlier writing in *Knowledge and Control* and to argue that historical work should be an essential ingredient of the study of school knowledge. He wrote of the need to understand the 'historical emergence and persistence of particular conventions (school subjects for example)'. By failing to situate the problems of contemporary education historically one is again limited from understanding issues of politics and control. He concluded that: 'one crucial way of reformulating and transcending the limits within which we work is to see ... how such limits are not given or fixed but produced through the conflicting actions and interests of men in history' (Young, 1977b, pp. 248–9).

New Directions for Studying School Subjects

The important work by sociologists of knowledge in defining research programmes for studies of school knowledge led on to an acknowledgment by some of them that historical study might complement and extend their project. In studying school subjects the enquiry has arrived at a new stage. Initial work in the early twentieth century has provided some important precursors to our work; sociologists of knowledge like Bernstein and Young, subsequently have played a vital role in rescuing and reasserting the validity of this intellectual project; in the process however, some of the necessary focus on historical and empirical circumstances has been lost. The task now being undertaken is to reexamine the role of sociological and historical methods in the study of curriculum and to rearticulate a mode of study for extending an understanding of the social history of the school curriculum and, in this work, particularly school subjects.

Beginning in 1985, *Studies in Curriculum History*, a series of books, was launched with this view in mind. In the first volume, *Social Histories of the Secondary Curriculum* (Goodson, 1985), work is collected together on a wide range of subjects: classics, science, domestic subjects, religious education, social studies and modern languages. These studies reflect a growing interest in the history of curriculum and, besides elucidating the symbolic drift of school knowledge towards the academic tradition, raise central questions about explanations of school subjects whether they be sociological of philosophical. Other work in the series has looked in detail at particular subjects, in McCulloch, Layton and Jenkins (1985) examined the politics of school science and technology curriculum in England and Wales since the Second World War. Subsequent work by Woolnough (1988) has looked at the history of physics teaching in schools in the period 1960 to 1985. Another area of emerging work is the history of school mathematics: Cooper's book *Renegotiating Secondary School Mathematics* (Cooper, 1985) looked at the fate of a number of traditions within mathematics and articulates a model for the redefinition of school subject knowledge; Moon (1986) meanwhile examines the relationship between maths in England and the United States and includes some very interesting work on the dissemination of textbooks.

Emerging work in the United States has also begun to focus on the evolution of the school curriculum studied in historical manner. Kliebard's (1986) writing on the curriculum in the United States from 1893 to 1958 discerned a number of the dominant traditions within the school curriculum, and as noted, comes to the intriguing conclusion that by the end of the period covered the traditional school subject remained 'an impregnable fortress'. His later set of essays usefully complements this theme (Kliebard, 1992). However, Kliebard's work does not go into the details of school life. In this respect Franklin (1986) provided some valuable insights in a case study of Minneapolis. Here the vital negotiation from curriculum ideas, the terrain of Kliebard's work, towards implementation as school practice is seen. In addition, a collection of papers put together by Popkewitz (1987) examines the historical aspects of a range of subjects: early education, art, reading and writing, biology, mathematics, social studies, special education, socialist curriculum, and a study of Rugg's work. Likewise, Apple's work has provided helpful studies of school texts (Apple, 1993).

In Canada, curriculum history has been launched as a field most notably by Tomkins' seminal work *A Common Countenance* (Tomkins, 1986). This work examines the patterns of curriculum stability and change in a range of school subjects in the nineteenth and twentieth centuries throughout Canada. Another volume (Goodson, 1987) which seeks to bring together some of the more important work emerging in different countries on curriculum history contains important articles on the history of school physics, on Victorian school science, on science education, on English, the Norwegian Common School, and on the development of senior school geography in West Australia.

Other work has begun to look beyond traditional school subjects to study broader topics. For example, Cunningham (1988) has examined curriculum change in the primary school in Britain since 1945. Musgrave (1988 and 1992) developed a sociohistorical case study of the Victoria University Examinations Board. Whilst R.W. Connell's ongoing work provides vital insights into the construction of the 'hegemonic academic curriculum' in Australia (Connell, 1985 and 1993; Connell et al, 1982). Here historical work begins to elucidate the change from curriculum content to examinable content which is such an important part of understanding the way that status and resources are apportioned within the school.

The study of the written curriculum of school subjects should afford a range of insights into schooling. But it is very important to stress that such inquiry must be allied to other kinds of study: in particular studies of school process, of school texts, and of the history of pedagogy. Hamilton (1989) has elegantly sought to capture some of these complexities as they intersect and interact. Schooling is composed of the interlinked matrix of these, and indeed, other vital ingredients. With regard to schooling and to curriculum in particular, the final question is 'Who gets what and what do they do with it?'

The preactive definition of school subjects is part of this story. That is not the same as asserting a direct or easily discernable relationship between the preactive definition of subjects and their interactive realization in classrooms. It is however, to assert that the written curriculum most often sets important parameters for classroom practice (not always, not at all times, not in all classrooms, but most often). The study of written curriculum of school subjects will firstly increase understanding of the influences and interests active at the preactive level. Secondly, this understanding will further the knowledge of the values and purposes represented in schooling and the manner in which preactive definition, notwithstanding individual, local and national variations, may set parameters for interactive realization and negotiation in the classroom and school.

To study school knowledge, a range of levels of analysis can be employed. This reader tries to cover some of the main areas and does so in ways that follow the main 'clusters' of my work. Hence, chapters 3 and 4 return to the early work conducted at the University of Sussex in the years 1975–1986. These two major research projects I was involved with were the Leverhulme Environmental Education Study (referred to earlier) which ran in the years 1974–1977 (chapter 3) and the Europe in the School Project which I directed in the years 1977–1982 (chapter 4). Chapter 3 reviews the evolutionary process of becoming a school subject and in doing so provides a sociohistorical path of analysis for capturing the social history of a subject. Chapter 4 looks in detail at the micropolitics of curriculum change at the departmental and school level.

In 1986 I left to work in Canada. The following three chapters grow from the Origins and Destinations Project funded by the Social Science and Humanities Research Council of Canada. This project provides an in-depth study of curriculum change in one school from 1916–1996. The full report of this project has been published in the book *Through the Schoolhouse Door* (Goodson and Anstead, 1993) but these three different levels of study are shop-windowed: — a school curriculum history focussing on an episode in curriculum change (chapter 5), another such study focussing on commercial education and exploring some aspects of the gendering of curriculum (chapter 6) and finally a study of the everyday life of schooling as seen through the prism of school subjects (chapter 7).

Alongside the Origins and Destinations Project, the Ontario Ministry funded a large million-dollar study of computers in classrooms. Here our study operated at both the level of classroom subject cultures (chapter 8) and at the level of changing rhetorics and ideologies in the arena of provincial policies (chapter 9).

The final chapters stay at the symbolic and ideological level whilst returning largely to the British context with a historical study of 'curriculum form' (chapter 10) and a review of the English National Curriculum (chapter 11).

References

APPLE, M.W. (1993) *Official Knowledge: Democratic Education in a Conservative Age*, New York: Routledge.

BARRACLOUGH, G. (1967) *An Introduction to Contemporary History*, Harmondsworth: Penguin.

BEN-DAVID, J. and COLLINS, R. (1966) 'Social factors in the origins of a new science: The case of psychology', *American Sociology Review*, **34**, 4, August.

BLUMER, H. (1969) *Symbolic Interactionism: Perspective and Method*, Englewood Cliffs, NJ: Prentice Hall.

BLUMER, H. (1976) quoted in HAMMERSLEY, M. and WOODS, P. (eds) (1976) *The Process of Schooling*, London: Routledge.

BOARD OF EDUCATION (1943) *Curriculum and Examinations in Secondary Schools* (The Norwood Report), London: HMSO.

BUCHER, R. and STRAUSS, A. (1961) 'Professions in practice', *American Journal of Sociology*, **66**, January.

BURSTON, W. (1966) *Principles of History Teaching*, London: Methuen.

BUTTERFIELD, H. (1951) *History and Human Relations*, London: Collins.

CONNELL, R.W. (1985) *Teachers Work*, London: Allen & Unwin.

CONNELL, R. (1993) *Schools and Social Justice*, Toronto: Our Schools/Our Selves Education Foundation.

CONNELL, R., ASHENDEN, D., KESSLER, S. and DOWSETT, G. (1982) *Making the Difference: Schools, Families and Social Division*, Sydney: Allen & Unwin.

COOPER, B. (1985) *Renegotiating Secondary School Mathematics*, London: Falmer Press.

CUNNINGHAM, P. (1988) *Curriculum Change in the Primary School Since 1945*, London: Falmer Press.

ESLAND, G.M. (1971) 'Teaching and learning as the organization of knowledge', in YOUNG, M.F.D. (ed.) *Knowledge and Control*, London: Collier-Macmillan.

ESLAND, G.M. and DALE, R. (eds) (1973) *School and Society* (Course E282, Unit 2), Milton Keynes: Open University.

FRANKLIN, B. (1986) *Building the American Community*, London: Falmer Press.

GOODSON, I.F. (ed.) (1985) *Social Histories of the Secondary Curriculum*, London: Falmer Press.

GOODSON, I.F. (1987) *International Perspectives in Curriculum History*, London: Croom Helm.

GOODSON, I.F. (1988) *The Making of Curriculum*, London: Falmer Press.

GOODSON, I.F. and ANSTEAD, C.J. (1993) *Through the Schoolhouse Door*, Toronto: Garamond Press.

HAMILTON, D. (1989) *Towards a Theory of Schooling*, London: Falmer Press.

HAMMERSLEY, M. and WOODS, P. (eds) (1976) *The Process of Schooling*, London: Routledge.

KLIEBARD, H. (1986) *The Struggle for the American Curriculum 1893–1958*, London: Routledge and Kegan Paul.

KLIEBARD, H. (1992) *Forging the American Curriculum: Essays in Curriculum History and Theory*, New York: Routledge.

KUHN, T.S. (1970) *The Structure of Scientific Revolutions* (2nd ed.), Chicago, IL: Chicago University Press.

LAYTON, D. (1972) 'Science in general education', *Trends in Education*, January.

McCULLOCH, G., JENKINS, E. and LAYTON, D. (1985) *Technological Revolution?*, London: Falmer Press.

MACDONALD, B. and WALKER, R. (1976) *Changing the Curriculum*, London: Open Books.

MOON, B. (1986) *The 'New Maths' Curriculum Controversy*, London: Falmer Press.

MUSGRAVE, P.W. (1988) *Whose Knowledge?*, London: Falmer Press.

MUSGRAVE, P.W. (1992) *From Humanity to Utility, Melbourne University and Public Examinations 1856–1964*, Melbourne: ACER.

MUSGROVE, F. (1968) 'The contribution of sociology to the study of the curriculum', in KERR, J.F. (ed.) *Changing the Curriculum*, London: University of London.

POPKEWITZ, T.S. (1987) *The Formation of School Subjects: The Struggle for Creating an American Institution*, London: Falmer Press.

SHIPMAN, M. (1971) 'Curriculum for inequality', in HOOPER, R. (ed.) *The Curriculum: Context, Design and Development*, Edinburgh: Oliver and Boyd.

TOMKINS, G.S. (1986) *A Common Countenance: Stability and Change in the Canadian Curriculum*, Scarborough, Ontario: Prentice Hall.

WALKER, R. and GOODSON, I.F. (1977) 'Humour in the classroom', in WOODS, P. and HAMMERSLEY, M. (eds) *School Experience*, London: Croom Helm.

WARING, M. (1975) 'Aspects of the dynamics of curriculum reform in secondary school science', unpublished PhD, University of London.

WILLIAMS, R. (1975) *The Long Revolution*, London: Penguin.

WOOLNOUGH, B.E. (1988) *Physics Teaching in Schools 1960–85: Of People and Power*, London: Falmer Press.

YOUNG, M.F.D. (ed.) (1971a) *Knowledge and Control: New Directions for the Sociology of Education*, London: Collier-Macmillan.

YOUNG, M.F.D. (ed.) (1971b) 'An approach to the study of curricula as socially organised knowledge', in YOUNG, M.F.D. (ed.) *Knowledge and Control: New Directions for the Sociology of Education*, London: Collier-Macmillan.

YOUNG, M.F.D. (1977) 'School science — Innovations or alienation', in WOODS, P. and HAMMERSLEY, M. (eds) *School Experience*, London: Croom Helm.

2   The Need for Curriculum History

The need for curriculum history arises from the view that recent modes of curriculum reform and curriculum study commonly share interlocking inadequacies. Both modes tend to share an obsessive contemporality allied with a belief that past curriculum traditions could, given conviction and resources, be transcended. One reason for the antipathetic relationship between curriculum reform strategies, curriculum studies and history (whether as a mode of study, as artefact, as tradition or as legacy) relates to the historical period of growth.

The great period of expansion in the United Kingdom both for curriculum reform initiatives and curriculum studies as a discipline ran from 1960 to around 1975 (Rubinstein and Simon, 1973, p. 105). This was a period of economic expansion and social optimism, of rapid reorganization into comprehensive schools and increasing public expenditure on schooling and universities. A period in short where previous traditions and legacies were subject to major challenge, where a common assumption was that a new world of schooling (and curriculum) was about to be constructed.

The documents and statements of the curriculum reform movement inaugurated in the 1960s reveal a messianic yet widespread belief that there could be a more or less complete break with past tradition. A belief that history in general and curriculum history in particular could somehow be *transcended*. Besides the all-pervasive term 'innovation' there was common reference to 'radical change in education', 'revolutionizing classroom practice' and 're-drawing the map of learning'. For instance writing in 1968 Professor Kerr asserted that 'at the practical and organizational levels, the new curricula promise to revolutionize English education' (Kerr, 1971, p. 150). Retrospectively there may seem something admirable, however misconceived, about such belief in contemporary possibility that history seemed of little relevance.

So at a time when traditional curriculum practice was thought to be on the point of being overthrown it was perhaps unsurprising that so many reforms paid scant attention to the evolution and establishment of traditional practice. In the event radical change did not occur. Curriculum study now requires strategies which allow us to examine the emergence and survival of the 'traditional' as well as the failure to generalize, institutionalize and sustain the 'innovative'.

The *transcendent view* of curriculum change infected many of those involved in researching schools and curriculum. The irony is supreme but for the best of reasons. Particularly 'infected' were those researchers involved in evaluation and case study work. Reflecting the participants' perceptions their transcendent bias is therefore partly explained by an historical climate of opinion where curriculum change was considered the order of the day. Hence Parlett and Hamilton (1972) in an influential paper, though claiming general application, focused on the evaluation of innovation. They wanted 'to study the innovatory project; how it operates, how it is influenced by the various school situations in which it is applied, what those directly concerned regard as its advantages and disadvantages'. The preoccupation with 'those directly concerned', with 'what it is like to be participating' were to characterize a major school of evaluators and case study workers. Indeed this posture characterized those researchers both most sympathetic and sensitive to the aspirations of the innovators. Above all they wanted to 'capture and portray the world as it appears to the people in it'. Some went even further 'in a sense for the case study worker what *seems* true is more important than what is true' (Walker, 1974).

Writing later, with a strong sense of personal disillusionment about curriculum reform, I saw the evaluator who had studied my school as merely confirming the participants' myopia:

> Focusing the evaluators' work on the charting of the subjective perceptions of participants is to deny much of its potential — particularly to those evaluators aspiring to 'strong action-implications'. The analysis of subjective perceptions is incomplete without analysis of the historical context in which they occur. To deprive the subject of such knowledge would be to condemn new evaluation to the level of social control — a bizarre fate for a model aspiring to 'democratic' intentions. (Goodson, 1977, p. 160)

Yet if many of those employing qualitative methods in evaluation and case study took a transcendent view of history they were not alone. By a peculiar convergence many contemporary interactionist and ethnographic studies were similarly ahistorical.

The experimental model of sociological investigation with its emphasis on single studies to test pre-selected hypotheses, whilst for long dominant, neglected participant perspectives and interactional processes. Paradoxically the interactionist and ethnographic models which were conceived in reaction to this model have often focused on situation and occasion with the result that biography and historical background have continued to be neglected. This is primarily because interactionist studies have built upon the perspectives and meanings that emerge in the interactive situation. The focus of inquiry then has been on the situation and the moment with a consequent disregard for historical background. Where this background is mentioned it is seldom finely detailed and linked to the process of interaction but is rather, presented as a set of general cultural or structural factors which underpin action. Hence in their valid reaction to the sociological determinists, interactionists may have severed the link between contemporary action and the historical economic and political backcloth. This danger can be best evidenced in those interactionist studies of micropolitical action (particularly in those studies which focus on 'resistance') where the actor is often invested with notions of autonomy and free agency which plainly fly in the face of the historical circumstances in which those actions are embedded.

The danger of breaking the links between interaction and historical circumstances can be well illustrated by studies of curriculum definitions and classroom practice. Through interactionist overreaction, practice in classrooms can be elevated to a pedestal where the curriculum is seen as presented and negotiated by the teacher as agent. Even where the curriculum, as in the National Curriculum, has been clearly politically designated elsewhere, interactionist and micropolitical studies hold on to the agency of the teacher.

This view conspires with the view of government regimes that say when learning fails to take place, the teacher as front-line agent must be, by definition, culpable (or incompetent). The preactive definition of the curriculum and of general historical circumstances is lost in the spectacle of classroom myopia.

In much of their work on curriculum philosophers have taken the curriculum as a given. Hence the historical environment in which knowledge is socially produced has been ignored. This ahistorical aspect of philosophy has defused its capacity to act as an antidote to the transcendence and immersed immediacy we have noted above.

Hirst (1967), for example, has talked about school subjects 'which are indisputably logically cohesive disciplines' (p. 44). In fact such a philosophical perspective is rooted in particular and rather contestable educational convictions. Most notable is the assertion that 'no matter what the ability of the child may be, the heart of all his development as a rational being, I am saying, intellectual' (Hirst, 1976). In accordance with these convictions Hirst (and also Peters) has argued that 'the central objectives of education are developments of mind' (Hirst and Peters, 1970, pp. 63–4). These objectives are best pursued by 'the definition of forms of knowledge' (later broadened to include 'fields of knowledge'). These forms and fields of knowledge then provide 'the logically cohesive disciplines' on which school subjects are based.

The philosophy of Hirst and Peters, therefore, provides an explanatory basis for the school curriculum as trying to promote the intellectual development of its pupils. In their model of school subject definition it is often implied that the intellectual discipline is created by a community of scholars, normally working in a university, and is then translated for use as a school subject. Phenix (1964) defines the intellectual discipline base in this way:

> The general test for discipline is that it should be the characteristic activity of an identifiable organised tradition of men of knowledge, that is of persons who are skilled in certain specified functions that they are able to justify by a set of intelligible standards. (p. 317)

When such a discipline has been defined, promoted and a university base has been established, it creates a cycle of virtuous self-fulfilment to argue that this is a bona fide academic form of knowledge. This academic discipline can then define and direct the 'academic' school subject. The model, by ignoring historical process entirely, celebrates this fait accompli in the painstaking creation of disciplines and associated school subjects. This model is devoid of explanatory potential because the stages in the promotion and emergence of disciplines and subjects are left unexplored, as are the reasons for the 'symbolic drift' towards academic forms. In fact, academic subjects tend to follow similar evolutionary profiles which tell us a great deal about the structuring of material interests and resources. By examining school subjects as 'professional communities' with clear 'missions' and underpinning material interests, we can begin to understand the symbolic drift of academic disciplines and school subjects towards common culminating patterns.

Of course the manner in which philosophical studies offer justification for the academic subject-based curriculum has been noted by sociologists. A major development in sociological studies, the sociology of knowledge, has sought to elucidate more fundamental patterns but such work has not presented the evolutionary, historical process at work. Studies have developed horizontally, working out from theories of social structure and social order to evidence of their application. Such an approach inevitably obscures, rather than clarifies, those historical situations in which 'gaps', discrepancies and ambiguities are created within which individuals can manoeuvre. More worrying where history has been considered it has often been 'raided', in Silver's elegant phrase, to prove a contemporary point (Silver, 1977, p. 17). I have evidenced elsewhere a 'raid' on David Layton's study *Science for the People* (Layton, 1973) and the use of his work to prove a contemporary political point about school science. In this case a disembodied historical snapshot is used in an attempt to further our understanding of certain basic assumptions about contemporary school science. I argued that, without direct parallels and with no evidence produced of continuities, it is difficult to move to *any* understanding of the basic assumptions of contemporary school science form the specific historical evidence presented from Layton's work. Clearly the danger of 'raiding' history is that such moves can span centuries of change at all levels of content and context. A more systematic *evolutionary* understanding of how the curriculum is negotiated is therefore needed (Goodson, 1983).

As we have noted historians of education have provided an important antidote to the ahistoricality of much curriculum study yet paradoxically a refined awareness of some of the problems cited above has led to an often over reactive posture to the sociological abuse of 'raiding' for contemporary or theoretical purposes.

Writing of the work of curriculum specialists with respect to historical perspective Marsden (1978) judges that they 'have often been deficient and can roughly be divided into those which are *ahistorical and unhistorical*, in so far as the categories can be isolated from one another'. He defines an ahistorical approach as:

> one which disregards the historical perspective, the writer perceiving it to be irrelevant and/or uninteresting. . . . Thus work proceeds, almost naively, in a temporal vacuum.

An unhistorical approach is characterised:

> as one inconsistent both in gross and in refined terms with the accepted canons of historical scholarship, purveying inaccurate, over-simplified and otherwise distorted impressions of the past. Attention is drawn to the past, not for its own sake but as a means of sharpening a particular contemporary axe. (pp. 81–2)

Alongside this 'misuse' of history Marsden places those curriculum studies 'in which the past is scanned for support of some broad sociopolitical interpretation or theory' (*ibid*, p. 82).

Historians have rightly reacted to the misuse of history for 'sharpening contemporary axes' or 'supporting broad sociopolitical interpretations or theories'. In my view that reaction has gone too far (understandable though it is if placed in historical context). The result is that history of education has often become rigidly 'periodized'; it has often pursued a policy of 'splendid isolation' from the messy and unresolved contemporary situation. This is to limit both its aspiration and its importance. History of education should clearly obviate any concern with 'sharpening contemporary axes'. But such a correct reaction should not be taken as disbarring concern with contemporary events. By my view history of education should set as an important criteria a concern, where possible, to elucidate the precedents, antecedents and constraints surrounding contemporary curriculum and practice. Likewise the reaction to theoretical enterprises should be conquered. Historical study has a valuable role to play in challenging, informing and sometimes generating theory. This role should not be emasculated through a fear of theoretical misuse by others.

Beyond the ambivalence to contemporary situations and theoretical enterprises much history of education shares a further characteristic which argues for a growing dialogue between historians and curriculum specialists. In many ways history of education has taken an 'external' view of curriculum focusing on political and administrative contexts and on general movements in education and schooling. Partly this is a reflection of the documents available which often relate to central regulations edicts or commissions on education and curriculum. This is a long way from curriculum as enacted, transacted, realized and received. Rudolph (1977) has warned that:

> The best way to misread or misunderstand curriculum is from a catalogue. It is such a lifeless thing. So disembodied, so unconnected, sometimes even intentionally misleading. Because the curriculum is a social artifact, the society itself is a more reliable source of curricular information.

The 'externality' of much history of education has led some scholars to argue for a major reappraisal: Franklin (1977) for instance:

> I see curriculum history as a speciality within the curriculum field, distinct from educational history. Its practitioners should be individuals whose primary training is in curriculum, not educational historians who happened to be interested in the nature of the course of study within the schools. (p. 73)

The reasons for the separation are made clear later:

> Because the concerns and foci of the two studies are different. Most important in this respect is that the educational historian's lack of training in curriculum

will lead him to either overlook or misinterpret those issues which are of most importance to the curriculum field. Above all this is because the educational historian focuses on those issues in curriculum most relevant to the general issues of education and schooling, rather than the other way round. (*ibid*, pp. 73–4)

One would not need to follow Franklin in advocating a separation of curriculum historians and historians of education to accept his diagnosis that much of the work of the latter is 'external'. Nor is the concentration of the 'external' necessarily a problem. It depends on the aspiration. If however an understanding of curriculum and curriculum change is given priority then a mode of study which focuses on and analyses 'internal' issues is of paramount importance. Partly the crucial nature of internal factors results from the way education and schooling are structured and relate to the broader economy and society. As Webster (1976) has pointed out: 'Educational institutions are not as directly nor as essentially concerned with the economic and social welfare of the community as, say, factories or hospitals. They are, therefore, particularly well equipped to weather any crisis that may be going on around them' (pp. 206–7). This relative autonomy explains the peculiar force of historical traditions and legacies in curriculum change. As a result as Waring reminds us 'it is hardly surprising that originality always works within the framework of tradition and that a totally new tradition is "one of the most improbable of events"'. Hence developing a sense of history will modify our view of curriculum. Instead of the transcendent expectation of basic change we look for alteration followed by regression, for change attempted and aborted in one place to emerge unexpectedly elsewhere. Through history we develop a longer view and with it a different timescale of expectations and presumably, range of strategies.

References

FRANKLIN, B. (1977) 'Curriculum history: Its nature and boundaries', *Curriculum Inquiry*, **7**, 1.

GOODSON, I.F. (1977) 'Evaluation and evolution', in NORRIS, N. (ed.) *Theory in Practice*, University of East Anglia, SAFARI Project, Centre for Applied Research in Education.

GOODSON, I.F. (1983) 'Subjects for study: Aspects of a social history of curriculum', *Journal of Curriculum Studies*, autumn.

HIRST, P.M. (1967) 'The logical and psychological aspects of teaching a subject', in PETERS, R.S. (ed.) *The Concept of Education*, London: Routledge and Kegan Paul.

HIRST, P.M. (1976) *The Educational Implications of Social and Economic Change in Schools Council Working Paper No 12*, London: HMSO.

HIRST, P.M. and PETERS, R.S. (1970) *The Logic of Education*, London: Routledge and Kegan Paul.

KERR, J. (1971) 'The problem of curriculum reform', in HOOPER, R. (ed.) *The Curriculum Context, Design and Development*, Edinburgh: Oliver and Boyd.

LAYTON, D. (1973) *Science for the People*, London: George Allen & Unwin.

MARSDEN, W.E. (1978) *Post War Curriculum Development: An Historical Appraisal*, History of Education Society Conference Papers.

PARLETT, M. and HAMILTON, D. (1972) 'Evaluation as illumination: A new approach to the study of innovatory programs', *Occasional Paper 9*, Edinburgh, Centre for Research in Educational Sciences.

PHENIX, P.M. (1964) *The Realms of Meaning*, New York: McGraw Hill.

RUBINSTEIN, D. and SIMON, R. (1973) *The Evolution of the Comprehensive School 1926–1972*, London: Routledge and Kegan Paul.

RUDOLPH, F. (1977) *A History of the American Undergraduate Course of Study Since 1636*, San Francisco: CA, Jossey Bass.

SILVER, H. (1977) 'Nothing but the past, or nothing but the present?', *Times Higher Educational Supplement*, **1**.

WALKER, R. (1974) 'The conduct of educational case study', in *Innovation, Evolution, Research and the Problem of Control: Some Interim Papers*, University of East Anglia, SAFARI Project, Centre for Applied Research in Education.

WEBSTER, J.R. (1976) 'Curriculum change and "crisis"', *British Journal of Educational Studies*, **214**, 3.

3   Becoming a School Subject

Sociological and Historical Perspectives

Contemporary accounts of school subjects arise from two major perspectives — the
sociological and the philosophical. Sociological accounts have followed a sugges-
tion made in 1968 by Musgrove (1968) that researchers should:

> examine subjects both within the school and the nation at large as social systems
> sustained by communication networks, material endowments and ideologies. Within
> a school and within a wider society subjects as communities of people, compet-
> ing and collaborating with one another, defining and defending their boundaries,
> demanding allegiance from their members and conferring a sense of identity upon
> them . . . even innovation which appears to be essentially intellectual in character,
> can usefully be examined as the outcome of social interaction. (p. 101)

Musgrove remarked that 'studies of subjects in these terms have scarcely begun at
least at school level'.

A more recent influential work in the field of the sociology of knowledge
was the collection of papers in *Knowledge and Control* edited by M.F.D. Young
in 1971. The papers reflect Bernstein's contention that 'how a society selects, clas-
sifies, distributes, transmits and evaluates the educational knowledge it considers
to be public, reflects both the distribution of power and the principles of social
control' (Bernstein, 1971). Young (1977) likewise suggests that 'consideration of
the assumptions underlying the selection and organization of knowledge by those
in positions of power may be a fruitful perspective for raising sociological questions about curricula' (p. 31). The emphasis leads to general statements of the following kind:

> Academic curricula in this country involve assumptions that some kinds and
> areas of knowledge are much more 'worthwhile' than others: that as soon as
> possible all knowledge should become specialized and with minimum explicit
> emphasis on the relations between the subjects specialized in and between spe-
> cialist teachers involved. It may be useful therefore, to view curricular changes as
> involving changing definitions of knowledge along one or more of the dimensions
> towards a less or more stratified, specialized and open organization of knowledge.
> Further, that as we assume some patterns of social relations associated with any
> curriculum, these changes will be resisted insofar as they are perceived to under-
> mine the values, relative power and privileges of the dominant groups involved.
> (*ibid*, p. 34)

The process whereby the unspecified 'dominant groups' exercise control over other presumably subordinate groups is not scrutinized although certain hints are offered. We learn that a school's autonomy in curriculum matters 'is in practice extremely limited by the control of the sixth form (and therefore lower form) curricula by the universities, both through their entrance requirements and their domination of all but one of the school examination boards'. In a footnote, Young assures that no direct control is implied here, but rather a process by which teachers legitimate their curricula through their shared assumptions about 'what we all know the universities want' (*ibid*, p. 22). This concentration on the teachers' socialization as the major agency of control is picked up elsewhere. We learn that:

> The contemporary British educational system is dominated by academic curricula with a rigid stratification of knowledge. It follows that if teachers and children are socialized within an institutionalized structure which legitimates such assumptions, then for teachers high status (and rewards) will be associated with areas of the curriculum that are (1) formally assessed (2) taught to the 'ablest' children (3) taught in homogeneous ability groups of children who show themselves most successful within such curricula. (*ibid*, p. 36)

Young goes on to note that it 'should be fruitful to explore the syllabus construction of knowledge practitioners in terms of their efforts to enhance or maintain their academic legitimacy'.

Two papers by Bourdieu (1971) in *Knowledge and Control* summarize his considerable influence on English sociologists of knowledge. Unlike many of the other contributors to *Knowledge and Control*, Bourdieu has gone on to carry out empirical work to test his theoretical assertions. His recent work — through concentrated at university, not school, level — looks at the theme of reproduction through education and includes an important section on 'the examination within the structure and history of the educational system' (Bourdieu and Passeron, 1977). Young (1977) also has come to feel the need for historical approaches to test theories of knowledge and control. He wrote recently: 'one crucial way of reformulating and transcending the limits within which we work, is to see . . . how such limits are not given or fixed, but produced through the conflicting actions and interests of men in history' (pp. 248–9).

Certainly the most undeveloped aspect of *Knowledge and Control* in respect to school subjects is the scrutiny of the process whereby unspecified dominant groups exercise control over presumably subordinate groups in the definition of school knowledge. Moreover if the dominant groups in question are related to the economy one would expect high status knowledge to be of the sort Apple (1978) refers to 'for the corporate economy requires the production of high levels of technical knowledge to keep the economic apparatus running effectively and to become more sophisticated in the maximization of opportunities for economic expansion' (p. 380). In fact high status groups have tended to receive 'academic' rather than 'technical' knowledge: a point that maybe contributes to the continuing dysfunctionality of the UK economy. We need to explore how this apparent contradiction developed and has been maintained in the school curriculum. Young's work, lacking in empirical evidence, develops horizontally in this exploration, working out from theories of social structure and social order to evidence of their application. Such macro-sociological theorizing is very different, although far from inimical, to studying social groups actively at work in particular historical instances. In this respect the examination of the process of 'becoming a school subject' should generate useful historical insights.

The second school of explanation, which might almost be called the 'establishment view', is essentially philosophical and has preceded and stood in contradiction to sociological perspectives. The philosophical view has been attacked by Young (1971) because, he argues it is based on 'an absolutist conception of a set of distinct forms of knowledge which correspond closely to the traditional areas of the academic curriculum and thus justify, rather than examine, what are no more than sociohistorical constructs of a particular time' (p. 23). Even if we largely accept Young's critique, however, it is important to know that in fact school subjects themselves represent substantial interest groups. To view subjects as 'no more than sociohistorical constructs of a particular time', whilst correct at one level, hardly serves to clarify the part played by those groups involved in their continuance and promotion over time.

The philosophical perspective is well summarized by the work of Hirst and Peters, and also Phenix. Hirst's position begins from a series of convictions that he defined in 1967 in a Schools Council Working Paper:

> No matter what the ability of the child may be, the heart of all his development as a rational being is, I am saying, intellectual. Maybe we shall need very special methods to achieve this development in some cases. Maybe we have still to find the best methods for the majority of the people. But let us never lose sight of the intellectual aim upon which so much else, nearly everything else, depends. Secondly it seems to me that we must get away completely from the idea that linguistic and abstract forms of thought are not for some people. (Hirst, 1967)

Hirst and Peters argue that 'the central objectives of education are developments of mind' and that such objectives are best pursued by the development of 'forms of knowledge' (a definition later broadened to include 'fields' of knowledge). From these forms and fields of knowledge so defined, school subjects can be derived and organized. Hence what is implied is that the intellectual discipline is created and systematically defined by a community of scholars, normally working in a university department, and is then 'translated' for use as a school subject.

This interpretation of Hirst's and Peters' work is commonly drawn, although not by the authors themselves. Other philosophers are more explicit. Phenix (1964) for instance states that: 'the general test for a discipline is that it should be the characteristic activity of an identifiable organized tradition of men of knowledge, that is of persons who are skilled in certain specified functions that they are able to justify by a set of intelligible standards' (p. 317). The subsequent vision of school subjects as derived from the best work of specialist scholars, who act as initiators into scholarly traditions, is generally accepted both by educationists and laymen. It is a view supported by spokesmen for governmental and educational agencies, subject associations and, perhaps most significantly, the media.

In questioning the consensus view that school subjects derive from the intellectual disciplines or forms of knowledge it is again important to focus on the historical process through which school subjects arise. This investigation may provide evidence of a considerable disparity between the political and philosophical messages which seek to explain and legitimize the 'academic tradition' of school subjects and the detailed historical process through which school subjects are defined and established. Once a discipline has established an academic base it is persuasively self-fulfilling to argue that here is a field of knowledge from which an 'academic' school subject can receive inputs and general direction. This version of events simply celebrates a *fait accompli* in the evolution of a discipline and associated school subject. What is left unexplained are the stages of evolution towards this portion and the forces which push aspiring academic subjects to follow similar routes. To understand the progression along the route to academic status it is necessary to examine the social histories of school subjects and to analyze the strategies employed in their construction and promotion.

Closer analysis of school subjects uncovers a number of unexplained paradoxes. First, the school context is in many ways starkly different from the university context — broader problems of pupil motivation, ability and control require consideration. The translation from discipline to school subject therefore demands considerable adaptation and as a result, 'many school subjects are barely disciplines let alone forms of thought. Many are unclear about their most fruitful concepts, forms of explanations and characteristic methodology' (Jenkins and Shipman, 1976, p. 107). Secondly, school subjects are often either divorced from their discipline base or do not have a discipline base. Many school subjects therefore, represent autonomous communities. The degree of isolation or autonomy of the school subject can be seen on closer analysis to be related to the stages of the subjects' evolution. Far from being derived from academic disciplines some school subjects chronologically *precede* their parent disciplines: in these circumstances the developing school subject actually brings about the creation of a university base for the 'discipline' so that teachers of the subject can be trained.

Layton has analyzed the development of science in England from the nineteenth century, suggesting a tentative model for the emergence of a school subject in the secondary school curriculum. He has defined three stages in this process. In the first stage:

> the callow intruder stakes a place in the timetable, justifying its presence on grounds such as pertinence and utility. During this stage learners are attracted to the subject because of its bearing on matters of concern to them. The teachers are rarely trained specialists, but bring the missionary enthusiasm of pioneers to their task. The dominant criterion is relevance to the needs and interests of the learners.

In the interim second stage:

> a tradition of scholarly work in the subject is emerging along with a corps of trained
> specialists from which teachers may be recruited. Students are still attracted to the
> study, but as much by its reputation and growing academic status as by its relev-
> ance to their own problems and concerns. The internal logic and discipline of the
> subject is becoming increasingly influential on the selection and organization of
> subject matter.

In the final stage:

> the teachers now constitute a professional body with established rules and values.
> The selection of subject matter is determined in large measure by the judgments
> and practices of the specialist scholars who lead inquiries in the field. Students are
> initiated into a tradition, their attitudes approaching passivity and resignation, a
> prelude to disenchantment. (Layton, 1972)

Layton's model warns against any monolithic explanation of subject and disciplines. It would seem that, far from being timeless statements of intrinsically
worthwhile content, subjects and disciplines are in constant flux. Hence the study
of knowledge in our society should move beyond the ahistorical process of philosophical analysis towards a detailed historical investigation of the motives and
actions behind the presentation and promotion of subjects and disciplines.

In examining the historical process of becoming a school subject the next
section provides a brief case study of geography. The subject's development is
traced largely through the publications of the Geographical Association, which means
that the focus of the study is on one aspect of the 'rhetoric' of subject promotion
rather than on the 'reality' of curriculum practice. The elucidation of the relationship between 'rhetoric' and 'reality' remains one of the most profound challenges
for future curriculum histories. (In one sense this relates to the broader problem of
the historians' dependence on written and published documentary sources). This
argues that subsequent studies are required to examine how far promotional activity effects the 'small print' of examination syllabuses and the content and practice
of classrooms. Earlier work has, I think, evidenced that the promotional rhetoric
employed by rural studies to validate its claims to be an academic discipline substantially modified the small print of an 'A' level syllabus.

The Establishment and Promotion of Geography

In the late nineteenth century geography was beginning to establish a place in the
curricula of public, grammar and elementary schools. The subject was emerging
from the initial birth pangs when it appears to have been little more than a dreary
collection of geographical facts and figures which MacKinder (1887) contended
'adds an ever-increasing amount to be borne by the memory'. This early approach
(which clearly precedes the somewhat idealized version of Layton's stage 1), has been

called the 'capes and bay' period. Very soon however the subject began to attract more inspired teachers, as a former pupil recalls: 'Later, however, in a London secondary school "capes and bays" were dramatically replaced by "homes in many lands" and a new world opened to us, through our non-graduate "specialist teacher"' (Garnett, 1969, p. 36).

The non-graduate label was at this time inevitable as geography remained outside the universities. It was partly to answer this problem that one of the founding fathers of geography, H.T. MacKinder, posed the question in 1887 'How can geography be rendered a discipline?' MacKinder was aware that the demand for an academic geography to be taught in universities could only be engendered by the establishment of a more credible position in schools. Essentially it was in the public and grammar schools that geography needed to establish its intellectual as well as pedagogical credibility.

In these schools, without full-fledged academic status, the subject's position as an established part of the curriculum remained uncertain. As a Rochester headmaster noted, 'the over-crowding in the school timetable makes it impossible to give more than one and at most two lessons per week in geography' (Bird, 1901). In the elementary schools geography was rapidly seen as affording utilitarian and pedagogic possibilities in the education of the children of working people. Hence the take-up of the subject grew considerably in the period following the 1870 Education Act. In 1875 'elementary geography' was added to the main list of class subjects examined in elementary schools.

Given the limited base in the elementary and secondary school sector the promoters of geography began to draw up plans for a subject association. Hence in 1893 the Geographical Association was founded 'to further the knowledge of geography and the teaching of geography in all categories of educational institutions from preparatory school to university in the United Kingdom and abroad'.[1] The formation of the Association in 1893 was extremely well-timed and it rapidly began to operate as a vocal lobby for the subject. Two years later the Bryce Commission reported and its recommendations were built into the 1902 Education Act. Further the 1904 Secondary Regulations effectively defined the traditional subjects to be offered in secondary schools; geography's inclusion in the regulations was a major staging-post in its acceptance and recognition and in the broad-based take-up of external examinations in geography in secondary schools. The emergence of external examinations as a defining factor in secondary curricula around 1917 is clearly reflected in the sharp increase in the Association's membership around this date. At this stage geography was included in many examination board regulations both at School Certificate and Higher School Certificate as a main subject. Certain boards, however, included geography only as a 'subsidiary subject'.

For those teachers involved in promoting geography the founding of a subject association was only a first stage in launching the subject; what was also required was an overall plan aimed at establishing the subject in the various educational sectors mentioned in the constitution. At a discussion on geographical education at the British Association in September 1903, MacKinder (1903) outlined a four-point strategy for establishing the subject:

Firstly, we should encourage university schools of geography, where geographers can be made . . .

Secondly, we must persuade at any rate some secondary schools to place the geographical teaching of the whole school in the hands of one geographically trained master . . .

Thirdly, we must thrash out by discussion and experiment what is the best progressive method for common acceptation and upon that method we must base out scheme of examination.

Lastly, the examination papers must be set by practical geography teachers. (pp. 95–101)

This strategy reads very much like a plea for monopoly rights or for a closed shop. The geography teacher is to set the exams and is to choose exams which satisfy the criteria of being acceptation' of the subject, (there is not even the facade that the pupils interest should be the central criterion); the teaching of geography is to be exclusively in the hands of trained geographers and the universities are to be encouraged to establish schools of geography 'where geographers can be made'.

In the immediate period following this pronouncement the Geography Association continued the earlier rhetoric about the subject's utility; a changeover was only slowly implemented. Thus in 1919 we learn that: 'In teaching geography in schools we seek to train future citizens to imagine accurately the interaction of human activities and their topographical conditions. . . . The mind of the citizen must have a topographical background if he is to keep order in the mass of information which he accumulates in the course of his life and in these days the background must extend over the whole world'.[2] Eight years later we hear that 'travel and correspondence have now become general; the British dominions are to be found in every clime and these facts alone are sufficient to ensure that the subject shall have an important place in the school timetable' (Board of Education, 1927).

Alongside the utilitarian and pedagogic claims, as we shall see, the Geographical Association began to mount more 'academic' arguments. But the problems of the more utilitarian and pedagogic emphases had by now surfaced. Thus in the 1930s the Norwood Committee was concerned by the way geography appeared effortlessly to change direction and definition, thereby intruding on the territory of other subjects and disciplines. Above all, the Committee was concerned with the temptation afforded by what it called the 'expansiveness of geography', for 'environment is a term which is easily expanded to cover every condition and every phase of activity which makes up normal everyday experience'. Hence, 'enthusiasts for geography may be inclined sometimes to extend their range so widely as to swallow up other subjects; in so doing they widen their boundaries so vaguely that definition of purpose is lost, and the distinctive virtues inherent in other studies closely pursued are ignored in a general survey of wide horizons' (Board of Education, 1943, pp. 101–2).

The results of such 'expansiveness' in school geography were later reported by Honeybone (1954) who argued that by the thirties geography 'came more and more to be a "world citizenship" subject, with the citizens detached from their physical environment'. He explained this partly by the spread 'under American influence' of 'a methodology, proclaiming that all education must be related to the everyday experience of children'. Hence, 'in terms of geography, they insisted that the approach must always be through life and the work of men. This is a premise with which many teachers of geography will agree, but when put in the hands of people untrained in geography or trained without a proper sense of geographical synthesis, it frequently meant that geography in school started with the life and work of man and made no real attempt to examine his environment'. Thus through the work of those teachers untrained or badly trained in the subject, 'by 1939 geography had become grievously out of balance; the geographical synthesis had been abandoned; and the unique educational value of the subject lost in a flurry of social and economic generalizations' (*ibid*, p. 87).

The central problem therefore remained the establishment of departments in universities where geographers could be made and the piecemeal changes in pursuit of pupil relevance and utility could be partially controlled. To further this objective the Geographical Association began to promote more academic arguments for the subject. By this increasingly academic presentation of the school subject provided more pressure on the universities to respond to the demand for the training of geography specialists. As a recent president of the Geographical Association has noted, 'the recognition of our subject's status among university disciplines . . . could never have been achieved without remarkable stimulus and demand injected from out of schools' (Garnett, 1969, p. 387). The contention, whilst correct, contains the origins of the status problems geography has encountered in universities. As David Walker (1975) has noted, 'some senior members of our ancient universities can still be found who dismiss it as a school subject' (p. 6). As a result until recently geographers remained a frustrated university profession because of what Wooldridge described as 'the widespread belief among our colleagues and associates that we lack academic status and intellectual respectability. What has been conceded is that geography has a limited use in its lower ranges. What is implicitly denied by so many is that it had any valid claim as a higher subject' (David, 1973, pp. 12–13).

Wooldridge hints, however, that acceptance at the lower level is the main threshold to cross: 'It has been conceded that if geography is to be taught in schools it must be learned in the universities' (*ibid*). The relevance of the school 'base' to university geography is well illustrated by St Catherine's College, Cambridge. The College has produced so many professors of geography for the country's universities that a conspiracy might be alleged. David Walker (1975) disagrees: 'In fact, to dispel the conspiracy, the reasons for this academic configuration are down to earth. St Catherine's was one of the first colleges to offer awards in geography: it established a network of contacts with sixth-form teachers, many of whom later were its own graduates, and with particular schools like the Royal Grammar, Newcastle'. Walker points to the personal nature of subject induction. 'Since the Second World War, moreover, many of the St Catherine's geographers who went on to become professors, readers and lecturers who were taught by one man, Mr A.A.L. Caeser, now the senior tutor' (p. 6).

The period following 1945 does seem to have been critical in geography's acceptance and consolidation within the university sector. Professor Alice Garnett explained in 1968 why this period was so important: 'Not until after the Second World War was it widely the case that departments were directed by geographers who had themselves received formal training in the discipline, by which time most of the initial marked differences and contrasts in subject personality had been blurred or obliterated' (Garnett, 1969, p. 368). At this point geography departments were established in most universities and the subject had a recognizable core of identity. By 1954, Honeybone could write a summary of the final acceptance and establishment of geography as a university discipline:

> In the universities, there has been an unparalleled advance in the number of staff and scope of the work in the departments of geography. In the University of London alone, there are now six chairs, four of them of relatively recent creation. Students, both graduates and undergraduates, are greater in number than ever before. Many of the training colleges and university departments of education are taking a full part in the progress; employers are realizing the value of the breadth of a university training in geography; and the Civil Service has recently raised the status of geo-graphy in its higher examinations. In fact, on all sides, we can see signs that, at long last, geography is forcing its complete acceptance as a major discipline in the universities, and that geographers are welcomed into commerce, industry and the professions, because they are well educated men and women . . .

So by the mid-1950s geography had achieved Layton's third stage in the acceptance of a subject. The selection of subject matter being 'determined in large measure by the judgments and practices of the specialist scholars who lead inquir-ies in the field'; the definition of the subject was increasingly in the hands of specialist scholars. The context in which these scholars operated was substantially divorced from schools; their activities and personal motivations, their status and career concerns were situated within the university context. The concerns of school pupils, thereby unrepresented, were of less and less account in the definition of this well established academic discipline. The situation within the schools themselves soon became clear. In 1967 the report on *Society and the Young School Leaver* noted that its young subject felt 'at best apathetic, at worst resentful and rebellious to geography . . . which seems to him to have nothing to do with the adult world he is soon to join' (HMSO, 1967, p. 3). The report adds:

> A frequent cause of failure seems to be that the course is often based on the traditional belief that there is a body of content for each separate subject which every school leaver should know. In the least successful courses this body of knowledge is written into the curriculum without any real consideration of the needs of the boys and girls and without any question of its relevance.

The threat to geography began to be appreciated at the highest level. A member of the Executive and Honorary Secretary of the Geographical Association recalls: 'Things had gone too far and geography became a too locally based regional thing

... at the same time the subject began to lose touch with reality ... geography got a bad name'.[3] A college lecturer, David Gowing, saw the same problem facing the subject and argued: 'One must recognize the need to take a fresh look at our objectives and to reexamine the role and nature of geography in school. It is not difficult to identify the causes of increasing dissatisfaction. Pupils feel that present curricula have little relevance to their needs and so their level of motivation and understanding is low. Teachers are concerned that the raising of the school leaving age and some forms of comprehensive reorganization may exacerbate the problems' (Gowing, 1973, p. 153).

The increasing definition of geography by the university specialists plainly posed problems for the subject in schools. To recapture the sense of utility and relevance of earlier days the subject would have needed to focus more on the needs of the average and below average school student. However, geography still faced problems of academic status within some universities and also among the high status sections of the secondary sector.

The advances in university geography after the Second World War partly aided the acceptance of geography as a subject suitable for the most able children, but problems remained. Marchant (1965) noted: 'Geography is at last attaining to intellectual respectability in the academic streams of our secondary schools. But the battle is not quite over' (p. 133). He instanced the continuing problem: 'May I quote from just two reports written in 1964, one of a girls' grammar school and the other on a well-known boys' independent school. First, 'geography is at present ... an alternative to Latin, which means that a number of girls cease to take it at the end of the third year ... there is no work available at A level'. Or second, perhaps a more intriguing situation: 'In the O level forms, the subject is taken only by those who are neither classicists, nor modern linguists, nor scientists. The sixth form is then drawn from this rather restricted group with the addition of a few scientists who failed to live up to expectations' (*ibid*).

To seal its acceptance by the universities and high status sixth-forms, geography had to embrace new paradigms and associated rhetorics. The supreme paradox is that the crisis in school geography in the late 1960s led not to change which might have involved more school pupils but to changes in the opposite direction in pursuit of total academic acceptance. This push for university status centred around the 'new geography', which moved away from regional geography to more quantitative data and model building. The battle for new geography represented a major clash between those traditions in geography representing more pedagogic and utilitarian traditions (notably the fieldwork geographers and some regionalists) and those pushing for total academic acceptance.

'New Geography' as an Academic Discipline

At the Madingley Lectures in 1963, which effectively launched the era of 'new geography', E.A. Wrigley (1967) contended: 'What we have seen is a concept overtaken by the course of historical change. "Regional" geography in the great mould has been as much a victim of the industrial revolution as the peasant, landed society, the horse and the village community, and for the same reason' (p. 13). To this problem Chorley and Haggett (1967a) proposed an 'immediate solution' through 'building up the neglected geometrical side of the discipline'. They noted:

> Research is already swinging strongly into this field and the problem of implementation may be more acute in the schools than in the universities. Here we are continually impressed by the vigour and reforming zeal of 'ginger groups' like the School Mathematics Association which have shared in fundamental review of mathematics teaching in schools. There the inertia problems — established textbooks, syllabuses, examinations — are being successfully overcome and a new wave of interest is sweeping through the schools. The need in geography is just as great and we see no good reason why changes here should not yield results equally rewarding. (p. 377)

The messianic nature of their appeal is shown when they argue that it is:

> Better that geography should explode in an excess of reform than bask in the watery sunset of its former glories; for in an age of rising standards in school and university, to maintain the present standards is not enough — to stand still is to retreat, to move forward hesitantly is to fall back from the frontier. If we move with that frontier new horizons emerge in our view, and we find new territories to be explored as exciting and demanding as the dark continents that beckoned any earlier generation of geographers. This is the teaching frontier of geography.

The Madingley Lectures proved a watershed in the emergence of the subject. Two years before, E.E. Gilbert (1961) — in an article on 'The idea of the region' — had stated that he regarded new geography in the universities as an 'esoteric cult'. After Madingley, this was no longer the case, as a college lecturer who was secretary of his local Geographical Association recalled: 'After Madingley my ideas were turned upside down . . . That's where the turn around in thinking in geography really started'.[4] But as Walford (1973) later noted, Madingley was 'heady to some, undrinkable brew to others' (p. 95). Following the second Madingley Conference in 1968, Chorley and Haggett sought to consolidate the changes they were advocating by a new book entitled *Models in Geography* (1967b). By this time opinions were becoming progressively polarized about the 'new geography'. Slaymaker (1960) wrote in support of the book:

> In retrospect, a turning point in the development of geographical methodology in Britain. After the exploratory and mildly iconoclastic contents of the first Madingley lectures, recorded in *Frontiers in Geographical Teaching*, a more substantial statement of the methodological basis and aims of the so-called 'new geography' was required . . . with the publication of this book (it is demonstrated that) the traditional classificatory paradigm is inadequate and that in the context of the 'new geography' an irreversible step has been taken to push us back into the mainstream of scientific activity by process of model building. The discussion of the relevance of new conceptual models in geographical research and teaching should serve as

a stimulus to participation in methodological debate to which, with notable exceptions, British geographers have made a disproportionately small contribution. It is therefore a major publication, both in achievement and potential.

Teachers of the subject received less enthusiastic advice from their journal, *Geography* and its anonymous reviewer 'P.R.C.':

> What ... is its object, and to whom is it addressed? These questions are avoided with perverse skill and in the absence of guidance, the conviction gradually takes root that, in fact, the authors are writing for each other! This may explain, though it does not excuse, the use in some papers of a barbarous and repulsive jargon. Is it then a joint expression of faith on the part of the new geographers? This would indeed have been welcome but a new faith is hardly likely to be attained by a frenzied search for gadgets which might conceivably be turned to geographical ends. The nature of those ends calls for solid thought, a task which cannot be delegated to computers. (PRC, 1968)

A year later the president of the Geographical Association pursued a similar opposition with a more explicit statement of the fears which new geography engendered. The new systematic geography, she argued, was:

> creating a problem that will increase in acuteness over the decades ahead for it leads towards subject fragmentation as fringe specialisms in systematic fields proliferate and are pursued independently to the neglect of the very core of our discipline — a core that largely justified its existence. Geography in our universities is in fact becoming so sophisticated, and its numerous branches in diverse fields at times so narrowly specialized, that sooner or later, the question must arise as to how much longer the subject can effectively be held together. (Garnett, 1969, pp. 388–9)

The implications of this analysis are clear:

> So my first plea to the academic teachers who will be the leaders of tomorrow must be: let there never be question (other than at an advanced postgraduate and research level) of the coexistence of two geographies, physical and social, regarded as one without reference to the other. University departments have a duty to ensure that, at least at the first degree level, the core of our subject is neither forgotten nor neglected, and that the synthesis of the specialist fields and their relevance to the core are clearly appreciated by our undergraduate students. In my mind, it is only on the foundation of a first degree course structure so designed that a geographer is basically qualified either to teach in our schools or to carry his studies further at a postgraduate research level. (*ibid*, p. 389)

The overwhelming worry reflected in this quote was that the myth of the discipline would be exposed. Geography was supposedly a unified academic discipline into which the school teacher initiated young pupils. If there was no obvious link between university and school geography this version of events — the Hirstian vision of school subjects — would stand exposed. Teachers themselves became very worried: 'Geography was in a state of ferment . . . it was moving too quickly . . . Let alone in the schools even many of the universities didn't have new geography';[5] and 'This new approach, however you felt about it, caused a sort of schism . . . both at university and at school level' (*ibid*).

Fears of this schism were expressed in a number of contemporary books. The gap between schools and universities, of which there is much evidence in previous periods, was thought particularly worrying:

> Techniques of study are changing more rapidly in modern geography than at any previous time in the subject's history. As a result there is a great need for a dialogue between research workers and those being admitted to the mysteries of the subject. Teachers provide the necessary link; and it is dangerous for the vitality and future health of geography that some teachers find current developments either incomprehensible or unacceptable. (Cooke and Johnson, 1969, p. 8)

Rex Walford (1973) made a similar diagnosis: 'The need for unity within the subject is more than a practical one of preparing sixth formers for their first lectures on campus; it is, I would assert, a basic requirement for the continued existence of the subject' (p. 97).

In spite of the opposition of teachers and academics, many of who saw regional geography as the 'real geography', there were strong pressures working in favour of the advocates of new geography. Beyond the problems in schools, the scholars in universities who controlled the new definitions of the subject were concerned to progress to the front rank of university academic disciplines. (Their concerns would of course be reflected in greater sixth form status.) New geography was conceived and promoted to achieve this end. The alliance between university status and school status ensured that ultimately the Geographical Association would embrace 'new geography'.

The perceived problems encountered by school geography were used as an argument for change. The change then moved in those directions most likely to satisfy geography's aspiration for the full acceptance as a first rank academic discipline in universities and sixth-forms. The changes emanating from universities were partly mediated through the Geographical Association to the schools. At stages where the gap between the two widened, the Association was always on hand to warn against too rapid redefinition and to exhort teachers to change and to encourage their retraining. In recent years fears about 'new geography' seem to have subsided and a period of consolidation has set in. Of the Cambridge base of Chorley and Haggett it was recently written, by David Walker (1975), himself a protagonist: 'The academic revolution of quantification which has battered traditional scholarship in fields like economic history and linguistics has taken its toll in geography in recent years, but the Cambridge Department which Professor Darby took over in 1966 remains on an even keel. The tripos system continues to offer a fine balance of specialization and liberal education' (p. 6).

Perceptions of the subject as being in crisis have considerably mellowed. A professor, who is on the Executive Committee and past holder of a number of positions in the Geographical Association stated: 'I see geography traditionally as a core to understand why places are as they are' but said of the present condition of geography: 'It isn't in flux . . . there is no end to the subject . . . of course the techniques by which you advance the subject will change . . . if the present emphasis on quantitative techniques helps our preciseness who could deny that it is an advance within the subject'.[6]

Ultimately the reconciliation with new geography was closely linked with geography's long aspiration to be viewed as a scientific discipline. In a previous decade Professor Wooldridge had written a book on *The Geographer as Scientist* (Wooldridge, 1956), but in 1970 Fitzgerald, reviewing the implications of new geography for teaching wrote: 'The change which many think is at the heart of geography is that towards the use of the scientific method in approaching problems' (Fitzgerald, 1973, p. 85). Similarly, M. Yeates (1968) wrote: 'Geography can be regarded as a science concerned with the rational development and testing of theories that explain and predict the spatial distribution and location of various characteristics on the surface of the earth' (p. 1).

At the twenty-first International Geographic Congress at New Delhi in 1968, Professor Norton Ginsburg identified *social* science as the 'fraternity' to aspire to. He saw: 'the beginnings of a new age for human geography as a fully-fledged member of the social science fraternity . . . the future of geography as a major research discipline will, I submit, be determined on the intellectual battlefields of the universities, where competition and conflict are intense; and where ideas are the hallmark of achievement' (Ginsburg, 1969, pp. 403–4). He considered that 'research has moved rapidly, albeit erratically, towards the formulation of general propositions and theories of organization and behaviour and away from preoccupation with patterns *per se*. In this sense geography's internal organization and intellectual apparatus have come to resemble those of the social sciences, whereas formerly they were markedly at variance with them'. Hence by 1970, geography had finished its 'long march' to acceptance as an academic discipline; from now on its future would indeed be determined not in the school classroom but on 'the intellectual battlefields of the universities'.

Conclusion

The establishment of geography — how geography was rendered a discipline — was a protracted, painstaking and fiercely contested process. The story is not of the translation of an academic discipline, devised by ('dominant') groups of scholars in universities, into pedagogic version to be used as a school subject. Rather the story unfolds in reverse order and can be seen as a drive on the part of low status groups at school level progressively to colonize areas within the university sector — thereby earning the right for scholars in the new field to define knowledge that could be viewed as a discipline. The process of development for school subjects can be seen not as a pattern of disciplines 'translated' *down* or of 'domination' *downwards* but very much as a process of 'aspiration' *upwards.*

To summarize the stages in the emergence of geography: in the earlier stages teaching was anything but 'messianic', for the subject was taught by non-specialists and comprised a 'dreary collection of geographical facts and figures'. The threshold for take-off on the route to academic establishment began with MacKinder's remarkably successful recipe for the subject's promotion drawn up in 1903. In the MacKinder manifesto the geography teacher is to set the exams and is to choose exams that are best for the 'common acceptation' of the subject, the teaching of geography is to be exclusively in the hands of trained geographers and the universities are to be encouraged to establish schools of geography 'where geographers can be made'.

The strategy offered solutions for the major problems geography faced in it development. Most notable of these was the idiosyncratic and information-based nature of school geography. Initially the subject stressed personal, pedagogic and vocational arguments for its inclusion in curricula: 'we seek to train future citizens' and moreover a citizen 'must have a topographical background if he is to keep order in the mass of information which accumulates in the course of this life' (1919). Later the subject was advocated because 'travel and correspondence have now become general' (1927). But the result of these utilitarian and pedagogic emphases was that comments arose as to the 'expansiveness' of the subject and the fact that it came 'more and more to be a "world citizenship" subject' (1930s).

The problem was that identified by MacKinder in 1903: geographers needed to be 'made' in the universities, then any piecemeal changes in pursuit of school relevance or utility could be controlled and directed. The growth of the subject in the schools provided an overwhelming argument for the subject to be taught in the universities. As Wooldridge noted later, 'it has been conceded that if geography is to be taught in schools it must be learned in universities'. Slowly therefore a uniformity in the subject was established to answer those who observed the chameleon nature of the subject's knowledge structure. Alice Garnett noted that it was not until after 1945 that most school departments of geography were directed by specialist-trained geographers but as a result of this training 'most of the initial marked differences and contrasts in subject personality had been blurred or obliterated' (one might say 'masked and mystified').

The definition of geography through the universities rapidly replaced any pedagogic or utilitarian promotional bias with arguments for academic rigour: and as early as 1927 Hadow had contended that 'the main objective in good geographical teaching is to develop, as in the case of history, an attitude of mind and mode of thought characteristic of the subject'. However, for several decades university geography was plagued both by the image of the subject as essentially for school children, and by the idiosyncratic interpretations of the various university departments, especially in respect to fieldwork. Thus, while establishment in universities solved the status problems of the subject within schools, within universities themselves the subject's status still remained low. The launching of 'new geography' with aspirations to scientific or social scientific rigour is therefore partly to be understood as a strategy for finally establishing geography's status at the highest level. In this respect the current position of the subject in universities would seem to confirm the success of new geography's push for parity of esteem with other university disciplines.

The aspiration to become an academic subject and the successful promotion employed by geography teachers and educationists, particularly in the work of the Geographical Association, has been clearly evidenced. We know what happened in the history of geography: less evidence has been presented as to why this should be so. A clue can be found in Garnett's presidential address to the Geography Association in 1968; a clear link is presented between 'the recognition of our subject's status among university disciplines' and 'the costly provision made available for its study'. Plainly the drive towards higher status is accompanied by opportunities to command larger finance and resources.

The close connection between academic status and resources is a fundamental feature of our educational system. The origin of this connection is the examination system created by universities from the late 1850s and culminating in the school certificate system founded in 1917. As a result the so-called 'academic' subjects provide examinations which are suitable for 'able' students whilst other subjects are not.

Byrne's work has provided data on resource allocation within schools. She discerned that: 'two assumptions which might be questioned have been seen consistently to underlay educational planning and the consequent resource allocation for the more able children. First, that these necessarily need longer in school than non-grammar pupils, and secondly, that they necessarily need more staff, more highly paid staff and more money for equipment and books' (Byrne, 1974, p. 29). The implications of the preferential treatment of academic subjects for the material self-interest of teachers are clear: better staffing ratios, higher salaries, higher capitation allowances, more graded posts, better careers prospects. The link between academic status and resource allocation provides the major explanatory framework for understanding the aspirational imperative to become an academic subject. Basically since more resources are given to the academic examination subject taught to able students the conflict over the status of examinable knowledge is above all a battle over the material resources and career prospects of each subject teacher or subject community.

The historical profile tentatively discerned for geography exposes certain omissions, in some cases misconceptions, within the main philosophical and sociological accounts. The philosophical perspective has provided support for the view that school subjects derive from forms or fields of knowledge or 'disciplines'. Of course, once a school subject has brought about the establishment of an academic discipline base it is persuasively self-fulfilling to argue that the school subject receives intellectual direction and inputs from university scholars. This version of events simply celebrates a *fait accompli* in the history of the school subject and associated disciplines. What is left unexplained and unrecorded are the stages of evolution towards the culminating pattern and the forces which push aspiring academic subjects to follow similar routes. By starting with the final historical product philosophical studies forego the opportunity to examine school subjects fully.

In a way, sociological accounts also celebrate the *fait accompli* and assume that university control of school subjects reflects a continuing pattern of pervasive domination. As we have seen the major agencies actively involved in constructing this pattern were the teachers of school subjects themselves — not so much domination by dominant forces, more solicitous surrender by subordinate groups. The stress on domination leads to an emphasis on teachers 'being socialized within institutionalized structures' which legitimate high status patterns of academic subjects. Far from this socialization in dominant institutions being the major factor creating the pattern we have examined, it was much more considerations of teachers' material self-interest in their working lives. Since the misconception is purveyed by sociologists who often exhort us 'to understand the teachers' real world' they should really know better. High status academic knowledge gains its adherents and aspirants less through control of the curricula which socialize than through re-established connection with patterns of resource allocation and the associated work and career prospects these ensure. The historical study of school subjects directs our attention to the development of patterns of resource allocation and I think shows how generative this approach might be in replacing crude notions of domination with patterns of control in which subordinate groups can be seen actively at work.

Notes

1 Manifesto of the Geographical Association printed on the inside cover of all copies of *Geography*.
2 Council of the Geographical Association (1919) 'The position of geography', *The Geographical Teacher*, **10**.
3 Interview, 30 June 1976.
4 Personal interview with college of education lecturer, 5 January 1977.
5 Interview, 30 June 1976.
6 Interview with a geography professor, 14 December 1978.

References

APPLE, M.W. (1978) 'Ideology, reproduction and educational reform', *Comparative Education Review*, **22**.
BERNSTEIN, B. (1971) 'On the classification and framing of educational knowledge', in YOUNG, M.F.D. (ed.) *Knowledge and Control*, London: Collier-Macmillan.
BIRD, C. (1901) 'Limitations and possibilities of geographical teaching in day schools', *The Geographical Teacher*, **1**.
BOARD OF EDUCATION (1927) *Report of the Consultative Committee: The Education of the Adolescent* (The Hadow Report), London: HMSO.
BOARD OF EDUCATION (1943) *Curriculum and Examinations in Secondary Schools* (The Norwood Report), London: HMSO.
BOURDIEU, P. (1971) 'System of education and systems of thought, an intellectual field and creative project', in YOUNG, M.F.D. (ed.) *Knowledge and Control: New Directions for the Sociology of Education*, London: Collier-Macmillan.

BOURDIEU, P. and PASSERON, J.C. (1977) *Reproduction in Education, Society and Culture*, London: Sage.

BYRNE, E.M. (1974) *Planning and Educational Inequality*, Slough: NFER.

CHORLEY, R. and HAGGETT, P. (eds) (1967a) *Frontiers in Geographical Teaching*, London: Methuen.

CHORLEY, R. and HAGGETT, P. (1967b) *Models in Geography*, London: Methuen.

COOKE, R. and JOHNSON, J.M. (1969) *Trends in Geography*, London: Methuen.

DAVID, T. (1973) 'Against geography', in BALE, D., GRAVE, N. and WALFORD, R. (eds) *Perspectives in Geographical Education*, Edinburgh: Oliver and Boyd.

FITZGERALD, B.P. (1973) 'Scientific method, quantitative techniques and the teaching of geography', in WALFORD, R. (ed.) *New Directions in Geography Teaching*, London: Longmans.

GARNETT, A. (1969) 'Teaching geography: Some reflections', *Geography*, **54**.

GILBERT, E.E. (1961) 'The idea of the region', *Geography*, **45**, 1.

GINSBURG, N. (1969) 'Tasks of geography', *Geography*, **54**.

GOWING, D. (1973) 'A fresh look at objectives', in WALFORD, R. (ed.) *New Directions in Geography Teaching*, London: Longmans.

HIRST, P.M. (1967) 'The logical and psychological aspects of teaching a subject', in PETERS, R.S. (ed.) *The Concept of Education*, London: Routledge and Kegan Paul.

HMSO (1967) *Society and the Young School Leaver*, Working Paper No 11, London, HMSO.

HONEYBONE, R.C. (1954) 'Balance in geography and education', *Geography*, **34**, 184.

JENKINS, D. and SHIPMAN, M.P. (1976) *Curriculum: An Introduction*, London: Open Books.

LAYTON, D. (1972) 'Science in general education', *Trends in Education*, January.

MacKINDER, H.J. (1887) 'On the scope and methods of geography', *Proceedings of the Royal Geographical Society*, **9**.

MacKINDER, H.J. (1903) *Report of the Discussion on Geographical Education*.

MARCHANT, E.C. (1965) 'Some responsibilities of the teacher of geography', *Geography*, **3**.

MUSGROVE, F. (1968) 'The contribution of sociology to the study of the curriculum', in KERR, J.F. (ed.) *Changing the Curriculum*, London: University of London Press.

PHENIX, P.M. (1964) *The Realms of Meaning*, New York: McGraw Hill.

PRC (1968) 'Review', *Geography*, **53**, 4, November.

STAYMAKER, O. (1969) 'Review', *Geographical Journal*, **134**, 2, September.

WALFORD, R. (1973) 'Models, simulations and games', in WALFORD, R. (ed.) *New Directions in Geography Teaching*, London: Longmans.

WALKER, D. (1975) 'The well-rounded geographers', *The Times Educational Supplement*, 28 November.

WOOLDRIDGE, S.W. (1956) *The Geographer as Scientist*, London: Nelson.

WRIGLEY, E.A. (1967) 'Changes in the philosophy of geography', in CHORLEY, R. and HAGGETT, P. (eds) *Frontiers in Geographical Teaching*, London: Methuen.

YEATES, M.H. (1968) *An Introduction to Quantitative Analysis in Economic Geography*, New York: McGraw-Hill.

YOUNG, M.F.D. (ed.) (1971) 'An approach to the study of curricula as socially organised knowledge', in YOUNG, M.F.D. (ed.) *Knowledge and Control: New Directions for the Sociology of Education*, London: Collier-Macmillan.

YOUNG, M.F.D. (1977) 'Curriculum change: Limits and possibilities', in YOUNG, M.F.D. and WHITTY, G. (eds) *Society, State and Schooling*, London: Falmer Press.

4 The Micro Politics of Curriculum Change: European Studies

European Studies: The Micropolitics of Curriculum Evolution

Many innovations are schools-based and attempts to generalize them and to create a wider 'structure' of change have to grapple with the problems experienced and perceived at school level. If such problems are substantial innovations are often 'contained' within the school and curriculum conflict remains local and idiosyncratic. One example of a new curriculum 'subject' which developed in the 1960s was European studies. Its subsequent development offers an opportunity to scrutinise the history of a 'contained' school innovation over two decades.

The concern in this chapter is less with the historical understanding of how European studies was structurally contained but more with how this containment was received and perceived by teachers of the subject. This pattern of reception and perception is, of course, part of the story of containment — for hostility at individual school level (and associated problems at personal career level) can defuse attempts to achieve broader structural changes in curriculum.

European Studies: Historical Background

European studies emerged as a fashionable curriculum innovation in the 1960s and originated from two quite unconnected events. Firstly, the growth of a movement aiming to develop European unity and European consciousness. In the forefront of this movement were agencies like the European Commission and the Council of Europe. For instance, a resolution passed by the Ministers' Deputies of the Council of Europe in October 1966 stated that 'at a time when Europe is becoming a reality it is the imperative duty of secondary eduction to inculcate into its pupils an awareness of European facts and problems'.[1] Essentially the messiahs of the new Europe were concerned to encourage an awareness of the Common European heritage. The European governments associated with the European Cultural Convention in 1966 were exhorted to 'do everything within their power to ensure that all disciplines concerned — for instance history, geography, literature, modern languages — contribute to the creation of a European consciousness' (Jotterand, 1966).

Secondly, the reorganization of the English secondary school system and associated changes in the curriculum encouraged the growth of European studies. The 1960s were a time of rapid change with the spread of the comprehensive system throughout the country. Interdisciplinary and integrated approaches were an important element in the curriculum reforms initiated in the 1960s to meet the new pedagogical demands of the comprehensive schools and the changes to mixed ability associated with ROSLA (1972).

As a solution to the problems engendered by the didactic teaching of traditional subjects in these new comprehensive classes curriculum reform groups such as the Goldsmiths team advocated organising schemes of work around interdisciplinary enquiries:

> We suggest ENQUIRY as the basic concept. We suggest this not merely as a technique but as the essence of the curriculum. Subject teaching to a syllabus restricts enquiry by the pupils. It is the teacher who has been creative, in making up the syllabus; what he has created then becomes the content of the syllabus, which is then *taught to* the class. Even if the teacher demonstrates the interrelationships of his subject with others at particular points, it is he who is being creative, not the children. The children are merely being *taught*.
>
> Teaching a theme embracing a number of subjects, despite its greater freedom, has the same limitations. It does not do what is essential too shift the emphasis from *instructing* to *active exploring*. (Goldsmiths College, 1965, p. 5)

Another curriculum project aimed at young school leavers underlined both the need to reappraise 'subjects' and to clearly define new pedagogic relationships. The Humanities Curriculum Project (HCP) began in 1967 with Lawrence Stenhouse as its Director. HCP pursued the pedagogic implications of curriculum reform through the notion of 'neutral chairmanship'. This meant: 'that the teacher accepts the need to submit his teaching in controversial areas to the criterion of neutrality . . . i.e. that he regards it as part of this responsibility not to promote his own view', and further that: 'the mode of enquiry in controversial areas should have discussion, rather than instructions as its core'.[2]

Alongside new definitions of pedagogy were new strategies for their implementation. Most commonly, 'team teaching' was seen as a mechanism for conducting enquiry-based or thematic integrated studies. David Warwick's book *Team Teaching* states that 'team teaching' and 'integrated studies' are very closely linked and argues that a new organizational format is replacing the subject-based curriculum:

> Most subjects have two or three single periods each week. They cannot spare the time for . . . experimentation and, if they could, forty minutes is totally inadequate. The practice of one man, one class, inevitably leads to departments often even individual teachers, working in complete isolation . . .
>
> . . . A whole new approach is coming into being. It entails complete afternoons given over to realistic fieldwork of all kinds, the availability of two or more members of staff simultaneously involved in one project: a breaking away from the conventional form of classroom divisions; and a 'blocking' of the school timetable to give the facilities and space required. It is a process that seeks to cast off the concept of the teacher as the '2–4–7 man' — someone most at home within the two covers of a text book, the four walls of a classroom and the seven periods of a school day. (Warwick, 1972, pp. 26–7)[3]

At the very time European studies teachers were seeing integrated or inter-disciplinary courses as the strategy for establishing their subject other voices were warning of the dangers inherent in the curriculum forms then being pursued. In 1969, Marten Shipman was warning about a new 'curriculum for inequality' (Shipman, 1971, pp. 104–5) but a year later at the British Sociological Association conference Michael Young extended Shipman's analysis, linking his two 'traditions' to status patterns inside the educational system. The academic tradition represented 'high-status knowledge' and the newer traditions 'low-status knowledge'. High status knowledge tended to be 'abstract, highly literate, individualistic and unrelated to non-school knowledge'. Low status knowledge was organized in direct contradiction to this pattern and was normally available only 'to those who have already 'failed' in terms of academic definitions of knowledge' (Young, 1971, p. 40).

Languages and the Comprehensive School — The Genesis of European Studies

The continuing division in British curricula between the two nations of 'the able' and the 'less able' is strongly in evidence when considering the emergence of European studies. A Department of Education and Science survey in April 1974 showed that 80 per cent of European studies courses in secondary schools in this country came under the aegis of modern languages departments. The most recent regional survey carried out in East and West Sussex confirms that 'the majority of teachers responsible for European studies are modern linguists'.[4]

With the introduction of the comprehensive system modern language depart-ments were faced by an enormous challenge: how to teach their subjects to the whole ability range. In the past three-quarters or four-fifths of the school population had gone to secondary modern schools. The 1963 Newsom survey noted that 'just under a third of the modern schools provided some foreign language teaching, mainly in French and largely confined ot the ablest pupils. Thus for the section of the comprehensive school population, somewhere over half the intake, defined as 'less able' learning a modern language was to be very much a new experience (CACE, 1963).

From the beginning it was clear that the low motivation to learn traditional academic subjects of 'the less able' was unusually potent in modern languages. Lambert and Gardner in their book on *Attitudes and Motivation in Modern Language Learning* (1975) noted that:

> the young person from a less advantaged background, without parental support, with relatively poor abilities and low achievement orientations is very likely to do poorly in academic work, including the study of Language.

What was needed, they argued, was to inform these pupils about the background and lives of the foreign people whose language was to be studied. Thereby the 'less able's' interest might be engaged and their motivation to learn enhanced. In edu-cational jargon they put it like this:

An integrative and friendly outlook toward the other group whose language is being learned can differentially sensitise the learner to the audio-lingual features of the language making him more perceptive to forms of pronunciation and accent than is the case for a learner without this open and friendly disposition. (quoted in Lawrence)

A number of teachers have tested out Gardner and Lambert's assertion. Though in a sense these teachers represent a 'second wave' in the introduction of European studies since their efforts are well documented they throw light on the general position of modern languages pioneers introducing the new subject. Basically they confirm Michael Williams' contention that:

Many European Studies courses have begun with the feeling of modern language teachers that a small 'pill' of language will be taken by weak pupils if it is strongly dissolved in a heavy surfeit of jam i.e. non-language study. (Williams, 1977, p. 18)

Williams also argues that:

Without doubt the teaching of European Studies to pupils in the first two years of comprehensive schools has become part of the debate over equality of curricula opportunity. If French is to be taught to one child then some would argue it should be taught to all. To make it palatable to the academically weaker pupils, especially when they are taught in mixed ability groups, much time must be spent arousing their interest, motivating them to learn the language, by using non-language studies. (*ibid*, p. 19)

The desire to use European studies as a vehicle for motivating the less able in languages lessons inevitable inverts the normal process by which school subjects are defined. In the traditional manner the 'intellectual disciplines' of the subject are defined and the pedagogic strategies with which to teach these disciplines are then formulated. European studies, introduced because pedagogic strategies to teach language could *not* be formulated, in desperation invoked pupil interest as the major criteria for content selection.

In each school we were, of course, dealing with separate subject ideologies. For French departments the effect (if not the stated intention) was often to quickly identify and displace the non-linguists (to use common school parlance in language departments). As a result the French teacher was then left with a small group of linguists to instruct for examination courses. European studies was then the other side of this coin: dependent on traditional subject fall-out for recruits.

Perceptions and Receptions 1979–84

The historical location of the origins of European Studies within the new comprehensive schools and with the focus on less able students of a traditional discipline point up the similarities with environmental studies. The latter, analyzed elsewhere, was able to mount a substantial challenge to the traditional discipline from below (See Goodson, 1993). In European studies this has not happened to the same extent and hence we have to focus our studies on the individual schools if we are to understand the history of 'containment'.

Teachers' contemporary perceptions of European studies focus on a range of episodes and constraints. It is possible to group these in the following manner: (i) views developed as the European studies courses were initiated; (ii) responses of colleagues; (iii) 'career' problems and possibilities; (iv) external opinions — parents, employers and universities.

Teachers' Perceptions of European Studies

The dominant perception amongst teachers recalling the beginning of their courses in the 60s and 70s was of haphazard and idiosyncratic reasons for introducing European studies. The following comment is rather typical:

> At the time I was Head of Geography in the Faculty of Social Studies. In the summer the headmistress suddenly decided we would have European studies. It was to be non-exam only.

Here we see two of the most common features: the rapid and essentially 'reactive' nature of the initiative and the concern for non-academic, non-examination pupils. In the English context of resource allocation the latter factor was of critical import from the earliest stages. The following comments extend on the dual characteristics of European studies courses:

> In my school languages were going down badly with whole sets of kids. The Deputy Head decided something new was needed . . . for the 'C' set anyhow . . .

> My Head of Languages gave me the responsibility for devising it (the European studies course). He wanted something fairly broad, fairly wide for the non-exams. Something to be taught from Macdonalds Atlas . . . that was the only book we had that was of any use . . . There were mutinies in the ranks . . . the teachers had seldom seen this band of kids. He introduced it just like that on the first day of September.

> I think it came from the staff originally, I mean the Head was very keen on it to start with and there were certain members of departments like myself, (i.e. liberal studies), history and modern languages and geography . . . Basically we were at the staff meeting talking about the less able students . . . saying 'we've done this for "n" years and it's running down' and that was the situation, universal apathy reigned and we just felt like giving them something else . . . and European studies came up, at the same time the Head was very helpful indeed and was looking for an expansion of the sixth-form option thing . . . we've got you know a very wide range of 'A' level students and we wanted one-year courses for the people who had a lot of free time . . .

A number of teachers described their awareness of the dangers which flowed from hasty considerations of what to do with the less involved pupils. In several instances this led to the development of a more positive view of the potentialities and position of European studies:

> Well you see . . . I think as far as we are concerned this was a conscious turning away from what was beginning to develop and that was people starting to say 'what are we going to do with the youngsters who are not learning French or German' . . . From the point of view of timetable convenience they ought to be doing something associated . . . 'let them learn about Germany, you know and what you have for tea in Brussels or something' . . . we were so frightened that this was what European studies was going to become, some sort of dustbin . . . I think we have consciously turned away from that and although I think we haven't go to lose sight of it eventually, I think we've got to come back to terms with this after we've done the other things . . . I think we've go to go ahead from our middle school into our sixth form first and get that thing right and get the subject established with status . . . then we may be able to add on these less able youngsters.

The origins of European studies as an impulsive, haphazard response to problems of involving 'less able' linguists meant that many courses were ephemeral, changing from year to year in opportunistic response to the character of pupil cohorts and reactions as well as to other institutional and timetable pressures. The most common teacher descriptions were of the following sort:

> Well, it may well be that in various years depending on the staff there, one of the CSE unit options will be a European studies course with geography, history and all the rest of it . . . but very hotchpotch and off-the-cuff.

> Well, when I became Head of Humanities they also made me Head of European Studies . . . which had been taught on and off for several years to the 'dumbos' in languages . . . So I organized a meeting to discuss it as a subject — only the young assistant teachers were interested. I went to the Head and asked for money, I was given £150.

> We drafted out a syllabus based on 'what can we reasonably do with them' — we then worked out a few aims . . . mainly based on bits of the local environment, like the ferries, identity cards . . . we were fighting to make it broad but sometimes we had to draw the line . . . glacial deposits, that was too technical. I didn't mind much what went on as long as the teachers could make it work. We built up our course mainly on the basis of what had worked in the first 'panic' year.

Once again we see the genesis of European studies as a response to the problems of what to do with 'them', 'the dumbos'. There seems solid evidence to substantiate some of Shipman's claims listed earlier of a development of a 'curriculum for inequality'.

Responses of Other Teachers

The responses from teachers of related disciplines were commonly the most hostile. As with environmental studies geographers were reportedly highly resistant to the new subject but so also were historians. Often this was expressed as a defence of the 'department':

> In a place like this departments are huge and they like to keep their legality. It's all a problem of trying to cross barriers which have been there for a long time. However well you get on with people it's still a thought in the back of their mind that their empire could be being chipped away at. Interdisciplinary studies are always going to be in that situation.

Often this emotional defence of 'subject' and 'department' has a rational basis for in fact new subjects will reduce numbers and hence resources. A Deputy Headmistress confirmed the point, 'I don't see why European studies shouldn't be out on its own but it would mean that probably history and geography numbers would go down. Fewer children would opt for them.'

The territorial defence of departments and subjects increases sharply in the fourth year with the defining of examination groups. These groups are closely related to the distribution of resources and graded posts in schools: subject interests and material interests now converge. For many of the integrated subjects who are happily conceded space lower in the school the dilemma is acute. A member of the school hierarchy put it this way:

> I see the strength of Bob's argument that European studies doesn't tread on history's and geography's toes in the second and third years so why suddenly discriminate at this level.

The micropolitics of subject defense move beyond special lobbying of heads and deputy heads. A good deal of interpersonal negotiation goes on between colleagues. The proponents of new subject contenders like European studies have to put up with a good deal of 'sniping'.

A Head of a very successful European Studies Department who was subsequently promoted listed the responses in the following manner:

	Type	**Response**
1	Hostile	'You're building a nice little empire'
		'Here comes Mr. Euro Studies'
2	Skeptical	'That sounds NICE'
		'Not more education'
3	Comparative	'It's not better than what we've got'
		'Other things are far more valuable'

4 Ignorance   'But we do French already'
                               'I suppose it'll help with their geography'

5 Personal   'It's beyond me'
                               'I'm a mathematician, not a social scientist'

6 Apathetic/   'It sounds a good idea but I'd rather not'
   lethargic

7 Suspended   'I really am too busy, you know'
                               'If you do get it off the ground then I might join you next year'

8 Situational   'How are you going to fit it in?'
                               'I can't see parents wanting their children to get a CSE in this!'
                               'Where are you going to get the money?'[5]

Career Problems and Possibilities

The school subject is, of course, the major reference point in the work of contemporary secondary schools. The information and knowledge transmitted in school is normally organized and defined through subjects. This centrality of the subject is crucial for the teacher's career because of the internal organisation of the school's curriculum. A number of teachers are usually required to teach each subject; these teachers are then grouped in a subject department. These departments provide the teacher with the milieu in which his/her career is pursued. Departments have 'graded posts' for special responsibilities and for acting as Head of the Department. In this way the teacher's subject defines the means whereby salary is decided, and career structure delineated.

But further the status of the subject is crucial in deciding the allocation of resources and posts to the department. 'Academic' 'O' and 'A' level subjects normally gain the most generous allocation and hence provide the best career routes.

New subjects have to battle against the vested interest and established examination status of 'traditional subjects'. The battle is heavily loaded against new contenders:

> the problem is that the children who adapt best to European studies in the lower school are the humanities-type children who obviously do history and geography. In the upper school they can get 'O' levels in history and geography so they're obviously going to opt for them. I can see that an 'O' level is going to be of far more use to them than a CSE which they can get for European studies so we're stuck between the devil and the deep blue sea.

One teacher of European studies, Bob, detailed his worries about the subject's status and survival. His comments typify those expressed by many European studies teachers:

> Really now we're held up by the exam boards because they haven't produced
> any worthwhile syllabuses. The subject has established itself . . . most schools now
> have European Studies Departments, but even so I'm still skeptical about its sur-
> vival simply because there are not public examinations to keep it moving. (. . .)
> We've got a CSE syllabus in the sixth form. It's a super syllabus but again it
> doesn't carry any weight.

The link between exams and the high or low status of a subject was more bluntly
stated by the Deputy Headmaster:

> I have every sympathy with Bob's need to get high status for the subject. The
> problem is the cash value of a subject. How marketable a subject is depends on
> the cashable value of its qualifications. The children are very aware of this.

The problem of being associated with a 'low-status' subject has career implications
which have become painfully clear to Bob himself:

> I'm very disillusioned about my own future. Well it hasn't given me a future after
> five years so I can't see that it will suddenly give me a future in the next few years.
> I don't think I could have done much more than I have done. I got involved with
> the county syllabus, had a lot of contacts with the European Resources Centre,
> one thing and another, and I thought this can only be of benefit to my career. But
> it's been going on and I've been doing things and doing things and it's done me
> no good whatsoever. You know I'm still where I was when I came here and that
> was seven years ago! I just don't know really . . . obviously I've become disillu-
> sioned, disheartened. I may have to move out of the subject altogether . . . go back
> to geography or the pastoral side. But it's not what I really want to do. (. . .) If
> you go looking for a job and say you've been Head of European Studies you don't
> get very far!

Because of his own experience Bob is rather pessimistic about the future of European studies not only in his own school but in general:

> European studies is always going to survive here I think . . . as long as I'm here,
> but I'm very doubtful about its future unless it becomes a common core subject.
> There's a lot of curriculum change going on at the moment and the possibility of
> the common core is very much the in-thing. European Studies appeared at a time
> when the rationale was for hugh, wide-open options which we still operate here as
> a matter of fact. The number of subjects available here is incredible yet they can
> only choose six to follow. As things start being chiselled down as it were, I think
> European studies has got to find its place as a free option soon otherwise it will
> disappear. I don't think it's got a tremendous future, if only because it won't be
> accepted by other departments . . . it's sort of . . . tainted in some way. It's got the
> mark on it (LAUGHTER) . . . the voodoo sign!

Bob's situation and his comments highlight what perhaps is the crucial factor
militating against any large-scale future development of European studies: that
being associated with a subject which has not achieved full academic respectability

and comparability with the established disciplines can adversely affect a teacher's career prospects and consequently his/her morale. This could result in the most energetic, committed and enthusiastic teachers such as Bob, reluctantly abandoning a subject they have painstakingly built up to return to former specialisms which seem to hold greater chances of future advancement (Goodson and McGivney, 1984).

External Opinions

New subjects to promote their case beyond the confines of the individual school have to persuade a wider 'external constituency' (*ibid*) made up of parents, employers and the universities.

All teachers involved in the introduction of European studies referred to the important role played by parental opinion. One of the problems consistently faced by new subjects in the secondary school is parental unfamiliarity and distrust:

> Well just to confirm the fact that there are difficulties to start with because when we offered this subject at first there was considerable resistance. Parents saying my child is not doing this new-fangled invention . . .

Several teachers speculated on the reasons for parental distrust:

> I think that people are suspicious you know . . . I think that they think this is not going to be academically acceptable . . . this is something that somebody had dreamt up, this is an artificial thing, contrived . . . it isn't something I can easily understand like geography or history, French and things . . .

> And I think another thing, I think people are tired of hearing things with studies on the end. I think we'll end up teaching something with a better title . . . we could do with a new term.

> The most common problem I had was parents saying my child is not doing this because it is a CSE and the fact that grade 1 is equivalent to 'O' level doesn't cut any ice . . .

> Above all the parents judge what's going on at school from their own experience and their own experience was the three 'Rs' plus if they were lucky drawing in the afternoon . . . and anything that's outside of that is extravagant.

Partly the parental opposition to innovational curricula was shared by the employers, partly indeed the parents' opposition derives from an awareness of employers likely antipathy.

> Our local employers have got a built-in prejudice against CSE — they want 'O's and 'A's to prove the child is good.

Several of the teachers appreciating the crucial importance of gaining parental support, opted for a policy of positive canvassing:

I campaigned in the third year at the parents open meeting . . . the Head always talks, not usually the staff . . . anyhow I stood up and talked about the new subject. I said it will offer an 'O' level pass for suitable candidates* in the option scheme beginning in the fourth year.

I went to the parents evening with copies of the aims and objectives of my European studies course. I handed it out at the door . . . well I had to make it sound attractive . . . the staff all made jokes, said it was the 'hard sell' . . . but it must have worked I got twenty-six children and at the time it was badly paired . . . 'A' band had 'O' level history paired against it.

European Studies as a 'Scholarly Discipline'

Many studies of school subjects have highlighted the substantial importance of the universities both (i) as 'customers' and 'recruiters' of those trained in a range of subjects at school and (ii) as definers of 'overarching disciplines' with high status.

These two aspects are often juxtaposed as the following quote illustrated. The university in question initially set up its own 'School of European Studies' but:

> after the mid-seventies once the attraction of 'new' universities started to decline we suffered a year by year decline in applications and in quality of applicants. We eventually changed the name of our school of European studies as a result of a new range of language-based courses. But we were influenced in reaching this decision by our own survey in selected secondary schools which almost universally demonstrated the 'low status' of European studies both amongst teachers and pupils. Our fortunes in both quantity and quality of applications have changed dramatically for the better since that time. (*ibid*)

As was noted in the case of environmental studies there was almost a chicken and egg game being played with regard to status. Essentially until the university develops a disciplinary definition of a new subject it will be perceived as an idiosyncratic school-based synthesis and hence of low status. This early stage can only be transcended if university scholars aid in the definition of a new synthesis. But as we can see in the quote above the initial stages of low status often act to 'warn off' such university scholars.

The conclusions of the state of the art with regard to European studies in higher education were recently drawn as follows:

> Certainly there is no single definitive model of a European studies course in universities, colleges and polytechnics although it is easy to identify the subjects which characteristically contribute most to such courses: languages, social sciences and history. There are in fact a number of different course models: European studies can for example provide a whole organising structure within which main

---

* This school, an East Anglian High School, offered the AEB exam.

degrees are provided (Sussex); it can be an integrated scheme composed of tightly focussed units deriving from European themes and leading to a single European Studies award (UMIST); it can be based on different subjects rather than themes, emphasize basic skills and have a vocational bias (Bath, Bradford). Several other models can be identified.

The range of possibilities, which is inevitable because of the scope of the subjects, led one speaker at a UACES conference in Lancaster in 1981 to refer to European studies as a 'humpty dumpty' subject; i.e. it can mean whatever people choose it to mean. Another participant pointed out that this can lead to the provision of too many course options which may not necessarily compose a coherent whole.

The haphazard and idiosyncratic nature of European studies in higher education at the current time is clearly evident. The reasons for this whilst partly related to social and 'political' factors also involve intellectual and epistemological considerations which are not dealt with herein. The important factor is that the implications of having no overarching 'scholarly discipline' definitions are crucial at school level. With such a vacuum at the 'top' effective change from the bottom is 'contained'. The universities in this case can act as final 'gatekeepers' and serve to ensure that restructuring innovations at subject level do not enter the educational system.

Without the prospect of any general definition and legitimation of a new subject at university level the new contender for subject status is left fighting a series of encapsulated battles within individual schools. Over time the micropolitical issues and perceptions summarized in this chapter will serve to ensure the initiative is not sustained over time. With no prospects of broadening the base beyond individual school definitions or isolated examination courses teachers draw negative 'conclusions' about the subject's viability and it's career-enhancing potential. A micropolitical 'war of attrition' leads to an inevitable defeat for the new contender.

Acknowledgement

This chapter arises from work carried out on the Europe in the School Project 1979–1984. My co-worker on this, Dr. V. McGivney, shared the work on this project and is in a real sense a co-author of this chapter.

Notes

1 Civics and European Education (6 October 1964), resolutions adopted by Minister Deputies at the Council of Europe.
2 *The Humanities Project: An Introduction* (1972) London, Heinemann, p. 1.
3 The 1982 edition has two misprints in the sector quoted.
4 *European Studies in East and West Sussex* (1977), an LEA survey.
5 See the work of John Meyer as reformulated for the English context by Reid (1984), pp. 67–75.

References

CACE (1963) *Half Our Future* (The Newsom Report), London: HMSO.

GOLDSMITHS COLLEGE (1965) *The Raising of the School Leaving Age, Second Pilot Course for Experienced Teachers*, London: University of London Press.

GOODSON, I.F. (1993) *School Subjects and Curriculum Change* (3rd ed), London: Falmer Press.

GOODSON, I.F. and MACGIVNEY, V. (1984) *Europe in the School, Research Project*, University of Sussex: mimeo.

JOTTERAND, R. (1966) *Introducing Europe to Senior Pupils*, Council for Cultural Cooperation of the Council of Europe.

LAMBERT, G. and GARDNER, N. (1975) 'Attitudes and Motivation in Modern Language Learning', quoted in LAWRENCE, F. (ed.) *Modern Languages and European Studies*, Falmer: University of Sussex.

SHIPMAN, M. (1971) 'Curriculum for Inequality', in HOOPER, R. (ed.) *The Curriculum: Context, Design and Development*, Edinburgh: Oliver and Boyd.

WARWICK, D. (1972) *Team Teaching*, London: University of London Press.

WILLIAMS, W. (1977) *Teaching European Studies*, London: Heinemann.

YOUNG, M.F.D. (1971c) 'Curricula as socially organised knowledge', in YOUNG, M.F.D. (ed.) *Knowledge and Control*, London: Collier-Macmillan.

5 On Explaining Curriculum Change: H.B. Beal, Organizational Categories and the Rhetoric of Justification

(*with Christopher Anstead*)

Introduction

This chapter focusses on one episode of curriculum change, in a Canadian school in the early twentieth century. The episode is part of a much broader matrix of social structure and change. Likewise, this chapter is part of a much broader study of schooling within the context of vocationalism and of early twentieth century Canadian society. In *Through the Schoolhouse Door* (Goodson and Anstead, 1993), we seek to provide a commentary on these wider contexts but here our focus is both time and context specific. The dangers in representing such a specific episode are clear: it may read like the story of one 'great man' (a dying genre) or of bounded internal curriculum change in one school. Nothing could be further from the truth: this is a story of agency *and* structure. This story then is part of our wider story and part of the wider social landscape and must be read against the background of this wider commentary and viewpoint.

But if the story feeds off wider contexts and commentaries, so too do the contemporary actors feed off wider definitions and directions. In a sense, this is an account of how internal school curriculum change is mediated by educational actors who employ the rhetorics and reforms which emanate from the wider society to pursue agendas within their workplace and locality. Leftist accounts of schooling often see the state or bureaucracy or industry as 'dominant interest groups' who legislate reforms for the schools. But such domination seldom reaches beyond the schoolhouse door — behind which the school change is mediated. In an earlier study Goodson argued 'it is perhaps useful to distinguish between domination and structure and mechanism and mediation' (Goodson, 1993, p. 192). So we believe is the case in this account.

An Episode in School Curricular Change

The turn of the century was a time of turmoil in Canadian society. Changes in the economic organization of society had brought cultural assumptions dominant since mid-century into question. In Victorian times, the liberal, respectable professionals and their emulators had dominated cultural discourse in Canada. Now a new group took the reins of the middle class. Though by no means a monolithic group, businessmen, with their emphasis on efficiency, management, and scientific rationality, began to challenge the cultural discourse of the professionals. Their views could more easily coalesce with those of increasingly vocal subordinate groups. Women, workers, and immigrants could support, or be brought to accept, a new consensus which included — besides 'business-like management' — social reform, domestic feminism, imperialism, and a combination of paternalism and coercion in industrial relations.[1]

Vocationalism — broadly, the idea that schools should prepare students for work, and specifically, for industrial work — appeared as the educational component of this world view. It brought scientific rationality to schools, while opening them up to the children of subordinate groups.[2] Vocationalism drew its theoretical support from the ideology of 'social efficiency' — a school of educational thought which first emerged in the 1890s, taking inspiration from F.W. Taylor's theories of 'scientific management'. According to this approach, efficient schools should fit students for their future lives in the workplace; efficient educators should determine what the local society and economy needed, find students most suited to these roles, and train them in their future functions, without any extra, useless education. Social efficiency supporters attacked the existing emphasis on university preparation in secondary schools as inefficient, and alienating to the vast majority of students. Once in place, an efficient school system would contribute to a stable society, in which many of the new evils arising in the cities could be eradicated (Kliebard, 1986). Of course, the focus on dividing student bodies through special programmes leading to disparate life outcomes demanded the sacrifice of individual equality of opportunity to the greater good of social efficiency. At the same time, the class, race and gender bias built into the sorting process made vocationalism more appealing to some supporters of the existing matrix of schooling.

Social efficiency educational reform developed through a 'coalition' of support. Three powerful constituencies have been discerned in the battle for vocationalism and social efficiency schooling at the provincial level, and in London. Firstly, capital was represented by the Canadian Manufacturers Association. The CMA was impressed with the potential of technical schooling to improve the productive skills of, and impose a form of institutional discipline on, the children of the working class. Yet it was also fearful that this type of schooling might reduce the distances between the social classes by expanding the opportunities of the working classes for socioeconomic mobility. Like their counterparts in Europe, the wealthy and the industrial and commercial bourgeoisie of Canada were willing to accept secondary schooling for the masses as long as it sharply distinguished between 'liberal' and practical styles of schooling. This, they hoped, would have the effect of perpetuating and legitimating the social differences among classes through schooling, that is, exploiting the capacity of educational systems to invest social distinctions with 'cultural meanings'.

Reformers among the educational bureaucracy also the supported social efficiency theory, although they were far from in a majority. Their agenda differed from the manufacturers in quite distinct ways as we shall see later. The educational reformers were concerned to obviate the status distinctions between vocational and academic schooling because they rightly saw that their career opportunities and material self-interest hinged on bridging this status divide. These educational groups tended to view the social efficiency movement as a new career opportunity and one with a promise of enhancement in personal and professional terms. Their concern, therefore, was to establish parity with academic forms of secondary schooling.

A third group comprised organized labour particularly as represented by the Trades and Labour Council. Organized labour, whilst extremely suspicious of the manufacturers, broadly supported the schooling which trained people in trades as long as it was placed under public control rather than undertaken privately in industrial organizations.

> The compromise among these three groups, the CMA, the educators and the TLC, smoothed the way for the Industrial Education Act, passed by the Ontario provincial legislature in 1911. In brief, the Act authorised municipalities to establish a form of amplified schooling which complemented the already existing programmes in manual training and domestic science at the elementary and secondary levels and commercial education in certain high schools. The most important feature of the Act was that it promised provincial funding for industrial education, enabling municipalities across the province to offer technical classes for adolescents beyond the school-leaving age of 14. (Goodson and Dowbiggin, 1991, p. 43)

In Ontario, those seeking to change education towards social efficiency ideals faced certain difficulties. Some members of the entrenched educational bureaucracy had not yet been won over by the move to business ideals. Instead, with individual exceptions, they clung to the world view which had brought them their power — a world view which tied directly back to Egerton Ryerson, the supreme Victorian authority in all matters educational.[3] For more than a decade, supporters of vocational education waged a relentless campaign for reform (Stamp, 1970). Eventually provincial and federal legislators, increasingly sympathetic to the calls for the efficient management of society, passed legislation which led to course realignment in myriad institutions, as well as the creation of dozens of new schools. While an important step, government funding for special programmes and institutions did not represent the broad victory sought by the vocational movement.

The story of Herbert Benson Beal, and his struggle to reform education in London, Ontario, provides one detailed example from the struggle for vocational education. Beal joined the London Board of Education in the dying years of the nineteenth century; over the next decade, he worked his way to the principalship of one of the city's elementary schools, and earned an administrative position at the city's Model School.[4] The most crucial aspect of his career was his experience as a student at Teachers College, University of Columbia, where Beal encountered some of the leading lights in the new social efficiency movement (Goodson and Dowbiggin, 1991, pp. 39–60; Kliebard, 1986). At this time, Teachers College was a major centre for the teaching and promotion of social efficiency ideas especially as seen in the work of David Sneddon.

Lobbied by Beal and like-minded supporters, the London Board of Education agreed to establish a terminal vocational secondary school in the city in 1912. The Board listed the London Industrial School's purpose as follows:

> ... the object of this school shall be to provide for those engaged in the local industries a broader training than it is possible to obtain in the shops under modern industrial conditions, by giving them the opportunity of gaining practice in a greater variety of processes than would be open to any one person under the modern system of production and by teaching the theory and principles underlying the trades and so prepare them for advancement in their chosen line of work.[5]

For more than two decades, Beal, as Principal of this School, under the nominal supervision of the Advisory Industrial Committee (AIC) — a Sub-committee of the city's Board of Education and a body which Beal in fact dominated — possessed wide powers to introduce changes in the curriculum, in the public discourse of schooling, and in the institutional framework as it affected his school. The way Beal took advantage of these opportunities reveals both the ideological and the practical sides of his nature.

At the level of the classroom, Beal sought to emphasize practical work, and to eliminate what he described as boring — and thus alienating — or simply unnecessary aspects of education. All students spent most of their time involved in practical subjects — which after 1921 included commercial studies. While Beal agreed with the necessity of teaching some traditional academic subjects, he instructed his staff to present them in a way related to the practical side of the curriculum. History lessons, for instance, should focus on the history of production.[6] Classroom teaching at the school remained committed to this sort of curriculum during the whole of Beal's twenty-three year tenure as Principal.

Beal departed from dominant norms of curriculum making in another way. He preferred to take his cue from local employers or workers rather than any self-proclaimed expert on curriculum. Before the establishment of regular courses, Beal frequently responded to groups of workers who requested classes in a specific aspect of their trade. As one example among many, in the fall of 1913, Beal approved new evening classes in theory of electrical work and sheet metal draughting on these grounds.[7]

Beal continually emphasized this commitment to lay participation in curriculum making. In 1921, he said:

> It has been the policy of the school to invite suggestions from manufacturers, superintendents and foremen, especially those who come in contact with the graduates of our school. The greatest attention is given to their opinions in order that our courses of study might be strengthened and adapted as far as possible to actual requirements . . .[8]

Three years later, he formalized this arrangement by appointing a 'coordinating officer' who visited former students at their workplace to see how the training at the school could be improved, by soliciting the opinions of the former students and their employers.[9]

While Beal sought to introduce these changes to the secondary curriculum, he also challenged the existing emphasis on liberal education aimed at a professional elite. His rhetoric, drawn straight from the social efficiency movement, constantly emphasized that his school aimed at efficiently training carefully selected students 'directly interested in Industrial occupations'.[10] Throughout his principalship, he maintained a continuous discourse of efficiency. The focus on efficient social goals is evident in such statements as the claim, in 1920, that: '. . . an analysis of the registration shows that the school is reaching the class of students to whose needs it is specially fitted to cater'.[11]

A decade later, Beal's reaction to the Depression illustrated his unchanged commitment to the doctrine of social efficiency.

What should be the policy in times of depression like the present? It would manifestly be unwise to carry out the full placement program during such times. Care should be taken to distinguish between unemployment that is caused by the depression and technological unemployment, by which is meant the unemployment caused by the replacement of man-power by machines and mechanical devices. This latter employment will not return and schools should no longer prepare students for occupations thus rendered obsolete, but unemployment due to the general depression is temporary, and wisdom would dictate that we make careful preparation for the return of normal times. (quoted in the *London Free Press*, 16 May 1933)

This attitude towards the school's purpose often set Beal's opinions apart from those of his more traditional colleagues; it meant, for instance, that Beal did not object to students quitting in the middle of their senior classes. In fact, he used figures for the destination of such students to claim aggressively that his school was doing its job, preparing students 'for success in productive occupations . . .'.[12]

This legitimating rhetoric did not only emanate from Beal, it found reflection in the support of outsiders, of most AIC members, and of his teachers. Through the latter group of intermediaries, the social efficiency argument made its way into the viewpoint of the school's students, as notebooks and yearbooks illustrated. Thus one student writing in the 1929 Yearbook, claimed that the workforce makes two demands of a young man: that he be proficient enough in some vocation as to be of immediate value to his employer, and that he has a general education which will allow him to become 'a sane conservative citizen' (LTCHS, 1929, p. 8). (What the workplace demanded of a young women went unexamined.)

Besides challenging existing curriculum and rhetoric, Beal's school at first seemed to provide a clear example for social efficiency thinking which questioned the structural framework of secondary education. For most of the first decade of the London Industrial School's existence, its staff did not arrange 'definite courses of study'. Students were separated by gender, but not by grade or major course followed. Subject boundaries remained vague. The school also followed critical attacks on the social value of university preparation courses by offering none. In fact, this had played a crucial role in the school's establishment. A powerful segment of London's social and economic elite still maintained a 'Victorian' world view, and supported the school because they saw it as a way of reducing crowding in the university preparation courses at the Collegiate Institute (Goodson and Dowbiggin, 1991). All the early proponents expected the London Industrial School to be a terminal institution preparing students for their lives in London's industrial economy.

Despite these beginnings, within eight years of the school's founding, its free and unstructured atmosphere had been replaced by all the traditional framework of grades, subjects and courses. This new format included the subjects and classes that had previously been used as part of generalized technical and industrial courses; it also included a new university preparation course. The matriculation course was aimed at those students possessing High School Entrance standing and intending to take engineering or domestic science at a university. The most noticeable innovations involved in this course comprised the addition of Latin and French to the subjects taken by technical students, and the extension of the course of study to five years.[13] Did this represent a defeat for Beal? To find the answer to that question, it is necessary to consider curriculum change in a broader way.

On Explaining Curriculum Change

The addition of matriculation courses at Beal School provides an example of curriculum change which was at odds with the early 'rhetorics of justification' for the school. Curriculum change which challenges foundational rhetoric is often associated with the power of 'external constituencies'. The notion of the power and influence of external constituencies or 'publics' is derived from the work of John Meyer. In his work:

> . . . external forces and structures emerge, not merely as sources of ideas, promptings, inducements and constraints but as definers and carriers of the categories of content, role and activity to which the practice of schools must approximate in order to attract support and legitimation. (Reid, 1984, p. 68)

Support and legitimation are often expressed through the existing patterns of structuration — in particular the way in which finance and resources are structured and allocated (Cohen, 1990).

The emergence and evolution of technical schooling however took place within an established 'matrix' of schooling in London. A new, somewhat messianic initiative like Herbert Beal's was able to establish a new school but the existing pattern of structuration provided a continuing logic of legitimation. Meyer (1980) has commented on the strategic requirement of legitimation if finances and resources are to be acquired and higher status achieved.

> The main problem for the administrator, if learning and participation are to be sustained, is to clearly link a particular educational organization or programme to this wider institutional system. The school must be wholly accredited in everyone's eyes, or commitment and resources will rapidly decline. Ideally, it should be accredited as properly within a nationwide category of schools of general meaning and substantial allocation power — for example, it is better to be a college than

a junior college, better to be a general high school than a vocational school, and so on. Much organizational activity must be devoted to maintaining institutional legitimacy. A stock of properly credentialed teachers is necessary, along with approved facilities and students who are themselves appropriately defined and credentialed. (p. 48)

Meyer argues that this pattern leads towards a conformity in the 'categorical' categories of schooling: 'As a result, schools and curricula and courses tend toward isomorphism with national systems of categories' (*ibid*, p. 49).

The force of categorical type and the tendency for innovations to 'regress' to the categorical norm can be illustrated in the case of Beal School. Here we can see evidence of a school founded to pursue a vocational rhetoric of social efficiency wrestling with the dominant system of status linked to academic 'high schools'. By 1918, Herbert Beal was beginning to realize the problems of status and resources which arise from innovation and categorical deviance. In an unpublished memo to the Chairman and members of the Advisory Industrial Committee of the Board of Education, he noted:

There are difficulties in the way of the school receiving the patronage of those who would profit from the courses provided that I should be lacking in my duty did I not bring them to the attention of the Committee at this time.

In the first place you will recognize the fact that habit is one of the strongest motives in our lives and there is an educational habit in this Province that has been confirmed by generations. It has been the custom for boys and girls to proceed from the kindergarten to the public school, thence to the high school and thence to the university. It was the boast of our educational system that it led from the kindergarten to the university. This time honoured habit is naturally followed by parents in selecting courses for their children in many cases without sufficient thought as to whether it is the most profitable course for the child to pursue. The problem is to induce the parent to select the course best suited to the needs of the child rather than to follow the custom referred to.

The second difficulty is to bring the parents of the city to the realization of the true character of the courses of study provided in a technical school. There is a popular idea that technical schools are for a class of more or less unfortunate pupils who are below the average mentally and that the courses judged from an academic standard are second class. Nothing could be further from the truth, but as long as this idea prevails the school will not receive the patronage it deserves.[14]

Beal School in its early years was therefore suffering from its deviance from the established understandings of external publics — at a certain age it was assumed that wherever possible a child would progress through to the high school and from there to the university. This structure was a 'time honoured habit', a traditional assumption.

Beal's dilemma therefore was to either defend its social efficiency, vocational principles and risk marginalization and a diminution of status and resources, or find a way of joining the categorical type, the 'high school'. But to join the high school category inevitably meant joining the 'matriculation' process. Curriculum change it seems was driven by the pursuit of resources and status, indeed by the very need for institutional survival. As early as 1917 Beal had argued:

> No school can be managed economically without a sufficient number of students to allow proper classification. This is impossible with our present accommodation. In order to have one class of boys and one class of girls for first year both technical and industrial each of the size required to economically handle them in academic subjects we would require to have thirty boys and thirty girls with High School Entrance standing and thirty boys and thirty girls without High School Entrance standing. This is 120 first year day students equally divided and this makes no allowance for shrinkage in the second year. This number could not be accommodated, but even this would leave no room for second and third year students. Classes of the same size in the second and third year are required to be economically carried on so that at the very least 200 to 300 students are required before anything like an economical classification can be made. At the present we have two academic class rooms provided for our use. You will see how impossible it is to economically conduct a school with our present accommodation especially when the Education Department requires that teachers with specialist qualifications shall be engaged.[15]

By this time then Beal faced three interlinked problems, stated very succinctly in a 1918 memo:

> The problem of the organization of the work for the new building for September next presents three phases, namely: — 1. What students will attend? 2. What courses of study shall be provided? 3. What instructors shall be secured? You will see that these questions are interdependent. The number and character of instructors required will depend on the courses to be provided and these in turn upon the number of students in attendance. The number of students will likewise depend on the character of the courses offered. Moreover competent teachers and instructors for technical schools are exceedingly hard to procure. They are required by departmental regulations to have all the qualifications of high school teachers and in addition to possess such a knowledge of industrial processes and practice as to be able to correlate the academic studies with the practical work. Such a combination is not easy to find and such instructors cannot be secured on a moment's notice. It is therefore necessary that the question of the organization of the school should be considered with the greatest care and definitely decided upon as early in the year as possible if the school is to be ready for opening in September next.[16]

Beal then goes on to itemize the kinds of students and courses he now thinks are required. For the first time this includes the requirement of matriculation courses. Three kinds of day school courses are listed:

1   We may expect to receive boys and girls from the higher grades of the public schools (Canadian state elementary schools) to whose needs the regular Public School curriculum does not directly cater. These are more numerous than is generally supposed. We have it on the authority of the Education Department that our industries are recruited mainly from the boys and girls who do not go

further than the sixth grade. This is a very serious handicap to the success of Canadian industries and to the life usefulness of the boys and girls who leave school so unprepared. By providing courses specially suited to the needs of these boys and girls their school life could be lengthened by from one to three years and their whole life career correspondingly improved. It was from the representation of the Superintendent of Education of this failure on the part of the public schools to hold boys and girls till they had received sufficient education to prepare them for a successful life career and useful citizenship that the Education Department decided to establish general industrial courses in connection with technical school.

2   The second class of boys and girls attending are those who now attend the collegiate institutes and high schools but who do not propose taking departmental examinations or prepare for the learned professions other than engineering and technology. It has been the experience of principals of collegiate institutes and educationalists in general that there is a pressing need for special courses for these students who are not employing their time as profitably as they might under present high school courses. They should be provided with a course which retains all the cultural value of the present high school course and combines with it a liberal allowance of technical work for boys and of domestic training for girls. In establishing these technical courses for boys and girls the question arose whether they should be given in collegiate institutes or in separate institutions, such as technical schools. The reasons for separating them were that while they were to retain all the cultural value of an academic course yet the technical work was of such importance and the whole course to fulfil its object, namely, to lead towards the higher directive positions in the industries, required distinctive courses. The teachers moreover, even of academic studies, must primarily have an interest in and a first hand knowledge of industrial conditions. The mathematics must be applied rather than demonstrated. The science must have direct application to industrial processes which could hardly be expected in an institution conducted primarily for cultural courses. The atmosphere of the courses must be such as to create an attraction towards and respect for industrial occupations. For these reasons technical courses in separate institutions for this class of students are advisable.

3   The third class of students attending should be boys with High School Entrance standing desirous of obtaining matriculation for the School of Practical Science and girls with the same standing desiring matriculation for the Household Science Departments of the university and those desiring to prepare themselves for higher technical institutions of university standing. A regular matriculation course combined with special draughting and mathematics courses and special home economics courses for girls should be provided for this class of students.[17]

Beal's strategy for course redefinition and curriculum change appeared then to be a response to two major problems he was encountering. Firstly, the limited and specific type of student the school was attracting which derived from 'the popular idea the technical schools are for a class of more or less unfortunate pupils who are below the average mentally'. Secondly, and associated with this problem, the obvious difficulty Beal was having in acquiring properly qualified teaching staff. Beal's response to these two problems which threatened the very survival of the school was clearly stated by 1918:

> The Education Department has insisted that the qualifications of teachers for technical schools shall be equal to that of collegiate institutes and the courses of study while different in character are in no way below the standard of collegiate institutes. It is indispensable to the success of your technical school that it is placed on an equality with other school in the estimation of the public. (*ibid*, pp. 114–5)

As we have seen, 'the public' had a view of high schools as an academic 'categorical type' leading on to university. Hence, to have any claim to the high school category and to 'equality of estimation', Beal had to develop matriculation courses. Hence, curriculum change resulted from a desire for 'parity of esteem' and equality of status resources and finance. Beal's memo of 31 January 1919, states the problem clearly:

> There will be a number of important problems to be considered by the Committee during the year. The first of these will be the ratification of the length and character of the classes of study. The arrangement of permanent courses of study was impossible under the conditions obtaining in the old building, but should be definitely decided and a proper calendar of the school issued this year. In order to do this, and from the fact that the most of the progressive younger teachers in the Province are teaching on interim certificates, which are made permanent by successful teaching experience in a school approved by the Educational Department, it is therefore of importance, if the school is to attract to its staff, the most desirable teachers, that it should receive the standing of a technical high school.

He therefore recommends 'that the Board of Education be requested to make application to the Department of Education for the school to be given the standing of a technical high school'.[18] Hence, Beal finally seals the campaign to join the categorical type of 'high school.'

Beal and the AIC had been expecting the Department to confer official high school status on the Technical School in the fall of 1919, a gesture that would have enabled the school to offer matriculation courses for students who wished to attend post-secondary faculties of engineering and domestic science, and hence improve its chances of enrolling students who might otherwise attend LCI. Yet the Department of Education hesitated to approve the measure because the new Headmaster, who served under Principal Beal, supposedly did not have the proper qualifications for his position. This can be clearly seen in comparing the memos of 19 May and 7 October (see appendices 1 and 2). The Department's delay provoked a heated response from W.N. Manning, the AIC Chairman. He complained to the Department that the delay jeopardized the Board of Education's recent effort 'to attract to our school some of those in the Collegiate Institute who would profit most by the technical school course'. More ominously, Manning stated, the Department's actions threatened to 'give aid to those who are opposing technical education in

London'. To Manning the risks the Department was taking were substantial. Its action, he argued:

> . . . has precipitated a crisis in the affairs of our (technical) school as the Board (of Education) has always had considerable criticism of its building programme and at the present time our Mayor is publicly advocating the use of the technical school building for academic high school work . . . I must frankly admit that the continuance of the school is seriously endangered at the present time and a continuance of hair splitting over regulations will tend to increase the likelihoods of the building being turned over to pure academic high school purposes and a discontinuance of any further attempt to provide technical and industrial education in London.[19]

Manning's letter coaxed the Department on 7 October 1919 into approving the Technical School's new Headmaster and the school became the London Technical High School (Goodson and Dowbiggin, 1991, pp. 39–60).

Thus Beal and his allies had to accept external definitions of institutional categories if they were to seek the resources that accompanied legitimacy; this did not, however, negate the whole social efficiency thrust of Beal's campaign. Though Beal did not do away with what some supporters of social efficiency saw as an irrelevant set of traditional structures, he did ensure that these structures supported his other ideals. In the new London Technical High School (granted that status in late 1919) Beal was supreme, his own status having been raised, as Principal of a high school. Thus, when Beal and the AIC considered establishing a Printing Department, they undertook the following tasks:

> . . . we have considered the local need for training boys to enter the printing trade, have visited the printing departments of other vocational schools, have consulted those engaged in the local trade, both as employers and employees and have considered the value of such training as a department of the present Technical High School course.[20]

When the Committee came up with a planned course, they submitted it to a 'representative meeting of employers and employees of the printing trade in the City' for approval.

Another piece of evidence supports the notion that Beal had little real commitment to the hegemonic structure he had accepted. If the changes of 1918/19 meant more than a simple accommodation to prevailing methods of legitimation, then the centrepiece was the establishment of a university preparation course, which took its first students in September 1919. Yet in reality, over the next two decades, few students took the programme, and few completed it. To start with, no more than 10 per cent of the first-year class of a given year enrolled in the matriculation course (see table 1). A very low rate of success exacerbated the initial lack of size. Each year saw wholesale decrease in the matriculation class through transfer, quitting and failure.[21] With this sort of attrition, the upper classes remained tiny. In 1924, the combined size of the third and fourth-year classes in the matriculation programme was only twenty-three students.[22] Obviously, Beal and his staff saw no reason to try to boost participation in this option.

Table 1: *Percentage of students entering first year of a general course, at four-year intervals*

Year	Technical	Commercial*	Matriculation	n =
1919	90.9%	—	9.1%	55
1923	54.4%	35.2%	10.4%	270
1927	37.1%	58.1%	4.8%	105
1931	49.5%	43.3%	7.3%	386
1935	61.1%	32.6%	6.3%	720

* Commercial Courses were not offered in 1919.
Source: SRC

Conclusion

What are we to make of these episodes in the evolution of the school which now bears Beal's name? Looked at from the viewpoint of Beal's original ideals, the end result seems an uneasy compromise. His school became a mix of socially efficient curriculum and rhetoric, resting ultimately on an 'inefficient' traditional framework. Yet a closer look leads to the impression that Beal, while certainly an idealist, was also strategically sophisticated. Beal accepted the cultural and political necessity of the traditional framework; he accepted that the rhetoric of justification had to include both social efficiency and institutionalized categories, despite the inherent contradictions.

Beal's actions seem to support Meyer's argument that it is easier to change some aspects of educational systems than others. In particular, institutionalized definitions of matters such as courses, types of students or subjects, are the most resistant to change. Beal, like other reformers, realized that the educational bureaucracy still maintained a high degree of control over the framework of schooling, if not over the actual practice of teaching. While Beal did not challenge the traditional structures, and indeed took advantage of them, he did make the changes which would have the greatest effects on the education of his students. As an informed actor, knowledgeable about some of the constraints upon him, Beal managed to achieve significant victories in building up his school programmes, in attracting resources and in acquiring status for both the teachers and the school.

Curriculum change then is embedded within wider patterns of structuration and strategic contestation. To understand the intentions of curriculum redefinition it is necessary both to explore the internal micropolitics of the school and the external manouverings for institutional and political legitimation. Each curricular change serves to reflect the mediation between internal and external milieu and to signify historic compromise according to the conditions of time and place. As such, curricular inquiry might best be conducted through socio/historical investigation — a form of investigation that has to date been somewhat underrepresented in a field that has too often viewed curriculum study as a mode of technical-rational implementation. Hopefully through historical study we can approach the complexity of the underpinning social and political process.

Notes

1 The foregoing description is not yet an accepted interpretation of Canadian history, though some Canadian historians, such as Lenskyj (1983) and Walden (1989), pp. 285–310, have moved in this direction. Instead, this interpretation draws from the example of American and British historians such as Smith-Rosenberg (1985), Blumin (1985) and Gray (1977).

2 Cremin (1961), Stamp (1970), Lazerson and Grubb (1974) Bowles and Gintis (1976), Lazerson and Dunn (1977), Kantor (1988) and Powers (1992).

3 On Victorian education in Ontario, see Gidney and Miller (1990), Houston and Prentice (1988) and Curtis (1988).

4 Board of Education for the City of London (1909a) *Annual Reports of the Board of Education for the City of London.*

5 Advisory Industrial Committee (AIC) of the London Board of Education (5 December 1991) *Minutes of the Advisory Industrial Committee* (typescript).

6 See, for example, AIC (1918) *Minutes of the Advisory Industrial Committee*, p. 113; London Technical and Commercial High School (1925) pp. 7–8 and (1933) pp. 6–7.

7 AIC (1913) *Minutes of the Advisory Industrial Committee* (typescript).

8 Advisory Vocational Committee (AVC) of the London Board of Education (1921) *Minutes of the Advisory Vocational Committee* (typescript), p. 55.

9 AVC (1924) *Minutes of the Advisory Vocational Committee* (typescript).

10 AIC (1919) *Minutes of the Advisory Industrial Committee* (typescript), p. 125.

11 AIC (1920) *Minutes of the Advisory Industrial Committee* (typescript), p. 167.

12 AIC (1922–3) *Minutes of the Advisory Industrial Committee* (typescript).

13 Board of Education for the City of London (1918a) *Annual Reports of the Board of Education for the City of London.*

14 AIC (1918) *Minutes of the Advisory Industrial Committee* (typescript), p. 114.

15 AIC (1917) *Minutes of the Advisory Industrial Committee* (typescript), pp. 78–9.

16 AIC (1918) *Minutes of the Advisory Industrial Committee* (typescript), p. 112.

17 *ibid*, pp. 112–13.

18 AIC (1919) *Minutes of the Advisory Industrial Committee* (typescript), pp. 132–3.

19 Board of Education for the City of London (1919b) *Minutes of the Board of Education for the City of London, London*, Board of Education, pp. 162–3.

20 AVC (1924) *Minutes of the Advisory Vocational Committee* (typescript), p. 36.

21 For instance, according to student record cards from the London Technical and Commercial High School, of the ninety-seven students entering the matriculation program, either directly in first year, or by transfer at more senior years, for the school years starting in 1927 and 1928, only nine completed the full five years, while another eleven completed the fourth year.

22 AVC (1924) *Minutes of the Advisory Vocational Committee* (typescript).

References

COHEN, I.J. (1990) 'Structuration theory and social order: Five issues in brief', in CLARK, J. *et al* (eds) *Anthony Giddens: Consensus and Controversy*, London: Falmer Press.

GOODSON, I.F. (1993) *School Subjects and Curriculum Change* (3rd ed), London: Falmer Press.

GOODSON, I.F. and ANSTEAD, C.J. (1993) *Through the Schoolhouse Door*, Toronto: Garamond Press.

GOODSON, I.F. and DOWBIGGIN, I.R. (1991) 'Vocational education and school reform: The case of the London (Canada) technical school, 1900–1930', *History of Education Review*, **20**, 1.

KLIEBARD, H. (1986) *The Struggle for the American Curriculum 1893–1958*, London: Routledge and Kegan Paul.

LONDON TECHNICAL AND COMMERCIAL HIGH SCHOOL (LTCHS) (1929) *The Tecalogue*, London: LTCHS.

MEYER, J. (1980) 'Levels of the educational system and schooling effects', in BIDWELL, C.E. and WINDHAM, D.M. (eds) *Analysis of Education Productivity, Volume 2 Issues in Macroanalysis*, Cambridge: Ballinger.

REID, W.A. (1984) 'Curricular topics as institutional categories: Implications for theory and research in the history and sociology of schools subjects', in GOODSON, I.F. and BALL, S.J. (eds) *Defining the Curriculum: Histories and Ethnographies*, London: Falmer Press.

STAMP, R. (1970) 'The campaign for technical education in Ontario 1876–1914', PhD thesis, University of Western Ontario.

APPENDIX 1

London, Ont.,
19 May 1919

Present:
W.N. Manning
H. Hayman
W.A. Reid
Mrs. A.T. Edwards
A.E. Silverwood
W.J. Tillman
R. Lawson
H.B. Beal

A letter from the Minister of Education, dated 7 April 1919, in reference to granting to the school the standing of a technical high school, was read.

Moved by Mr. Silverwood, seconded by Mr. Lawson and carried that the Secretary be instructed to notify the Minister of Education as follows:

That the conditions stated by the Minister of Education in his letter of 7 April, requiring the appointment of a teacher as Headmaster of day classes who holds a High School Principal's Certificate and who is approved by the Minister in order to give the school the rank of a technical high school by accepted; it being understood that the Minister requires that the Headmaster of day classes shall be responsible to the Department of Education, to the Advisory Industrial Committee and to the Board of Education through Principal of the School and that the Principal of the School be held responsible by the Department of Education, the Advisory Industrial Committee and the Board of Education for the policy and management of the School.

That if necessary, the Chairman of the Committee interview the Minister of Education in regard to the matter.

Moved by Mr. Hayman, seconded by Mr. Silverwood that the Principal be instructed to advertise for a Science Specialist with High School Principals qualifications, the salary to be up to $2500, according to experience.

The design for the tablet to mark the official opening of the School was submitted by the Dennis Wire & Iron Works Co. Moved by Mr. Hayman, seconded by Mr. Lawson that the Chairman and Principal be empowered to place order.

APPENDIX 2

7 October 1919

A meeting of the Advisory Industrial Committee was held in the City Hall at 4.15 this afternoon. The following members were present: Messrs. Silverwood, Lawson, Udy, Barnard, Manning, Mrs. Edwards, R.M. McElheran and H.B.B.

On motion the report of Mr. Manning was adopted:

TO THE MEMBERS OF THE ADVISORY INDUSTRIAL COMMITTEE:

I would report as follows:

That during the month the Chairman of the Board received a communication from the Department in regard to the standing of the school as a Technical High School.

I communicated with Dr. Cody and he sent Dr. Merchant to finally settle any misunderstanding. Dr. Merchant arrived this morning.

I discussed the resolution of the Advisory Industrial Committee of 19 May with him and found that he quite agreed with the resolution of the Advisory Industrial Committee as we understood it, but so that there should be no possible misunderstanding he suggested that the resolution be worded as follows and this being done the Department, on receiving notice thereof, would grant to the school the standing of a Technical High School:

That the conditions stated by the Minister of Education in his letter of 7 April, requiring the appointment of a teacher as Headmaster of day classes who holds a High School Principal's Certificate and who is approved by the Minister in order to give the school the rank of a Technical High School be accepted; it being understood that the Minister requires that the Headmaster of day classes shall be responsible to the Department of Education through the Director of Technical Education and the Principal of the school and to the Advisory Industrial Committee, and to the Board of Education through the Principal of the school and that the Principal of the School be held responsible by the Department of Education, the Advisory Industrial Committee and the Board of Education for the policy and management of the school.

I would therefore advise that the resolution as worded be passed and sent to the Board for ratification.

Sgd. W.N. Manning
Chairman,
Advisory Industrial Committee.

6 Subject Status and Curriculum Change: Local Commercial Education, 1920–1940

(with Christopher Anstead)

The first four decades of the twentieth century saw substantial transformations in systems of secondary education throughout North America. Social, economic and legislative changes brought new clienteles and new courses to schools — both state and private — in all regions of the continent. In Ontario, for instance, total secondary school enrollment increased from 21,723 in 1900 to 119,652 in 1940, while the number of secondary schools rose from 131 to 489 — among the latter were fifty-nine vocational institutions, symbolizing the changing orientation of North American education.[1] These adjustments inevitably altered the professional status of teachers and educators associated with particular disciplines. In cases where their status declined, some subject teachers and administrators employed curriculum change as a way to increase the material or symbolic resources available to them.

A case study of commercial studies in London, Ontario, illustrates this intersection of curriculum change and subject status. During the middle of the 1920s two major changes transformed commercial studies at the London Technical and Commercial High School. This chapter argues that these curriculum changes represented a response to declining subject status. During the quarter century preceding these changes, commercial studies in London declined from its position as a high-status department in the prestigious Collegiate Institute, being first marginalized in that institution and then transferred to the technical school. These changes took place at a time when the subject's student clientele had become feminized and, with the transfer to the technical school, proletarianized. Commercial educators viewed the change in student characteristics as causing the decline in their subject's status (and thus in their own professional standing). They introduced two new courses in an attempt to change both the class and gender characteristics of commercial students. In the end, these initiatives led to an educational experience increasingly segregated and structured by class and gender characteristics.

The period of change in North American education from the 1890s to the 1930s has attracted a good deal of scholarly attention; a 'post-revisionist' interpretation[2] provides a framework for understanding curriculum change in London, Ontario — a city of roughly 70,000 people (in 1930) with an economy based on brewing, manufacturing and financial services. In particular, the works of Herbert Kliebard, Harvey Kantor and David Labaree have provided clear elucidations of the patterns of conflict between various social and ideological forces involved in the construction of early twentieth-century American education (Kliebard, 1986; Kantor, 1988; Labaree, 1988).[3] Kantor and Labaree have both drawn attention to the semi-independent roles played by educators and students in the construction of curriculum; neither group acted simply as puppets of external interests.[4] Both studies are particularly relevant to the present investigation: Kantor's because it examines the vocational movement, including commercial education; and Labaree's because it is firmly grounded within a case study of a particular school. In addition, Jane Gaskell and Nancy Jackson (1987) have produced a short study of commercial education in two Canadian provinces which provides crucial background to our exploration (pp. 177–202).

The concept of subject status used in this chapter emerges from a definition used by researchers dealing with the status of individuals; this definition sees status as deriving from ownership of and control of access to material and symbolic capital (Bourdieu and Passeron, 1977; Deever, 1990, pp. 33–4). Subject status essentially represents the collective professional status of subject teachers.[5] Its material side may consist of remuneration in cases where teachers in different departments receive different salaries. It can also cover career prospects, which may increase, for instance, when a subject earns departmental status. The material capital of a subject also consists of the collective resources in terms of buildings, classrooms and equipment which determine the working conditions for subject teachers. The symbolic side of subject status includes the authority or respect accorded to the subject, as well as the extent to which it controls access to a form of knowledge deemed valuable. This knowledge can be described in terms of cultural capital or credentials; its value reflects the degree of desirability of the opportunities for future prospects opened to the subject's students (Bourdieu and Passeron, 1977; Labaree, 1986, pp. 42–57 and 1988; Deever, 1990, pp. 3–5; Giroux and Penna, 1983; Ringer, 1987). This chapter further argues that, in the early twentieth century, a discipline's symbolic capital derived partly from the perceived value of the student body, and could change as a result of transformations in student socio-economic characteristics.

Commercial studies, which moved from the Collegiate Institute[6] to London's technical high school in 1920, underwent a major curriculum revision in the middle of the decade; as a result, the commercial course evolved from a single common general course, into three courses of different lengths, with different emphases, aimed at different groups of students. The discipline had already experienced one major change at the start of the decade, when the Provincial Department of Education ordered its extension from two to three years. According to Principal Herbert Benson Beal, this allowed students to train for 'the higher positions in mercantile life'.[7] At the same time, the school allowed students the choice of leaving after two years with a 'junior diploma' which Beal described as adequate preparation for 'junior and stenographic positions'.[8] At this point, though, all commercial students enrolled in the same general course. The first major exception to this rule took the form of a one-year 'special commercial' course created in 1924. This course admitted only those students who already had several years of secondary school experience. It served to attract dozens of young women (and smaller numbers of young men) who had finished their academic education at one of London's prestigious academic schools — styled as 'Collegiate Institutes' — or, in a few cases, other schools. Because these students had already obtained a grounding in academic subjects at their previous school, the special one-year course featured only strictly vocational classes.[9]

In 1926 the school announced the formation of a 'special business course for boys', (which became a 'general business course for boys' in 1933).[10] This new course had a different focus from the general commercial course; while the older course trained students to take general office positions, the new course trained male students for positions at wholesale firms and financial institutions, or in sales. As Beal pointed out, the course would prepare young men to work in places where they could find 'ample opportunity for advancement'.[11]

Why did these changes come about? One obvious hypothesis, that the provincial government insisted on their introduction, does not fit the evidence. Certainly, in both cases the provincial department allowed or authorized these changes, but they did not demand them. It was a purely local decision to take advantage of these options, and one which Principal Beal seems primarily to have made. Neither the local Board of Education nor the Advisory Vocational Committee — which oversaw the school's operations — urged Beal in this direction; instead they simply reacted to his decisions.[12] On the other hand, a lack of documents makes the question of whether Beal felt some pressure from commercial teachers in the school unanswerable, though that seems a reasonable contention.

Why did Beal (probably acting in conjunction with commercial teachers in his school) decide to introduce these courses, and what interests did they serve? If the new courses were to serve the interests of the students, then they should have changed the school experience in some way. In fact, the two innovations did little to alter existing practices. The special commercial course did not change anything for students at the technical school, since they could not take it. Instead of making improvements for an existing student clientele, the course sought to attract another group of students. Had this new group consisted of young people who would otherwise have left the educational system, the change would have represented a laudable attempt to build on the school's original mandate. The new course, however, did not seek out the otherwise unschooled, but instead aimed at attracting educated youths away from private business colleges or even from the collegiates.

On the other hand, the creation of separate courses for males only marked the public confirmation of a pattern that had existed for years. From the first years of commercial courses at the technical school, the classes had a slightly different curriculum for each gender. The new course promised an emphasis on penmanship, business correspondence, accountancy, investment math and salesmanship; yet the male classes in the general commercial course already featured more of an emphasis on accountancy than did those for females. The existing separate classes in other subject for each gender would have allowed for an emphasis on penmanship, business correspondence or investment mathematics if desired. The only real change in curriculum came with the introduction of a class in salesmanship; the introduction of a brand new course was primarily a feat of legerdemain.[13]

The existing gender differences in curriculum fit into a wider pattern in the school (and of course wider patterns beyond the school); although all Ontario schools were premised on the American model of coeducation, female students at the technical school followed a different curriculum from males.[14] Besides the obvious differences in the technical subjects taken by each gender, males at the school took algebra throughout their course, whether they had entered a general technical, matriculation or general commercial stream, while only those few females enrolled in the matriculation course took algebra, and they only took it from second year. In the technical department, females took art but males did not.[15]

Since the two new courses in no way responded to student demands, they seem to have been created mainly for the educators themselves. Commercial teachers did have definite occupational concerns at the time. In particular, they faced a clear decrease in the status of commercial studies, which occurred during the period from the turn of the century to the 1920s.

During the late nineteenth century commercial studies managed to amass substantial symbolic and material resources in the Ontario school system. From mid-century classes in such business subjects as bookkeeping and penmanship became standard in the province's secondary schools. As demand for this sort of professional training grew during the second half of the nineteenth century, private business colleges proliferated, emphasizing a purely practical curriculum and guaranteed placement for graduates. The Ministry of Education also responded to this demand, introducing a one-year commercial course in 1885, and extending it to two years in 1896.[16]

In London at this time, commercial subjects made up part of the general academic curriculum at the city's Collegiate Institute. Commercial studies commanded increasing authority, and in 1895 became a separate department, with a distinct course of study, at the Collegiate Institute. In 1899 the Commercial Department moved to a new four-room building adjacent to the older CI building. From that point on, reports of attendance at the school listed students in the Commercial Department separately.[17] Both of these actions point to an acknowledgment of the amount of symbolic capital controlled by commercial education at the end of the nineteenth century; departmental status provided material resources in terms of additional teaching positions up to and including department head, while the new building represented a high standard of working conditions. Indeed, the incoming Chair of London's Board of Education confirmed this status in 1899 when he declared the primary role of the local system to be the provision of 'a good English and business education'.[18]

The success of commercial studies in the late nineteenth century reflected the association of office work with middle class male respectability. Middle-class men in the late nineteenth century viewed clerical work as the first, obligatory, rung on a ladder of commercial success. Young men who wanted to make up the next generation of merchants, bankers or entrepreneurs, knew they had to serve their time as clerks, bookkeepers or secretaries. Many educators, worried about the movement of young women into the high schools, saw commercial courses as a way to make school more relevant and attractive to these male students (Gidney and Millar, 1990, p. 294; Jackson and Gaskell, 1987, pp. 182–3).

Though the achievement of departmental standing, and quarters in a new building, resulted from commercial studies' high status at LCI, the physical and administrative separation from academic subjects made the department much more vulnerable to marginalization as its cultural authority decreased during the opening decades of the twentieth century.[19] At this time the symbolic capital associated with the value of the subject dropped throughout North America; thus the 1900 annual report of Ontario's Minister of Education quoted the opinion of the President of Harvard University on commercial courses, which he saw as 'hopelessly inferior to other courses . . .' (cited in Jackson and Gaskell, 1987, p. 193).

The physical resources which contributed to the status of commercial studies reflected the subject's large enrollment at the turn of the century; a province-wide decline in enrollment in the early twentieth century accelerated the decrease in subject status. In 1902, 11,334 students in Ontario secondary schools took bookkeeping among their subjects. By 1922, that number had fallen to 6524. The increase in absolute enrollment made the relative decline in the attraction of commercial studies even greater. Almost half (46 per cent) of Ontario's secondary students took bookkeeping in 1902; twenty years later, the proportion had fallen to less than 15 per cent.[20]

In London, the decline in commercial education's status led to marginalization, beginning early in the new century with the establishment of domestic science classes in the commercial building, thus reducing the material resources controlled by commercial teachers. Domestic science classes were held in the commercial building from 1903, and by 1907 the commercial building had become too crowded.[21] In 1908 the 'severe overcrowding' had reached the point where one commercial class consisted of sixty-two pupils sharing eleven typewriters. Some of the pressure eased later that year with the transfer of domestic science classes to the basement of the main building.[22] The commercial building remained crowded as it aged, and teaching conditions worsened. In 1915 the Principal reported an average class size of forty-nine, despite provincial regulations limiting class size to thirty. By that point, the Principal was talking of 'separating the Commercial Department from the rest of the Collegiate work.'[23]

After the end of the war, overcrowding at the commercial building reached a crisis point. In 1918 the Board authorized the removal of a staircase so classes could be held in a hallway, and the creation of a new classroom in the attic.[24] Finally, in 1919 the Board decided to act. At first they considered a new building in a site distant from the CI since in their opinion, 'it would be preferable to have the commercial classes entirely separated from the Collegiate Institute.'[25] When the City Council refused to allow the funds for this, the Board decided to move the commercial classes into an old, decrepit, elementary school building, used by the military during the war; academic classes would move into the former commercial building. Even these poor quarters did not provide immunity for the commercial department; in September 1919 academic classes which could not fit in the other two buildings took over one of the Department's six classrooms.[26]

The transfer of the Commercial Department to the London Technical High School in the early 1920s represented another stage in the subject's downward trajectory. The Technical High School had a remarkably different status from the

Collegiate Institute, a difference based in the symbolic, rather than the material, realm. One of the chief factors behind the formation of the 'London Industrial School' (later the 'London Technical and Commercial High School') in 1912 was a desire to ease overcrowding at the Collegiate Institute by the transfer of students who only attended the school for a year or two, before entering the industrial workforce. Enthused by the claims of the movement for social efficiency, London educators undertook the implementation of a school which would prepare these students for their expected careers (Goodson and Dowbiggin, 1991, pp. 43–4).[27]

Thus, from the start, the technical school suffered under the image of an institution for less desirable students. The school's first Principal, and prime mover in its creation, Herbert Benson Beal, did not take this complacently; instead he fought to raise the public's estimation of his school by attracting students who had achieved high school entrance standing. Beal wanted to challenge, and, in the end, destroy a widespread perception of technical schools as 'the natural dumping ground for all backward and defective children'.[28]

The willingness of both federal and provincial levels of government to fund technical schooling handsomely at this time provided an important boost to Beal's campaign, and brought control over considerable material resources to the school. The construction of a brand new building (completed in 1918) filled with up-to-date equipment, seemed to signal Beal's complete victory, and caused many traditionalists, led by the *London Free Press*, to attack the technical school on a variety of issues, all underpinned by a feeling that this new form of schooling presented a serious challenge to the cultural dominance of traditional elite academic education (Goodson and Dowbiggin, 1991, pp. 47–56).

The last of the campaigns of opposition took place in 1923 and early 1924. This campaign started with a series of attacks by the newspaper and Council members which maligned the school in terms of its standards of teaching. Opponents also described the school as an inefficient part of the local system, claiming that it was too expensive and too little used.[29] The climax of this campaign came with a movement to convert the technical school into a comprehensive high school, combining academic and technical streams. While this would have prevented the resulting school from challenging the Collegiate Institute on status grounds, it also promised to eliminate another problem — the growing need for some kind of secondary school in the city's predominantly working class east end. The combined weight of technical education supporters, spokespeople for the east end community who wanted their own CI, and provincial officials opposed to the comprehensive plan, finally scuttled this movement.[30]

Despite victories like this, and the early burst of funding from provincial and federal sources, any increase in status experienced by the technical high school proved short-lived. Neither of these factors led to any great increase in symbolic capital, since the key distinction between practical and academic forms of knowledge remained firmly in place. In 1926 the Board eliminated all the manual training and domestic science classes from the city's collegiate institutes (by that point the city had three CIs), making the distinction between these schools and the technical school more sharp.[31]

Despite Beal's efforts, his school remained starved of symbolic capital. A teacher who arrived at the school in 1930 remembered how a 'general feeling' existed 'that you were rather an inferior type if you attended Beal Tech. It was for the people who just didn't have the ability or didn't belong to the right class of people'. Or, put another way, '. . . if you weren't very bright you went to Tech. And (you also went) . . . if your family was poor'.[32]

In 1920, this Technical Institution, burdened with continuing status problems, became the new home of the Commercial Studies Department formerly associated with the Collegiate Institute. The destruction by fire in April 1920 of the CI building only hastened the implementation of existing plans to move the commercial students to the technical school. Within days of the disaster, administrators worked out a new arrangement; academic classes from the burned-out building moved into the classrooms occupied by commercial courses, and commercial courses moved to the technical school building. Though the Commercial Department remained administratively connected to the Collegiate for several months, the move proved permanent; the Commercial Department became an official part of the Technical School a year after the fire and emergency move.[33] Commercial education, once a highly respected component of the LCI curriculum, had now been consigned (along with domestic science and industrial education) to the technical school building.[34]

In 1924, facing this situation of declining status, commercial educators embarked on a set of curricular changes to increase the material and symbolic resources of their department. They had the full support of Principal Beal, constantly concerned with his school's status, which had been seriously threatened in the previous eighteen months. One way to increase the material resources of the discipline was to increase enrollment, resulting in a greater number of paid positions available to teachers of the subject and a greater voice in the distribution of other material resources. The provincially-ordered expansion to a three-year course in 1921 had certainly contributed in this vein, but such an increase in bodies seemed to have little effect on symbolic wealth. The reforms initiated at the middle of the decade, by contrast, aimed to increase material resources, with more students and more courses, but they also evinced a concern with symbolic resources, through the recruitment of new student clienteles. This underscores the beliefs of the educators involved that student characteristics had an effect on subject status.

Taking the second reform first, the creation of a gender-segregated course represented a reaction to the observation that commercial classes, like commercial work, had become dominated by females. A perception that this fact had negative status implications caused commercial educators throughout the continent to seek some means of redressing the balance. Many business teachers sought to model their subject on the increasingly-prestigious professional schools, which laid a heavy emphasis on masculinity; the presence of a female student body seemed to threaten this goal (Weiss, 1978, pp. 176–7). Of course, such concerns were unique to neither commercial studies nor North America. For instance, Brian Doyle (1989), examining English studies in the United Kingdom, concludes: '. . . during the inter-war period English was . . . securely established as a stable and male-dominated professional field despite the presence of a majority of female students (p.71). In

London, these concerns led to the decision to offer a special course to attract more young men.[35]

In the twentieth century, the respectable and male aura of commercial studies started to diminish as more and more positions for women opened up in clerical work. The Canadian economy underwent great changes in the generation surrounding the turn of the century. A fairly sudden transformation from entrepreunerial to corporate forms of capitalism meant the volume of clerical work increased, and offices became the central directing agencies of huge economic entities. In an effort to rationalize these new phenomena, and maintain power in the hands of managers, clerical tasks became specialized and routinized. The new positions did not call for a few generalists with a wealth of skills, but for various specialists with limited skills; thus they paid poorly and offered little chance of advancement. These jobs did not suit the aspirations of most males entering the business world, but they did seem a step above traditional female paid work as a domestic or factory worker; female clerical workers flooded into the Canadian office in the first thirty years of the twentieth century (Lowe, 1986; Jackson and Gaskell, 1987, pp. 184–5; Kantor, 1988, p. 62; Labaree, 1988, pp. 166–8). By 1931, women held almost half of all clerical jobs in the country; over half of these women worked as typists and stenographers. In these junior positions, women outnumbered men by a ratio of more than 20:1.[36]

Commercial education itself changed in reaction to these transformations. The addition of new subjects like stenography and typewriting around the turn of the century showed a curriculum adaptation to new circumstances. The commercial student body also reflected this new reality; by the time commercial education was widely and successfully established in the province, the majority of students enrolled in such courses were probably female. Young women ignored the wishes of mainstream educational reformers, who proclaimed the merits of domestic science, and eagerly sought the training which prepared them for the flood of new clerical jobs.[37] In an unpublished study, Gail Posen (1980) has found that women outnumbered men by a of 3:1 in Toronto's High School of Commerce, from 1911 through to the Second World War.[38] In 1930, the six strictly commercial high schools operating in the province all reported a similar dominance of female students, who made up over three-quarters of the 6721 students enrolled at those institutions. These figures tie the Ontario experience to that of American schools which also saw a female majority in commercial classes appearing in the first decades of the twentieth century.[39]

London was not immune to these provincial, national and international trends. Increasingly in the twentieth century, women took jobs in the city's clerical workforce. A comparison of the census figures for 1911 and 1921 provides a small illustration of this movement. In 1911, London's banks employed 121 male clerks and twenty female clerks, while its insurance offices employed fifty-three male and thirty-six female clerks. By 1921, the number of male bank clerks had increased by only one, and the number of male insurance clerks dropped by twenty-four; over the same period, the numbers of female bank and insurance clerks increased by eighty-one and eighty-two, respectively. Twenty years later, 2393 women held commercial positions in London.[40]

At the same time as women became a fixture in London's offices, their younger sisters started to change the matrix of local secondary education. From the start of the new century, girls frequently outnumbered boys at the Collegiate. Many of them ignored the domestic subjects, introduced to the local curriculum in 1902.[41] Instead they chose to take commercial studies, leading to a female dominance in the subject. Commercial studies had certainly become feminized by the time the program came to the technical school in 1920. A list of commercial diplomas awarded by the school in the first year of commercial studies included twenty-eight female names and only six male names. In 1923 the group of students entering the first year of the commercial program numbered seventy-one females and only nineteen males.[42] A similar ratio continued to mark the commercial program through the next two decades. In 1930 the number of students enrolled in commercial classes included 462 young women and 105 young men. In 1940 the school awarded eighty-five intermediate certificates in commercial studies, of which seventy went to young women.[43]

The possibility that this female influx had major repercussions for subject status resides in the nature of gender roles and relations at the time. In education, as in so many areas of early twentieth-century life, the experience of London's women and girls differed markedly from that of the city's men and boys. A wealth of evidence supports this interpretation at the level of the Board of Education and, especially, at the level of the teaching staff; it must have held true at the level of student.

Women in London had little representation on their Board of Education — the locally-elected body which supervised the city's schools. Although one female trustee did serve a single term at the end of the nineteenth century, women only started to achieve sustained representation on the Board from 1919. Though the 1920 Board included four women out of fourteen trustees, for the next few years the Board included only one or two women at a time. In 1928 the Board reduced itself to six members. The number of women members on this Board stayed constant at one or two until at least 1940. Women trustees took another important step with the election of the first female Chair of the Board in 1929, followed by two more women in that office in 1933 and 1934.[44] Although the representation of women on the Board did increase over time, it never reached an equality with that of men in this period, despite the fact that both streams of feminism — maternal feminism and equal rights feminism — had an interest in education. One of these pioneer female trustees reflected the prevailing denigration of women's experience when she concluded her report of an annual convention to the Board by regretting that no male trustee from the city had attended the convention and adding: 'My report is only from a woman's viewpoint.'[45] The deadpan delivery of sixty-year-old minutes prevents us from listening for any trace of sarcasm.

Women teachers experienced vastly different professional lives from those of their male colleagues. As in other places, London's female teachers faced discrimination in terms of status, both through official decisions on things like salaries or promotions and in the general level of treatment they received. A definite and formal gender differentiation appeared in the salaries paid teachers. As an example, the 1932 salary schedule for the London Board paid female elementary school

Table 2:   Percentage of students entering first year of any commercial course, by gender

	1923	1927	1931	1935
Male	21%	20%	21%	24%
Female	79%	80%	79%	76%
n =	91	325	292	406

Source: LTCHS Student Record Cards.

teachers with a first class certificate a maximum of $1800 a year, while those with a second class certificate could receive up to $1600; the corresponding maximums for male teachers stood at $2500 and $2400 respectively. The terms for teachers in secondary schools were more equal, but a formal difference remained; thus teachers in the highest category received $3400 a year if male, and $3200 if female.[46] Of course, this latter statistic had little meaning for the majority of women teachers, clustered at the elementary level.

In terms of promotion, women could not move above the level of classroom teacher. Technically the Board did allow female principals in schools containing less than eight rooms, but in practice this meant that one teacher in each of the schools (only two operated in 1928) which had only two full-time teachers, received the title of Principal, with little increase in pay or status.[47] In the secondary schools, women could not become a department head outside of the female technical subjects.[48] Advertisements for job openings always sought candidates in terms of gender; the Board ignored any women who applied for a male job unless they could find no suitable man. One teacher recalled her experience at being hired during the Depression: '. . . they wanted a commercial specialist, they wanted a man; but apparently they couldn't get a man, so they took me' (Fallona interview).[49]

Simply stated, school authorities treated female teachers as second-class employees. The Board expected women teachers who married to give up their positions, and would only consider hiring a married woman, even for a substitute position, in an emergency.[50] When a Chair of the Board of Education spoke in favour of introducing mandatory retirement, he saw no problem in suggesting that men retire at 65 and women at 55 years of age.[51] Of course, this all took place in a society that by and large took such things for granted. Many female teachers themselves felt it was simply logical that men have higher pay, that only men became principals, and that women should drop out when married, and turn their attention to raising a family (Fallona interview).

The creation of a special commercial course for boys in 1926, then, represented an attempt to alter the slide in subject status through the recruitment of a more socially valued student clientele; did it succeed? Did the introduction of the course actually change the gender split in the subject? The answer has to be negative. Table 2, below, outlines the gender division in new commercial students, taking all commercial courses into account, at four-year intervals. Despite the introduction of the new course in 1926, males made up roughly 20 per cent of new commercial students in 1927 and 1931, as they had in 1923. It is only in 1935 that even a minor change in ratio is detectable.

Table 3: Parental occupations, london secondary schools, 1922

	C.I.	Tech. H.S.
Non-manual	66.3%	21.5%
Manual skilled	30.1	58.2
Manual unskilled	3.6	20.3
n =	880	423

Source: Ontario, Minister of Education, *Annual Report* (1922) pp. 228–9 and 260–1.

Despite the apparent failure of the new course to significantly alter the gender ratio in the commercial department, it still may have helped with the symbolic status of the discipline, since the mere presence of this course on the books provided evidence for commercial studies' importance. In an attempt to raise the status of commercial classes generally, the staff at Beal pointed to gender differences in education, and in particular, to the presence of young men in segregated classes. By contrast, the school did not refer to other commercial courses as being 'for girls', indicating the low status of a female clientele, and leaving the impression that all commercial courses contained some males.

While the introduction of a specifically gender segregated course reveals an obvious attempt to manipulate student characteristics, the introduction of the special one-year course demands closer inspection. In fact, the special commercial course also sought to attract a new group of students — students with a different socioeconomic background from those normally associated with the technical school. The move of the commercial department to the technical school (a result of the decrease in status associated with the gender characteristics of students) had started a further round of devaluation associated with the socioeconomic background of pupils; gender and class patterns began to interact in a vicious downward spiral. In the 1920s and 1930s, new patterns of attendance brought about by legislative and economic changes tied technical schools more and more firmly to a working class student body, perceived to have less academic ability (Jackson and Gaskell, 1987, pp. 193–4; Kantor, 1988, pp. 123–48).

The composition of London's technical school's student body differed dramatically from that of the more academically-oriented Collegiate. A comparison of the occupational status of student families at the Collegiate Institute and the technical school shows this discrepancy. Table 3, below, reveals that two-thirds of the pupils in the Collegiate came from families headed by men or women employed in white collar positions, while only a fifth of technical school pupils came from this group. The figures for manual occupations are reversed.[52]

Once established at the technical school, commercial studies drew from its pool of students. Table 4, below, identifies student socioeconomic status on the basis of the parental occupation listed on student record cards from the technical school. This table reveals the similarity in the socioeconomic status of students in the two general courses. The data shows that a slight difference in class characteristics of female students taking the general technical and commercial courses existed in 1927, but vanished thereafter. For 1931 and 1935, the patterns of representation seem

Table 4: Socioeconomic characteristics of female students in selected courses

	General Technical	General Commercial	Special Commercial
1927			
Non-manual	19%	30%	53%
Skilled manual	40%	36%	28%
Unskilled manual	40%	33%	19%
n =	67	129	58
1931			
Non-manual	25%	24%	39%
Skilled manual	37%	38%	42%
Unskilled manual	38%	38%	19%
n =	92	105	69
1935			
Non-manual	30%	33%	60%
Skilled manual	33%	35%	30%
Unskilled manual	37%	32%	10%
n =	81	135	83

Source: LTCHS Student Record Cards.

almost identical. Thus, at least in the 1930s, class had no bearing on patterns of enrollment in the two general courses, and commercial studies thus suffered the double disability of a student body undervalued both in gender and in class terms.

The special one-year course sought to remedy this problem. Because the course demanded at least two years high school standing for admission, it enrolled only students who transferred from another secondary school, which meant in practice usually one of the collegiate institutes, though a few came from private schools or rural continuation schools. Many of the students entering this course had already achieved junior or senior matriculation; in a few cases, young women even attended this course after graduating from university.[53] The special commercial course thus drew students not from the general pool of students entering the technical school, but from a pool of those who had entered the collegiate institutes or other secondary institutions.

The presence of the new group of students changed the socioeconomic composition of the Commercial Department. Table 4 shows how the socioeconomic status of these students contrasted with that of the students in the two general courses discussed above. Where the non-manual segment of the general courses varied between a fifth and a third of all students, in the special commercial course it varied from two-fifths to three-fifths. At its minimum, it still exceeded the maximum for either of the other two courses.

These two new courses, then, emerged at the technical school to help raise teachers' professional status; while doing so, the courses also increased lines of segregation within the student population based on ascribed, involuntary characteristics. The creation of a course restricted to males added to the formal distinction between the genders in school society. The special one-year course produced similar, if less obvious, effects. While the new course did succeed in attracting a more highly valued clientele, in doing so it created a new division in the student body, which corresponded to a difference in socioeconomic status.

While the class-based segregation imposed by the new course did not upset proponents of social efficiency, it did mark an unintended, if acceptable, outcome. Although Beal himself did attempt to minimize the social distance between the special commercial pupils and those from the general courses by organizing school-wide recreational activities (Morgan interview), these social events did nothing more than mask the systematic stratification being worked at the level of curriculum.

As is so often the case in historical research, the authors have to wonder whether their edifice of argument and evidence appears to others as little more than a house of cards. Direct evidence supports the following assertions. First, during the period 1900 to 1920, commercial studies in London, Ontario, suffered from a trend of increasing marginalization in the Collegiate Institute, which culminated in a transfer to the Technical High School — an institution with a much less enviable reputation. Second, this marginalization occurred at the same time as the subject's student body underwent a process of feminization. Third, at the Technical School, the commercial studies student body quickly became identical, in social class terms, to the technical student body, and different from that of the Collegiate Institute. Fourth, during 1923 and 1924 the school underwent a series of attacks led by the conservative local newspaper and City Council members. Fifth, soon after these attacks ended, school officials decided to introduce two new courses which made little difference to existing students. Sixth, the first of the new courses aimed to attract CI students and resulted in a different class composition in the student body. Seventh, the other new course aimed at attracting males, thus directly seeking to change the student body profile.

This chapter has tried to tie these seven phenomena together in one particular and specific sense by arguing for the importance of the notion of subject status. Since subject status played a major role in determining professional career status and prospects, the personal interests of commercial teachers demanded attempts to elevate the discipline's status. One way to do so involved changing the characteristics of the student body, since at this time subject status rested to a degree on the perceived value of the students enrolled. In particular, student social characteristics of gender and class acted as crucial determinants in setting the status of a particular subject. The curriculum change of the mid-1920s sought to achieve this restructuring.

In the end, the struggle for professional status resulted in a major increase in stratification and segregation in the technical school. While educators acknowledged the gender segregation, the more circumspect class segregation provided similarly potent mechanisms for structuring student experience in the school. The result was a distinction by class and gender in the credentials student received from their secondary schooling. The fact that these changes took place under provincial authority, seems to indicate that London's situation was far from unique, and might have reflected a province-wide concern with the status of commercial studies. This suggests strongly that the 1920s witnessed increased socioeconomic segregation in secondary school commercial courses throughout Ontario — a conclusion which matches recent interpretations of the so-called 'vocational era' in the history of education (see, for example, Lazerson and Dunn, 1977).[54]

Notes

1   Ontario Legislative Assembly (1902) p. iv; and (1942) p. 111.

2   The 'post-revisionist' approach challenges both the traditional, celebratory understanding of this period and the later revisionist interpretation. The former school is represented by Koos (1927) and Cremin (1961). The revisionist approach is best seen in Katz (1968), Bowles and Gintis (1976) and Lazerson and Dunn (1977).

3   See also Weiss (1982), pp. 613–38 and Powers (1992). For comparison, Harold Silver's British work is of great utility in discerning patterns of vocational education (see Silver, 1983).

4   This point is supported by Jane Gaskell's convincing contemporary analysis of the perceptions of female students in commercial courses (see Gaskell, 1987).

5   The social construction of subject status has been studied in some depth by historians (see Goodson, 1988).

6   From the 1870s, the Ontario school system included two types of secondary schools: high schools and collegiate institutes. Both taught the normal academic curriculum, with high schools teaching modern languages to males and females, and collegiate institutes teaching the classical languages, mainly to young men. By the twentieth century, this distinction no longer existed. High schools and collegiate institutes enrolled students of both genders, whom they taught an academic curriculum on a college preparatory model, though most graduates went into the workforce, not to higher education (see Gidney and Millar, 1990).

7   London Board of Education, Advisory Vocational Committee (AVC) (1992) *Minutes*, p. 4. The AVC was also known as the 'Industrial Advisory Committee' at one point, but for consistency this title will not be used in this chapter.

8   AVC (1924) *Minutes*, p. 3. Beal's comments reveal his concern with slotting students into specific occupations — a major goal of the efficiency movement. On Beal's own commitment to social efficiency see Goodson and Dowbiggin (1991) pp. 39–56.

9   London Board of Education (1924) *Annual Report*, p. 77; AVC (1925) *Minutes*, p. 3; London Technical and Commercial High School (LTCHS), student record cards, H B Beal secondary school archives; interview with Margaret Fallona, 1990. Fallona was a student at the school in the 1920s, and a teaching in the Commercial Department in the 1930s.

10   London Board of Education (1926–33) *Annual Reports*.

11   AVC (1927) *Minutes*, p. ; and (1928) p. 3. Similar courses were introduced elsewhere in North America. See Kantor (1988) p. 63 for evidence from California.

12   London Board of Education (1920–1930) *Minutes*; AVC (1920–1930) *Minutes*.

13   LTCHS, student record cards. See also Jackson and Gaskell (1987), p. 192.

14   See Goodson and Dowbiggin (1989). Of course, even in the home of coeducation itself — the USA — a similar pattern held true (see Rury, 1984, pp. 36–8; Tyack and Hansot, 1990; and Powers, 1992).

15 LTCHS, student record cards; London Board of Education for the City of London (1921) *Annual Report of the Board of Education for the City of London, London*, Board of Education, pp. 86–8.

16 Jackson and Gaskell (1987) pp. 186–7. On commercial education in the United States, see Weiss (1982), Rury (1984) pp. 29–34 and Powers (1992) chapters 4 and 10.

17 Dickinson (1935), pp. 7–8; London Board of Education for the City of London, Advisory Vocation Committee (AVC) (1898–99) *Minutes of the Board of Education for the City of London*, pp. 25–6, 38 and 87.

18 London Board of Education (1899–1900) *Minutes*, pp. 2–3.

19 For a parallel account describing how the separate physical location of a department allowed for a separate status see Labaree (1988) p. 164.

20 Ontario Minister of Education (1914) *Annual Report of the Minister of Education*, Toronto, Legislative Assembly, pp. 84–6 and (1922) pp. 260–3.

21 London Board of Education (1902–3) *Minutes*, pp. 44 and 52; and (1907) p. 196.

22 London Board of Education (1908) *Minutes*, pp. 315–16 and 355.

23 London Board of Education (1915) *Minutes*, pp. 53 and 130–1.

24 London Board of Education (1918) *Minutes*, p. 140.

25 London Board of Education (1919) *Minutes*, p. 53.

26 *Ibid*, pp. 84–5, 134–5, 138, 141 and 183.

27 The best analyses of social efficiency and its effects on education can be found in Kliebard (1986) pp. 89–122 and Franklin (1986) pp. 83–118.

28 AVC (22 January 1918) *Minutes*. See also London Board of Education (1912) *Annual Report*, pp. 24–38. The problem was unavoidable though, since the original justification for vocational schooling emphasized its role in making education interesting to those who were not interested in, or suited to, academic work. On this point see Kantor (1988) p. 115.

29 London Free Press, 29 December 1923, 2–9 January 1924 and 5 February 1924.

30 London Free Press, 29 January-8 February 1924; London Board of Education (1924) *Minutes*, p. 26 and 41–3.

31 London Board of Education (1926) *Minutes*, pp. 350–2.

32 Fallona interview; see also R I Mann (n.d.) 'Quo vadis domini?', clipping found in H B Beal secondary school archives. Gary McCulloch has drawn my attention to a similar expression of opinion in a local rhyme from Christchurch, New Zealand: 'with hob-nailed boots and unwashed neck, they don't come in here, they go to tech'.

33 London Board of Education (1920–21) *Minutes*; Dickinson (1935) p. 8.

34 This happened throughout the province, though other places did not have the excuse of a spectacular fire. See Jackson and Gaskell (1987) p. 194.

35 There is some evidence that local educators had tried to increase male attendance through earlier advertising campaigns. Documents from the period 1914 to 1917 contain a series of references to programs of publicity for commercial education, on the part of the Principal of the CI and the Commercial Advisory Committee, and with the approval of the Board of Education. Yet, during the same period, the same men (and they were all men) complained that the facilities for commercial classes had become strained to the limit. Why did such an oversubscribed course generate campaigns of recruitment, when other courses did not? A logical answer (though one unsupported by surviving direct evidence) is that the campaign aimed at males, rather than at seeking to increase the absolute numbers of commercial students. See, for example, London Board of Education (1914) *Minutes*, p. 140; (1915) p. 53; (1916) p. 146; (1917) p. 115; and (1918) p. 140.

36   Canada (1931) *Census of Canada*, Ottawa, King's Printer, v. 7, p. 74.
37   On the philosophy behind domestic science, the alternate vocational option for young women, see Pedersen (1981) pp. 178–94; Danylewycz, Fahmy-Eid and Thivierge (1984) pp. 106–12; Crowley (1986) pp. 520–1. The Canadian movement was informed and inspired by similar campaigns in Britain and the United States. On these see Purvis (1985); Yoxall (1913); and Rury (1984) pp. 21–44.
38   Posen (1980). We wish to thank Jane Gaskell for supplying us with a copy of this paper. See also Ontario Minister of Education (1920) *Annual Report*, p. 250; (1925) p. 216; and (1930) p. 352.
39   Ontario Minister of Education (1930) *Annual Report*, p. 352; Weiss (1982) p. 627; Rury (1984) pp. 30–3; Powers (1992) pp. 113–27.
40   Canada (1911) *Census of Canada*, v. 6; p. 340; (1921) v. 4, pp. 432–4;, (1941) v. 7, p. 238.
41   London Board of Education (1902/03) *Minutes*, pp. 5–9 and 52.
42   London Board of Education (1921) *Annual Report*, p. 1989; LTCHS, student record cards. For data from 1927 and 1929 see Goodson and Dowbiggin (1989) p. 32–3.
43   Ontario Minister of Education (193) *Annual Report*, p. 353; London Board of Education (1940) *Annual Report*, pp. 72–3. This feminization of commercial studies clearly took place at the expense of domestic technical subjects. In 1923 almost twice as many first year female students chose commercial studies as chose the general domestic curriculum. In later years the discrepancy grew; the almost 500 young women enrolled in commercial classes in 1930 contrasted sharply with only 147 registered in domestic technical courses. In 1940, the seventy female winners of commercial certificates for outnumbered the twenty-one female students who took certificates in home economics. LTCHS, student record cards; Ontario Minister for Education (1930) *Annual Report,* pp. 352–3; London Board of Education (1940) *Annual Report*, pp. 72–3. These statistics differed markedly from the rough estimates presented by Danylewycz, Fahmy-Eid and Thivierge, who claimed that twice as many young women took domestic subjects as commercial studies in technical schools at this time (see p. 103).
44   London Board of Education (1898–1940) *Annual Reports.*
45   London Board of Education (1920) *Minutes*, p. 93.
46   London Board of Education (1931) *Minutes*, appendix.
47   See London Board of Education (1923) *Minutes*, pp. 43–51; and (1928) pp. 30–4.
48   London Board of Education (1915) *Minutes*, p. 143; Fallona interview.
49   See also London Board of Education (1921) *Minutes*, p. 201.
50   London Board of Education (1933) *Minutes*, p. 58; Fallona interview.
51   London Board of Education (1905) *Minutes*, p. 95.
52   The tables was constructed from the Minister of Education's *Report* as follows: 'Non-manual' on the table represents the sum of the *Report* categories titled 'commerce', 'law, medicine, dentistry and the church' and 'teaching'. 'Skilled manual' is identical to the category title 'the trades' while 'manual unskilled' in the same as the category 'labouring occupations'. The categories 'agriculture', 'other occupation' and 'no occupation' from the *Report* were ignored in the construction of the table.
53   LTCHS, student record cards; Fallona interview; interview with Pearl Morgan, 10 June 1989. Morgan taught in the Technical School at the time.
54   See, for example Lazerson and Dunn (1977). For similar American interpretations consult Lazerson and Grubb (1974); Kantor and Tyack (1982); Labaree (1988); Kantor (1988); and Powers (1992).

References

BOURDIEU, P. and PASSERON, J.C. (1977) *Reproduction in Education, Society and Culture*, London: Sage.

DEEVER, B. (1990) 'Curriculum change and the process of hegemony in an Appalachian community', paper presented at the annual meeting of the American Educational Research Association, Boston, April.

DOYLE, B. (1989) *English and Englishness*, London: Routledge.

GIDNEY, R.D. and MILLAR, W.P.J. (1990) *Inventing Secondary Education: The Rise of the High School in Nineteenth-Century Ontario*, Montreal: McGill-Queens University Press.

GIROUX, H.A. and PENNA, A. (1983) 'Social education in the classroom: The dynamics of the hidden curriculum', in GIROUX, H. and PURPEL, D. (eds) *The Hidden Curriculum and Moral Education*, Berkeley, CA: McCutchan.

GOODSON, I.F. and DOWBIGGIN, I.R. (1991) 'Vocational education and school reform: The case of the London (Canada) technical school, 1900–1930', *History of Education Review*, **20**, 1.

JACKSON, N.S. and GASKELL, J.S. (1987) 'White collar vocationalism: The rise of commercial education in Ontario and British Columbia, 1870–1920', *Curriculum Inquiry*, **17**.

KANTOR, H.A. (1988) *Learning to Earn: School, Work and Vocational Reform in California 1880–1930*, Madison, WI: University Wisconsin Press.

KLIEBARD, H. (1986) *The Struggle for the American Curriculum 1893–1958*, London: Routledge and Kegan Paul.

LABAREE, D.F. (1986) 'Curriculum, credentials, and the middle class: A case study of a nineteenth-century high school', *Sociology of Education*, **59**.

LABAREE, D.F. (1988) *The Making of an American High School*, New Haven, CT: Yale University Press.

LAZERSON, M. and DUNN, T. (1977) 'Schools and the work crisis: Vocationalism in Canadian education', in STEVENSON, H.A. and WILSON, J.D. (eds) *Precepts, Policy and Process: Perspectives on Contemporary Canadian Education*, London: Alexander Blake.

LOWE, G.S. (1986) 'Women, work and the office: The feminization of clerical occupations in Canada, 1901–1931', in STRONG-BOAG, V. and FELLMAN, C.A. (eds) *Rethinking Canada: The Promise of Women's History*, Toronto: Copp Clark Pitman.

POSEN, G. (1980) 'The office boom: The relationship between the expansion of the female clerical labour force and the response of the public education system, 1900–1940', Toronto, OISE, photocopy.

RINGER, F. (1987) 'Introduction', in MULLER, D.K., RINGER, F. and SIMON, B. (eds) *The Rise of the Modern Educational System*, Cambridge: Cambridge University Press.

WEISS, J. (1978) 'Education for clerical work: A history of commercial education in the United States since 1850', EdD thesis, Harvard.

7 Subjects and the Everyday Life of Schooling

(*with Christopher J. Anstead*)

In 1986 Chad Gaffield noted that Canadian history of education, as it then existed, paid little attention to students and their experience, especially at the level of the classroom. Although Neil Sutherland's description of elementary school life did come out that same year, little has been done since to answer Gaffield's challenge to produce a 'comprehensive perspective on the actual experience of sitting in a classroom' (Gaffield, 1986, p. 116). In fact, Harold Silver has recently accused historians of education in Britain and the United States of exactly the same failing (Silver, 1992, pp. 97–108). The following description of the day-to-day experience of schooling as it took place at the London Technical and Commercial High School (LTCHS) between 1920 and 1940 is an attempt to answer at least part of the challenge (Barman, 1984). The image painted here emerged primarily in a series of interviews held with twenty-four former students and two former teachers of the school.[1]

The London Technical and Commercial High School marked London's contribution to the vocational movement in education. The early twentieth-century campaign for vocational schooling influenced all areas of North America, as well as most European states and their colonial empires. At first historians on this continent interpreted the movement as the arrival of democracy in education (Bennet, 1926 and 1937; Cremin, 1961; Patterson *et al*, 1974). A reaction to this interpretation arose in the late 1960s and 1970s, when revisionist researchers argued that vocational education represented an attempt by dominant interests to subordinate and control those groups which seemed to threaten existing society (Katz, 1968; Lazerson and Grubb, 1974; Dunn, 1979). More recently, scholars such as Herbert Kliebard (1986), Harvey Kantor (1988) and David Labaree (1988) have challenged the simplicity of each of the earlier interpretations, arguing that major educational reforms result from a process of conflict between social and ideological forces.

The history of LTCHS does reveal a pattern of contestation involving more than simply domination and resistance; elements in the school mediated and co-operated in the construction of the schooling experience. We have argued elsewhere (Goodson and Dowbiggin, 1991, pp. 39–60; Anstead and Goodson, 1993, pp. 459–81; Goodson and Anstead (1993); and chapter 5 in this volume) that teachers and their Principal at LTCHS sought, in part, to turn the rhetoric and resources of vocationalism to their own ends. Yet the fates of both external domination and internal mediation rested on the reaction and actions of students — a group conspicuous by either its absence or its passivity in most histories of the vocational movement.

In presenting a piece focussed on the daily life of students, the writers might seem to be engaging in 'history as description' — something that history professors tell their freshest undergraduate students to avoid. Yet Annaliste's 'total history', Foucault's 'geneologies' and postmodernism's emphasis on letting other voices speak, all seem to indicate some intellectual support for the future of 'history as description'. At the same time, such an approach bridges the gap to popular culture's construction of 'history'.

Beyond this, a description of the commonplace practices of a typical day at a particular school furnishes glimpses of the underlying structures and mediating practices of educational experience. As Anthony Giddens (1981, 1984 and 1991) and Roy Bhaskar (1979) have pointed out, structures are constituted by human social practices, often institutionalized practices, which they themselves have shaped. The human actors are always knowledgeable about some of the conditions of the surrounding system, though the consequences of their action may be unforeseen. Structures both constrain and enable practice, so that all structures offer some institutional space for transformative action.

The work of Giddens and Bhaskar provides a theoretical foundation for researchers seeking to reconstruct the everyday human actions that contribute to the maintenance — or downfall — of a social system predicated on an uneven balance of power (see also Barman, 1984). In some cases the more extreme structuralism present in the work of Giddens and Bhaskar has led to an interpretation of everyday life and practices as merely the 'superficial' consequences of underlying factors. For instance, Cooper (1985) argued in his study of mathematics curriculum practice: 'Observed events and their correlations are the superficial consequences of underlying structures and relationships' (p. 6). In this chapter we take a more dialectical view and seek to develop the generative insights provided by de Certeau (1984) in his pioneering work on the practice of everyday life. We see institutionalized practices and social structures and relations as mutually constitutive. In the context of a school case study, these ideas lead us to consider the relationship between structures and institutionalized practices within the school, as well as the role of the various sorts of people implicated in these practices.

Each day at the London Technical and Commercial High School started with the arrival of the students. In wintertime, most would travel to school on foot, many of them walking several miles a day. Yet 'shank's pony' did not provide the only means of transport; in better weather, flocks of bicycles appeared as the day started. Before the building of the gymnasium, students used a basement room to store their bikes during the day; later, they had to leave them in outside racks (Hopkins). For those students who lived near its route, the street railway provided an easier means of travel — it stopped just outside the school. A few students from the town of St. Thomas and the surrounding area took the London and Port Stanley railway every day into the centre of London, and then walked to the school (Buchwald). Finally, a handful of students arrived by car. Few families in London had an automobile, and only a minority of them had one which a teenager could take. Those students who drove could sometimes park on school property, in an area behind the building. On days when this lot was full or closed, parking was available nearby; there was no shortage of parking spots on the residential streets of London between the wars.

The teachers arrived in much the same way. Many walked, while most of the male teachers, at least, rode bicycles in suitable weather. Some teachers arrived on the street railway, while a select few brought their automobiles.

When they arrived at school, students congregated outside their assigned external doors, with boys at one end of the school, and girls, almost a block away, at the other — starting the daily segregation of the genders. A different segregation also took effect: students could not use the central front doors, which were reserved for teachers and office staff. As they stood around, students took care to stay off the grass lawns in front of the school; even cutting across a corner of the lawn served as grounds for a reprimand (Geddes).

The students all arrived wearing their school clothes, which they had to take off when they returned home; the same dress or shirt and pants might be worn for several days in a row before going into the wash (particularly during the Depression). For boys — whether in commercial or technical programs — proper dress included dress pants (often of worsted wool) sweaters, shirts, and ties. In the 1930s, some of the specialized technical students wore more appropriate clothing, such as denim overalls for motor mechanic students (Cushman). For girls, a dress or skirt was normal. For much of the period, an unofficial female uniform predominated, with girls wearing navy blue pleated skirts and 'middies' — white blouses trimmed with sailor's collars (Stamp, 1975; notes the same 'uniform' in Calgary).

After entering the school, students moved to their lockers to discard coats and drop off some of their books before reporting to their homeroom. Every homeroom contained roughly forty students, which represented one class in the commercial side but comprised two classes of twenty students each, for technical students. Each class sat in alphabetical order. After conducting a roll call, the homeroom teacher made up a class list, which one student carried from room to room until mid-afternoon, when he/she dropped it off at the office. This gave teachers in each subject a chance to add any comments until that time (Hopkins).

Until the fall of 1928 (when a school auditorium was built), the completion of the morning roll call signalled the commencement of the first class of the day; in the years after that, a different order was followed. After the roll call, the students left their books and moved down to the auditorium for morning exercises. The whole school went in; each class had its own place to sit, though members of the school orchestra scurried to their pit ahead of the others, and struck up their polished version of *Finlandia* or some similar piece (Brooks). On a typical day, the assembly would feature the Royal anthem, a hymn or two (with the words projected onto a screen), prayers, school announcements — concerning both official policy and extracurricular activities — and perhaps a short speech. Principal HB Beal — a short, red-headed man who favoured 'English' vests and tweeds — often took the duty of leading this assembly, which frequently was the only contact a student had with the Principal. According to one student, Beal 'wasn't a big guy, physically, and his voice wasn't very big either. It's a wonder that the words got to the back of the auditorium' (Brooks).

Normally the auditorium session lasted for some fifteen or twenty minutes, but on occasion — generally about once a week — the assembly lasted for an hour or longer and featured different kinds of educational entertainment. Sometimes the show consisted of a skit put on by a particular grade or class. At other times it might be a visiting speaker, a musical programme or a short film. After the assembly, the students returned to their classroom and started the day's lessons, some of them remaining in their homeroom while others collected their books and headed elsewhere.

At this point in the day, the sharp distinction between commercial and technical students became apparent. Very little mixing took place between commercial and technical students. Even non-vocational classes, such as academic subjects or physical training, were taken separately. In fact within the two sides, other distinctions existed, such as that between special and general commercial students recalled by one student in the former group:

> We never really got to know them (general program students); we just were our own class, and we all stayed together . . . Admittedly they hardly recognized us, let's put it that way. We'd come in and when we were at Collegiate anybody you met you said, 'Hi'. Well there, if I didn't meet my own classmates, most of them didn't know who we were even. I think they probably thought we shouldn't even be in there. (Allison)

(The other secondary schools in London, which featured an academic, college preparatory program, were titled 'collegiate institutes' at this time.) The fact that the special commercial students tended to be in classrooms on the other side of the building from the general commercial students, closer to the technical students, reinforced this division (Brown).

The subjects which students took during the school day had, for the most part, already been chosen by the administration; students rarely had any options. This meant that the same group of students remained together as a class for the whole day. To assign students to a class at the beginning of the year, teachers in each course divided their students by gender and then lined them up alphabetically. They would then count off the required number for each class. In some cases, the leftovers from each gender would be combined into one class, which then sat with the boys and girls separated in the classroom. Each class moved as a group from room to room in single file, while the teachers stayed in their own rooms. The weekly schedule meant that each day differed in the order students took subjects, with the pattern repeating each week. In the classroom, each student sat in the same seat all year long, generally in alphabetical order. In commercial studies, the same group tended to go though the whole three or four years together, while in technical studies specialization changed class composition after the first or second year.

A survey of old records reveals that the constraints of official timetables were not forged of unbreakable steel. Instead school administrators made accommodations for some students, especially those in senior years. For instance, some students who held jobs attended only in the morning or the afternoon and had special timetables as a result. Technical students in the fourth or fifth year of the matriculation course exercised some choice in the matter of extra subjects, with more than one female matriculation student taking a few periods of commercial subjects. Senior students in the general technical course also had some leeway in choosing other subjects to complement their specialization (SRCs; Kennedy).

For most students the particular subjects that they took still depended on the course and year. In first year, for example, students in the technical side's three-year general course received an introduction to the range of specialities available. Thus young men in the 1921/22 school year took classes in woodworking, machine shop, electricity, building construction and drafting. Over the next two decades, motor mechanics, printing and sheet metal work augmented this list.[2]

The young men entering first year would be expected to produce a variety of standard projects in each of these subjects. When they arrived at the machine shop, for instance, on the first day of the year, they would listen to a lecture on safety. (In fact, the safety lecture was standard in each technical subject, and for every class of students.) Then came the specific projects. One early machine shop project started as a piece of cast iron, five-eighths of an inch thick, and about three by four inches. Students first drilled three-eighths inch holes in the corners, and then drilled a number of connecting small holes in the middle until they could drop the centre out. Next they had to trim the piece in the shaper. The teachers had some students do this drilling and shaping in the opposite order, so that not all were waiting for the same machine.

Students then moved on to the second project; they had to:

> . . . turn a piece of iron in the lathe. The piece of iron, of course, was just a round piece, eight or nine inches long and about an inch and a half in diameter, which you first of all had to drill a centre hole in each end, and then put it in the lathe and turn it smooth, to a set diameter — for which you were checked and marked. And eventually it ended up as a piece which had a taper on it and you put a thread on it in the lathe. (Hopkins)

Students had to complete this second project in time for the Christmas break. Along the way, students also received more didatic training, in the form of delivered lessons, reinforced with blackboard notes, on such things as sharpening tools, the proper use of tools, and the names of the various parts of their tools (Hopkins).

A typical shop class would number fifteen to twenty students under one teacher, who spent most of his time going from pupil to pupil to check their work. The layout of the technical department frequently meant that two such classes would share a room. In this case the two teachers involved would work together, though the work of each class remained distinct. The two classes might each use a separate part of the shop room, divided by 'an invisible line' (Hopkins). Such team teaching was a common feature of technical education at the school. In many cases the two teachers had complementary strengths, one teacher having a stronger teaching background, and the other having more practical experience in the industry.

For their second or third year, male technical students picked one subject in which to specialize.[3] In the 1930s, when the decision to specialize was made at the start of second year, students also picked a second, complementary, area to do a minor concentration. Students who had picked a specialization generally spent roughly half their time in the subject, at times taking trips to relevant local industries. Technical students also took some academic classes.

The projects of the senior students were by reason of specialization much more complex than those of first year students. Indeed, the projects were frequently much more 'practical' in the sense that they attended to the needs of the school itself: students in woodworking built all the teachers' desks; printing students provided all printed material the school needed, from standard forms to report cards and even school yearbooks; electricity teachers assigned specific students to keep a close eye on the back-up batteries used for the school's emergency lighting system; other electricity students ran the lighting for school assemblies and evening events; and all senior students and teachers were ready to pitch in and repair any piece of school equipment which broke down.

In motor mechanics teachers emphasized a 'craftsman ethos' in their approach to this vocation. Students took pride in fabricating replacement parts, which included difficult processes such as pouring moulds. Each class followed a series of practical requirements to get through the course. For instance, they were required to take a week to overhaul an engine (Walsh). At first students learned on practice engines. When the teacher felt they had mastered the basic skills, they would be allowed to work on real cars — cars sent by teachers, students or their families, who received free repairs, except for the cost of parts. Students in the auto course used a current automotive repair manual, from one of the major manufacturers, as a textbook. They studied it from cover to cover, and even had homework assignments based on it.

The motor mechanics classroom had a seating area, but most of it comprised a shop, practice engines, workbenches, and a huge tool room. The tool room operated under very specific rules, as one student recalled:

> We had all the tools in a big tool room; every week . . . one of the students was assigned to the tool room, and he was in charge of tools. I mean you'd go for tools and there was a board and your number — you had six tags on each peg. Say my number was 26, well there'd be six '26' tags there. Now, if I wanted some tool they'd go and get me my tool and hang my tag where they took the tool off, and that was the way they'd keep track of it. And we never left there at night, until every tag was back on that board. If there was a tool missing, the whole class was looking for it. (Walsh)

Drafting took place in three rooms on the third floor, including a small blue-print room, and two rooms with drafting tables. Drafting courses usually started with students each receiving an article, such as a spindle table leg. Each student had to measure the article, make a quick hand sketch, and then produce a full-size drafting blueprint. The point of the middle step was to teach students to take their own measurements and make interim sketches in case they lost access to a particular item.

In the printing shop, the first lesson involved learning how to set type, as well as how to find type in the special print job cases. 'On the very first day, you were supposed to set the type for your name, your street address, and the city. And then go over and ink the form, and put a piece of paper in and roll it off. And you were marked on that' (Hopkins).

The woodworking shops, on the second floor, featured lots of machines, including half-a-dozen wood lathes. In first year, each student had the same project; they had to learn to use a hand plane, saw and chisel on wood — mostly straight hand work. The Department bought rough lumber, which they stored in a special area, sometimes used to teach students about materials. Some wood went into a small room with a steam radiator for drying it out. Before use, the teachers put the lumber through a planer (Hopkins).

The Electricity Department consisted of three rooms: a store room, with switchboard and engines; a lecture room with lots of chalkboards; and a third room containing a wooden structure, representing a building under construction, which was used for practice wiring. When the framework became too filled with holes, woodworking students would rebuild it.

While boys in the technical courses went through these areas, female technical students studied domestic subjects. In these domestic classes, teachers taught cooking, sewing skills, and spent a lot of time discussing efficient methods of housekeeping, including particular dusting, sweeping or floor washing techniques.

Sewing class featured various forms of needlework: sewing, crochet, embroidery, and petit-point. The students' first projects usually involved making petticoats and lampshades. Some teachers had to improvize: 'We all couldn't afford knitting needles at times, and (the teacher) went to Anderson's butcher shop by the market and got us skewers that you put in meat, and string, and that's what she taught us on' (Brown).

The school provided three rooms on the third floor for the cooking side of domestic science. Each had a couple of big stoves, along with gas burners for each student. (Later they were replaced by electrical burners.) The teacher would announce the day's work, give a demonstration, and then, depending on the teacher, either sit quietly at the other end of the room, or roam from student to student. In season students would learn to can peaches. They also made lots of cream soups — 'not what you would cook for a working man' (Darnell). The class seemed to spend a great deal of their time cleaning up.

One special course taught in the technical side, the only one open to both males and females, was art, taught by a certain Mrs Cryderman — a flamboyant figure 'known for her hats' (Carter). Although her class emphasized the fine arts, Cryderman taught more commercial applications, such as sign painting, as well.

She taught, we did, make silk batik work, don't recall that we did watercolour work, which was not my forte. But I don't recall using oils. For the first year it was a lot more varied crafts really than, in conjunction with art. Like the silk batik work. And she was good at all of those things. And of course we did life drawing, with these plaster casts, we didn't have any nude models then. (Carter)

Art students also took technical subjects, such as sewing and dressmaking for the young women, as well as basic drafting.

In contrast to the variety of trades taught in technical courses, commercial courses focussed on three subjects: typing, shorthand, and bookkeeping. Passing the year depended on adequate speeds in typing and shorthand, so classes involved a lot of drills and tests for speed. One typing teacher encouraged his students to type to music, using a given piece, instead of a stopwatch, to time their work (Allison). Others used blindfolds on their students (Brown). The school provided plenty of typewriters, so that each student had one, though the exact model varied. Procedures and type of equipment were all as up-to-date as a typical office of the time, though the typewriters were allowed to age before they were replaced. Students also took lessons in skills such as filing, and could earn special certificates in these skills, sponsored by various office supply companies (MF). A class in business machines involved the whole group sitting in front of hand-cranked adding machines, and totalling long columns of figures.

Commercial students also took rapid calculation — a special course on techniques for adding columns of figures. The teacher who taught that subject had a tendency to start his classes somewhat abruptly, as one student recalled:

> Of course, when we'd get to his room, we'd all start to talk, naturally . . . He carried a three foot ruler and he'd come in that back door and bang that on the wall and just about scare us out of our wits. (Smith)

This teacher spent many classes in speed tests, with students required to add a column of figures in a given period of time. Unfortunately, his habit of banging his pointer to mark the halfway point caused some students to jump and completely forget the sum they were carrying in their heads (Cull).

Teachers in this course also offered lessons on proper office etiquette and behaviour. Women in the commercial courses were taught to be quiet and listen. They were not taught to be aggressive or independent, qualities not welcomed by employers of female office help (Geddes; MF).

General commercial students had to take some time in technical subjects — domestic studies for girls and shop for boys. (Special commercial students did not take these subjects.) Commercial students also took academic subjects — but a limited menu, with no languages, for instance.

The same group of teachers taught academics to pupils from each section of school. Most academic teachers put the day's work on the board, and then went up and down the aisles to check each student's progress, and, often, to confirm that they had done the assigned homework. If teachers wished to include any additional information as part of the lesson, they delivered it in the form of a lecture while standing at the front of the room. The students stayed in seats when talking; they did not have to stand (Walsh). The walls of the classroom tended to be very bare, with just the blackboards and a picture of the king and queen. Where the teachers at the Collegiate were very formal, and called students by their last name, at 'Tech' the teachers used students' first names.

Homework was considered very important at the school; students got homework every night, and the load increased as exams got closer. These exams took place at Christmas, Easter, and in June, and covered academic subjects as well as theory related to practical subjects. Students had to pass every subject; those who failed one — vocational or academic — failed the year. Those who earned three or more 'honours' on their report card (out of thirteen or so subjects) had their name published in the local newspaper. This list was divided into groups by the number of honours won. It was a 'big thrill' for many students to wait and see their name listed in the paper (MF).

An account of one teacher's math classes illustrates the highly structured pedagogy often practised. Each day this teacher would start by sending ten students (of the twenty in the class) to put their solutions to homework problems on the blackboard. Those who did it one day knew they would not do it the next, since he alternated the same groups of ten all year. However, if the teacher thought certain students had not done their homework, then he might send them to the board on a day they were not expecting it. Those students who could not achieve a correct solution did not face recriminations if they had made an honest effort. Instead, the teacher would interrogate their answer and help them reach a correct one. This teacher spent the whole period on his feet in this manner, and then ended the day with new homework assignments. While sticking with this very structured style, the teacher tried to make the content interesting. Thus he used baseball scores and players' statistics as a way to teach mathematics to his class of senior boys, requiring his pupils to bring in the scores from the paper each day (Hopkins).

Not every teacher followed this plan; the English teachers in particular tended to employ a different teaching style, inviting class discussions, which sometimes led to 'pretty hot arguments' (Walsh). Even in this case, most of the teaching came from the front of room, though one particular teacher preferred to move to the back of her room.

Students in English class spent a lot of time reading out loud or reciting memorized passages. They generally used modern renditions of Shakespeare, along with other British works — George Eliot, Sir Walter Scott, and collections of the standard poets. One student described an English teacher this way: 'She used to make books come alive. She would give us all a part and we'd have to act it out' (Richardson). Another teacher also encouraged his students to immerse themselves in Shakespeare's plays, having some of the boys fence with yardsticks at the front of the room. At time he did the acting himself, running into the hall, pounding on the classroom door and then rushing inside to recite *The Highwayman* (Mitchell). Yet this process could be a source of terror for some students, who had what we now know as learning disabilities (Cull). Even some teachers had difficulty with this form of pedagogy. One English teacher, a 'very nervous man', had his students take parts in Shakespeare's plays and then 'raced up and down the aisles', before grabbing a handful of aspirins and chewing them. If his supply ran out, he would send one of his students to a nearby drugstore for more (Carter; Pruss).

Some academic subjects were taught with content considered more relevant to technical or commercial students than what the collegiates taught. Both maths and sciences were taught from special texts aimed at technical schools.

> The physics was geared (towards) mechanics, and they went into far more detail on mechanics than they did in the collegiates. I think we had more on gearing and pulleys and inclined planes and wedges and so on, more experiments and so on, which was geared to our future work situations. (Mitchell)

The content of the first year history course in the mid-1920s also reflected this impulse. The course started with civics — first studying local government, then the provincial government, and finally federal institutions. That took from September to December. In the next term students studied the history of industry, which culminated in one or two field trips to a factory or a foundry. This version of the history course only lasted for about four or five years, then teachers curtailed the field trips and reduced the concentration on the history of industry (Hopkins). Focus in later years reverted to British history, 'especially the battles' (Geddes).

Other academic subjects included: geography, where students spent a lot of time drawing maps of different countries; physiography, a mixture of geography and science, with the emphasis on physical geography and climate; chemistry, with an emphasis on conducting experiments; and French, learned through books rather than conversation (Brown; Champness; Brooks).

Students in every course took physical training, though classes did not take place as frequently as for other subjects. Students would change into a gym outfit, with shorts and sometimes a change of tops. At first, the school did not have a gymnasium, so students took their classes outside in good weather. This meant exercises on a cinder court between wings of the school — many students would return home on those days with cinders in their knees. In worse weather, students had the use of a small room in the basement, full of pipes and plumbing (Cull; Hopkins). Later, expansion allowed for two gymnasia — a boys' gym and a girls' gym. The school still had no proper playing field.

Most physical training classes were spent either in floor games (like basketball) or, more frequently, in gymnastic exercises — doing exercises, running, tumbling or using various pieces of equipment. One student recalled:

> Our gym teacher . . . was an ex-Royal Navy man. . . . He had a cane — a bamboo cane — he called his 'persuader.' . . . Now they had ropes tied to the roof of the gym, and you went up them hand over hand. He'd always demonstrate it first, and then you were expected to go up those ropes. Eventually, (you were expected) to get up there at the same time as he could, and if you didn't make it, he'd let you go so far and then you'd get a whack across the rump with the 'persuader'.
>
> Now there were always two bells at the end of the class. The first one was a warning bell, which meant that you had to start getting changed out of your gym clothes. And, boy, you had better be out of that change room by the time that second bell rang, because he was in there with that cane. (Kennedy)

In the early years, the school also supported a cadet corps. This was mandatory for all male students, who wore a woollen khaki uniform to practice drill either in the school courtyard, or at the nearby armouries. Cadet training took place during school hours. Female students did not take part, and had no alternative activity of a similar sort offered to them (Champness).

For some students, a few additional subjects added variety to their week. Female students in the technical program took a period or two of art each week, though male students did not. Some students, particularly those enrolled in the matriculation program (a part of the technical side of the school) spent some time each week in the library. In academic terms, these extras carried little weight; students (aside from those in the special art course) received no marks for their achievements in gym, library, or art classes (SRCs).

The day's round of classes was broken by the lunch hour, though, through time, the exact arrangements changed both in terms of the length of lunch hour and in the provisions of eating areas. In the earliest years of the school, lunchtime was quite lengthy, lasting one hour and forty-five minutes. Many students went home at lunchtime, often getting a hot meal; those who did not go home ate packed lunches at school. In the 1930s, they could buy chocolate milk, at the cost of two tickets for a nickel (Geddes). The physical arrangements changed frequently, with students eating at times in designated classrooms, in special lunchrooms, in the auditorium, or in one of the gyms. Some years saw the boys and girls separated, while other years saw them mixed together. This provided other experiences too; if a boy and a girl sat together at the back of the auditorium, it meant they were exploring a relationship — often a whole new world. Only a few couples would be brave enough to do this, as the other kids in the hall '. . . would be thinking that it just wasn't the proper thing to do' (MF).

After completing their meals, students left the school building and mixed with their friends, often walking the streets of downtown London for an hour or so. Students had no choice about leaving the building:

> . . . we weren't allowed to roam in and out of the school at random at lunch hour
> — the doors were locked. We had time to eat our lunch, and whatever, and then
> the doors were locked. And you had to stand outside 'till they were open again.
> (MF)

During the mid-1930s, the lunch time break was quite long for some senior students. This did not please nearby merchants, who felt that the students were a disruption. The storekeepers convinced the city police department to assign two or three constables to walk the area during the lunch break to discourage horseplay and shoplifting (Cull).

A few students did stay in during the whole lunch period. The technical shop teachers allowed their students to work on their projects during the lunch hour. Often this meant the whole senior class in these subjects would work these extra hours together (Mitchell).

The school day ended as it had begun, with students walking, riding or driving home; in some years, however, not every student left at the same time. The reality of the Depression and the rhetoric of government spending policies meant that the middle years of the 1930s saw overcrowding in the school. The student body had risen steadily throughout the 1920s and continued to do so in the early 1930s.[4] Since the provincial Department of Education was unwilling to finance any additional expansion to the school, Principal Beal introduced 'the staggered system of classes' in September of 1933. The 'staggered system' changed the temporal structures of the school day. Rather than having all of the school's students spend the same eight periods a day in the building, Principal Beal and his staff arranged for a twelve period day. Each student attended for eight of the twelve periods, with the senior students starting early or ending late, while each teacher only taught the same number of periods as usual. Noon hour was still a common time, and first year students had their eight periods scheduled during the traditional teaching hours. After two years the staggered system disappeared as the crisis faded.[5]

The teachers did not leave in concert with their charges. Most stayed behind to finish paperwork or marking, or prepare for the next day. In addition, many of the teachers seemed willing to take some extra time to help particular students. If any students showed that they were serious about tackling a particular problem, or getting extra experience that would help their job prospects, teachers would devote some of their own time after school to help. As one student remembered: 'Nothing was too much trouble for them' (Hopkins).

While the prescribed structures, accepted pedagogy and delivered curriculum described above merit examination in any survey of school experience, revisionist historians and sociologists of education have drawn attention to what they call the 'hidden curriculum' — the rules of behaviour enforced at a taken-for-granted level (Jackson, 1968; Vallance, 1973/74). In the London Technical and Commercial High School this aspect of the school experience was pervasive and in fact openly emphasized — rather than hidden — by school administrators. Discipline at the school was considered to be enforceable in the classroom, between classes, as well as before and after school. Students who misbehaved might receive extra homework, one or more detentions, or (in the case of gym classes) be made to run laps or do extra calisthenics. Others found themselves sent to the Principal's office, where they might face the strap, or receive detentions along with a lecture on proper behaviour (making the Principal primarily a figure of discipline for many students) (Sutherland, 1986, also discusses contemporary elementary school discipline).

> Only major misdemeanours had expulsion from the school, and they had to be major — destroying property or equipment or something, malicious damage, or an incorrigible person, who they couldn't discipline . . . Fighting, swearing, vulgarity and smoking were all sort of medium misdemeanours. You might get up to a week's detention or two week's detention if it was really something horrible, or something you repeated. (Cushman)

Attendance too was a regulated behaviour. Students who had good or perfect attendance received a bonus of up to 5 per cent on their final average mark, while being late to school was a sure ticket to the detention room (MF).

Classroom discipline followed certain common rules throughout the school, but ultimately individual teachers had their own definitions of proper behaviour, and their own means of providing censure. 'We were always very scared of our teachers. . . . We wouldn't say "boo" to them, because they were an authority' (Richardson).

Of one particular teacher, only bad memories seem to remain among all the students interviewed:

> He was a bully, and I don't think he was right, his personality was warped, I'll put it that way. He started every class by slamming a metre stick on the front work table . . . and that was the way he'd run his class from start to finish, with a loud yelling voice. And he took no — there was no jokes, no kidding, no laughing in his class. He taught very well, because you were scared of him literally, because he would smack fellows on the side of the head and so on like that. I've seen him knock fellows right off their stool. But, he didn't give many detentions, he handled it all himself in his classroom. I didn't, nobody liked him. I guess he taught us — I guess we learned our subject — but it wasn't because he put it across to us in any way of a gentlemen. He was a boor and a bully. (Mitchell)

Another student remembered how a different teacher handled misbehaviour: 'If you cut up — goofed off — you got a cuff alongside the head' (Champness). At the same time, former students insist that these heavy-handed sorts were in the minority at LTCHS.

One aspect of behaviour constantly brought to students' attention was the habit of calling their elders 'sir' or 'ma'am'. The slogan 'Get the "yes, sir" habit' appeared on signs in classrooms throughout the school, and was repeated constantly by teachers. Many of them told their students that this habit represented a key to the successful reputation of the school, and its consequent ability to place students in employment situations.

Discipline extended beyond the classroom walls. As the students moved through the halls in single file, teachers would come out to ensure that order was maintained, and that no one was speaking. One of the perennial monitors brought his yardstick with him to enforce his power, though the other teachers refused to follow his example. Principal Beal himself also frequently appeared in the halls to watch his charges. Students caught speaking in the line between classes would be pulled from the line, either silently or with much commotion — depending on the teacher — and sent for punishment.

At times discipline reached even further. As one former student recalled:

> It was a no-smoking school; after school you had to be at least two blocks from the school (before you could smoke). How they built in these kinds of restrictions . . . But that was life as it was then; nobody seemed to think this was a hardship. That's just what the rules were. (Cushman)

Despite the teachers' efforts, not all students conformed to their idea of disciplined behaviour. Some skipped school, others exchanged notes as they passed silently in the halls, while the most outspoken acted disruptively in the classroom. One of the most popular means of misbehaviour was to throw things (peanuts for instance) at the teacher when his/her back was turned (Brown). Writing rude things on the blackboards or other places in the classroom also proved popular. Nicknames, too, indicated a quiet rebellion. Mr. T.W. Oates became 'Timothy Wheat

Oats', while Mr. Wheeler, who 'had a game leg' was called 'side-wheeler' behind his back (Pruss). Students in many courses would try to get away with practical jokes, though the technical students usually had the most access to materials which could serve their pranks. Thus students in the automechanics course would take some carbide (used in early automobile lamps) and drop it into water to generate an awful, pervasive, odour (Cushman).

Other forms of resistance to teachers existed; some used the internal mechanisms of the school:

> We had a Mr. O'Donell, from Dublin. He taught French . . . So him and I got into an argument one day, so he put me in the hallway, and I thought 'I'm not putting up with this', so I went right upstairs to the office to the Principal. And next thing you know, this Mr. O'Donell is standing looking through the door, so the Principal calls him in and he said, 'Mr. Pruss will not be in your class any longer'. He said, 'what's your problem?'. I said 'well you can't understand the man when he talks the king's English, so how do you understand an Irishman from Dublin, teaching you French?' I said 'it sounds like something from some other foreign country'. I said 'I just don't get along with him, you leave me in there, why I'll just be in a problem all the time with him'. So the rest of them, they caught on, so there's a lot of them got out of the class doing the same thing. Get in an argument with him, and then get out of it. (Pruss)

Students also rebelled at times against the general codes of behaviour, such as that which barred smoking on school grounds:

> We used to smoke in the boiler room. In those days, you know, it was just, girls were just beginning to smoke and that sort of thing. And the man who was in charge of the boiler room, he was very understanding, he let us smoke in there sometimes. (Carter)

The washrooms too often 'reeked of smoke' though students would deny their behaviour when challenged by a teacher (Cushman).

The more relaxed atmosphere of physical training class allowed for other forms of rowdy conduct. One student recalls a row of 'travelling rings' hanging from the gymnasium ceiling. He and his classmates used to swing from the rings

> . . . like a monkey, going from one end to the other. Our objective was to see if we could get up enough speed at the end rings to be able to get our feet up onto the balcony and grab the rail. Of course this was forbidden, but it was fun. We used to try it. (Cushman)

Even the popular Mrs. Cryderman and her loosely structured art classes did not prove immune from this sort of statement.

> We had a great many life sized plaster casts of ancient Greek gods, Mercury and Zeus. And sometime when she must have been out of the room . . . some of the boys went in and they painted strategic spots with bright colours green. I always

remember the fig leaf on — of course there were fig leaves on all of them because it was a school — the leaf on Mercury who is you know, bright bright green, and I've never seen anyone so angry. She just went into orbit. And I'd never heard her really raise her voice, and she screamed and yelled at us, and stormed up and down the room . . . and until whoever did it confessed, she wasn't having anything to do with us, she wouldn't even talk to us. (Carter)

At times, student resistance to certain classroom management techniques left other students as victims:

We knew we had a squealer in the (science) class. So this day, some of them got in ahead and they went up and got a piece of phosphorus out of the water, and they put it in this kid's desk . . . (The teacher) comes whistling and this kid's sitting there and all of a sudden the smoke started coming out of his desk. So he took the kid out in the hall and punished him. But we did it because this kid was squealing on us. (Pruss)

Physical fights between students also broke school rules of conduct, though the immediate reasons were no doubt more personal. Such disputes occurred regularly, but usually consisted only of a few blows; more serious fights were often broken up by other students (Cushman).

Finally, not all students were concerned with their performance at school. Other interests, including outside work, often claimed more of their attention (for instance, Brooks).

While students spent their school day in the company of the same group of classmates (usually of the same gender), extracurricular activities allowed students from different years, different classes and different courses to meet. Some extracurricular activities, such as sports participation, remained segregated by gender, but others provided opportunities for boys and girls to mix, either as participants, or as spectators.

Before the building of the gym and auditorium, the school offered little in the way of extracurricular activities. Unlike later years there were no sports, dances, or musicals. Despite this, teachers did try to organize a few leisure activities, such as hikes, sleighrides or skating parties (Smith; Brown).

In later years, extracurricular sports included basketball, both for boys and girls, track and field, sometimes baseball, and boy's hockey (with very little in the way of protective equipment). The school boasted no football team, though. Most sports took place after school; neither players nor spectators were excused from lessons for games. The lack of field facilities meant many of the activities took place at nearby schools with better facilities. Despite these drawbacks, there was still a lot of enthusiasm. In addition, sports participation allowed student athletes a chance to travel to nearby communities for games (Brooks).

Activities concerned with more cultural pursuits also brought students from various courses together. Some thirty-forty students made up the large school orchestra, while the glee club and the literary society provided similar forms of activity. The best-known cultural activities, though, were the annual school shows which commenced with the building of the auditorium. These shows involved hundreds of students, including a large cast, the orchestra, and scores of workers. The facilities available through the technical side of the school — especially carpentry and painting — made the school shows much more impressive than those of other secondary schools in the city. The annual show ran for several nights each spring, and usually attracted sell-out crowds. At first this had not seemed likely, since the stage did not come with any lighting at all. Teachers and students had to coax the authorities just to allow them to put up a single trough of white lights behind the curtain; it did not take long for the students to rewire this simple system so that it operated as three separate banks of different coloured lights (Hopkins).

After the building of the school gym, dances became a regular fixture of the social calendar. The school orchestra would provide the music for waltzes, foxtrots or jitterbugs. The teachers, acting as chaperones, would lead by example and dance themselves. Strict adolescent social rules governed the behaviour of students at these affairs:

> There'd be a line of boys along one wall and a line of girls along the other wall . . . They wouldn't think anything of going over and asking a girl to dance. The girls . . . didn't ever ask the boys. The girls were not aggressive . . . You waited 'till a boy asked you. If you didn't get asked you were considered a 'wallflower'. (Geddes)

For a while the school ran annual picnics. Everyone would go to the school building, where the teachers took attendance. Then they jumped on the open-sided street railway cars which were waiting, lined up outside the building. The school body reached Springbank park by about ten o'clock in the morning. Following lunch, a program of sports and games took place. In the late 1930s, individual class picnics replaced the more embracing school picnics, and often involved more distant destinations, such as Port Stanley on Lake Erie (Cushman).

For senior students, much of their last days at school were occupied with thoughts of the next stage: entrance to the world of work. Even here school structures were important, since the school handled placement duties for many of its students, though not every student benefitted. Generally teachers sent a small group out to interviews after being contacted by an employer needing to fill specific positions. At other times the school put enquiries around to local employers, to see if they would take students. A teacher involved in the relevant area would then decide who to send out for the interviews; obviously such arrangements added immeasurably to the power available to some teachers, who could exert some control over the subsequent careers and earnings of their charges.

The students chosen would be called to the office and given a couple of days warning. As part of this process, students received instruction on how to behave themselves in interviews. In some cases, the preparation was on an individual basis. But near the end of the year, one of the teachers would address each class of senior students: '. . . the girls were to dress like ladies, and our nails were to be clean, and our hair was to be clean — and the boys were to wear a suit' (MF).

Another sort of placement was available to graduates of the early years of the school, as it expanded. The top students in the commercial course were offered positions in the school office, while students in some of the technical courses might also receive school job offers as maintenance workers or electricians (Brown). Later, senior-year commercial students were used as temporary help in the city, thus giving them office experience for two weeks or so, without jeopardizing their school work (Cull).

Conclusions and Complexities

While the foregoing appears primarily as a mass of thick description, some observations emerge from the account. One central theme in the recounting of the tales of everyday life is the importance of structures in the school. Students spent their day segregated by gender, year and course. Their experience in academic and commercial classrooms was bound by tight rules of discipline and formal modes of pedagogy. The period under study here includes that of the Great Depression — when the economy of Canada suffered a collapse just as total as that affecting the United States. The Depression did cause some students to attend LTCHS — either because they (or their parents) felt a vocational course offered a more solid economic future, or because alternate career paths which involved expensive education or training had moved out of reach. The depressed economy also reduced students' chances of finding work at the end of their schooling (Geddes; Pruss). Yet, in general, the Great Depression had little consequence on the daily structures of classroom life. In this sense, the period 1920–1940 is marked more by continuity, than by change. The building of the gym and auditorium wing actually marked the most notable experiential change, as it allowed for the dissolution of some structures of segregation in terms of sports, the school show, dances, and other extracurricular activities.

The conclusion that schools are highly-structured environments is not revolutionary; in fact, for many people, no other phase of life ever comes under such rigid rules. Yet all the structures of schooling had to be continually re-created through the practices of human actors. All the people who spent time in the school — the Principal, teachers, students and support staff — contributed to the ongoing structuration of school life, as did people who never physically entered the school on a typical day — parents, board officials, employers and the great mass of people with no direct connection to LTCHS but with a firm sense of what education involved.

In most cases, it is far easier to see teachers and administrators as the agents whose practices reinscribed particular structures, but student behaviour — passive or active — also played a role. Thus the structured maintenance of gender divisions through course selection, curriculum variation and coercive control over much student activity also received support from student practices such as wearing gender-distinctive clothing, or lining up on opposite walls at the start of school dances (see also Connell, 1987). Similarly, teachers employed at least three distinct pedagogic styles, and a number of different pedagogic practices, yet they all shored up the structured relationship between teacher and pupil; most students accepted the authority of this relationship, and even allowed it to govern their behaviour up to two blocks away from the school, before or after formal school hours.

A good deal of the daily action surrounding practices can be represented as ritual (Bernstein, 1971). Many writers have commented on the similarities between schools and churches. The process begins with the pilgrimages to the site and then involves a variety of ritual processes, incantations, and ceremonies. In schools we may have the secular and socialising succession to the religious mission.

Finally, it is clear that all students (and all teachers) were able to act for themselves in some ways, despite the surrounding structures. Student 'misbehaviour' can be interpreted in a variety of ways. At one level, acting up served to challenge existing structures, encouraging teachers to abandon some of their role constraints and react as individuals. Such behaviour is part of the continuous bargaining between students and teachers which is crucial to the reproduction or transformation of lived classroom structures. At the same time, student misbehaviour also served to justify, and thus reproduce, the massive disciplinary structures of the school.

Yet dropping phosphorus into a 'squealer's' desk, or throwing peanuts at a teacher were only the least subtle forms of agency; at a day-to-day level the senior male students on the technical side had the greatest control over the conditions of their schooling, as each tended to work on an individually chosen project, or tackled a different problem as they fixed teachers' cars or tended to the school's practical needs. It is interesting to note that the one example we have of a student challenging fundamental school structures (Glen Pruss' successful campaign to move out of a particular teacher's French class) involved a young man enrolled in the general technical course.

The conclusion that students in shop courses had the greatest control over the conditions of their schooling offers an intriguing sidelight on the normal perception of vocational education. This might explain some of the continuing ambivalence about vocationalism, as opposed to the ongoing acceptance and promotion of more 'academic' versions of schooling, among those lobbies which equate social control with education. Certainly these insights suggest how generative studies at the level of individual schools, particularly those with vocational and academic missions co-existing, can be. Such studies show how structures are not timeless and immutable but are in Williams' words both 'structures of feelings' and 'structures of intentions' at once constraining and negotiable, produced and reproduced in an ongoing social process (Williams, 1977).

Acknowledgments

This research was supported by a grant from the Social Sciences and Humanities Research Council of Canada. We wish to thank Patrick Burman for his comments on an earlier version of this chapter.

Notes

1 Information on the interview subjects is contained in the appendix to this chapter. In this text, any direct quotation or other evidence provided by a single informant is noted by the use of a reference to that person's name without a date. We have previously discussed the problematic nature of oral testimony as a source (Goodson, 1992) and the issue of ethical procedures in the study of teachers' lives (Goodson and Walker, 1991). Where 'SRCs' are cited, this refers to information found on student record cards, available for the whole period.

2 London Technical and Commercial High School (LTCHS) (1921) *Curriculum: Industrial, Technical and Matriculation Courses*, London, LTCHS; LTCHS (1923), (1925), (1933) and (1938) *Announcements*, London, LTCHS.

3 Students made this decision before entering third year until the last 1920s (LTCHS, 1925) and before second year from the late 1920s through the 1930s (SRCs).

4 Attendance peaked at 1714 in September 1935, before levelling off for the rest of the decade.

5 London Board of Education for the City of London (1933), (1934) and (1935) *Minutes of the Board of Education for the City of London*, London; Beal (1934), pp. 7–8.

References

ANSTEAD, C.J. and GOODSON, I.F. (1993) 'Subject status and curriculum change: Commercial education in London, Ontario, 1920–1940', *Paedogogica Historica*, **29**.

BARMAN, J. (1984) *Growing up in British Columbia: Boys in Private School*, Vancouver: University of British Columbia Press.

BENNET, C.A. (1926 and 1937) *History of Manual and Industrial Education* (2 vols), Peoria, IL: Bennett.

BERNSTEIN, B. (1971) 'On the classification and framing of educational knowledge', in YOUNG, M.F.D. (ed.) *Knowledge and Control*, London: Collier-Macmillan.

BHASKAR, R. (1979) *The Possibility of Naturalism: A Philosophical Critique of the Contemporary Human Sciences*, Brighton: Harvester Press.

BURMAN, P. (1988) *Killing Time, Losing Ground: Experiences of Unemployment*, Toronto: Wall and Thompson.

CONNELL, R.W. (1987) *Gender and Power: Society, the Person, and Sexual Politics*, Cambridge: Polity Press.

COOPER, B. (1985) *Renegotiating Secondary School Mathematics*, London: Falmer Press.

CREMIN, L.A. (1961) *The Transformation of the School: Progressivism in American Education, 1876–1957*, New York: Knopf.

DE CERTEAU, M. (1984) *The Practice of Everyday Life*, Berkeley, CA: Berkeley University Press.

DUNN, T.A. (1979) 'Teaching the meaning of work: Vocational education in British Columbia 1900–1929', in JOHES, D.C., SHEEHAN, N.M. and STAMP, R.M. (eds) *Shaping the Schools of the Canadian West*, Calgary: Detselig.

GAFFIELD, C. (1986) 'Coherence and chaos in education historiography', *Interchange*, **17**.

GIDDENS, A. (1981) *A Contemporary Critique of Historical Materialism, Vol 1*, London: Macmillan.

GIDDENS, A. (1984) *The Constitution of Society: Outline of the Theory of Structuration*, Cambridge: Polity Press.

GIDDENS, A. (1991) 'Structuration theory: Past, present and future', in BRYANT, C.G.A. and JARY, D. (eds) *Giddens' Theory of Structuration: A Critical Appreciation*, London: Routledge.

GOODSON, I.F. and ANSTEAD, C.J. (1993) *Through the Schoolhouse Door*, Toronto: Garamond Press.

GOODSON, I.F. and DOWBIGGIN, I.R. (1991) 'Vocational education and school reform: The case of the London (Canada) technical school, 1900–1930', *History of Education Review*, **20**, 1.

JACKSON, P. (1968) *Life in Classrooms*, New York: Holt, Rinehart and Winston.

KANTOR, H.A. (1988) *Learning to Earn: School, Work and Vocational Reform in California 1880–1930*, Madison, WI: University of Wisconsin Press.

KATZ, M. (1968) *The Irony of Early School Reform*, Cambridge, MA: Harvard University Press.

KLIEBARD, H. (1986) *The Struggle for the American Curriculum 1893–1958*, London: Routledge and Kegan Paul.

LABAREE, D.F. (1988) *The Making of an American High School*, New Haven, CT: Yale University Press.

LAZERSON, M. and GRUBB, W.N. (1974) *American Education and Vocationalism: A Documentary History 1870–1970*, New York: Teachers College Press.

PATTERSON, A. *et al* (eds) (1974) *Profiles of Canadian Educators*, Toronto: DC Heath.

SILVER, H. (1992) 'Knowing and not knowing in the history of education', *History of Education*, **21**.

STAMP, R. (1975) *School Days: A Century of Memories*, Calgary: McClelland and Stewart West.

SUTHERLAND, N. (1986) 'The triumph of "formalism": Elementary schooling in Vancouver from the 1920s to the 1960s', in McDONALD, R.A.J. and BARMAN, J. (eds) *Vancouver Past: Essays in Social History*, Vancouver: University of British Columbia Press.

VALLANCE, E. (1973/74) 'Hiding the hidden curriculum', *Curriculum Theory Network*, fall, **4**.

WILLIAMS, R. (1977) *Marxism and Literature*, Oxford: Oxford University Press.

APPENDIX: INTERVIEW SOURCES

Teachers

Name	Subject	Starting year
Fallona, Margaret	Academics	1930
Morgan, Pearl	Academics	1922

Students

Name	Course	Years at LTCHS
Allison, Marjorie	Special Commercial	1930–1
Brooks, Tom	General Commercial	1931–3
Brown, Gaye*	General Commercial	1920–3
Buchwald, Art	General Technical	1925–8
Carter, Nora	Art	1931–5
Champness, Tom	General Technical	1920–3
Childs, Joyce*	General Commercial	1927–30
Cull, Helen	General Commercial	1922–5
Cushman, Russ	Special Auto Mech.	1934–5
Darnell, Helen	Night School, Cooking	1921–2
'MF'	General Commercial	1935–8
Fisher, Ben	General Technical	c. 1930
Geddes, Irene	General Commercial	1930–3
Hopkins, Norman	General Technical	1924–8
'MK'	Special Commercial	1927–8
Kennedy, Harold	General Technical	1935–40
MacDonald, Evelyn	General Commercial	1932–5
Maclaren, Hilda	General Commercial	1928–31
Mitchell, Fred	General Technical	1937–40
Pruss, Glen	General Technical	1933–6
Richardson, Edna	General Commercial	1921–4
Smith, Edith	General Commercial	1924–8
Spence, Gladys	Nursing and Diet.	1930–1
Walsh, George	General Technical	1932–5

* These two students also took secretarial positions at LTCHS after graduating.

8   Subject Cultures and the Introduction of Classroom Computers

(with J. Marshall Mangan)

One of the most prominent features of present-day school systems is the rapid introduction of computers into classrooms. This ubiquitous innovation has been linked
to a number of processes which seek to restructure and reform North American
education. Not surprisingly, it has also sparked a corresponding wave of research,
with masses of data and analysis being accumulated, covering a wide array of issues
related to both technical and pedagogical processes (Sutton, 1991, pp. 475–503;
Bangert-Drowns *et al*, 1985, pp. 243–56).

What has often been missing in this research, however, is a developed analysis of the challenge which microcomputers in classrooms may present to the
well-established cultures and sub-cultures of schools, and in particular to subject
sub-cultures. A range of work has reported on educational change generally (see
Fullan, 1993; Hargreaves, 1993) but here we report on recent research in which
we attempted to assess some of the reciprocal effects of classroom computing and
the context and culture of schooling.

The Research Project

'Curriculum and context in the use of computers for classroom learning' was a
three-year research project, funded by the Ontario Ministry of Education, and conducted by researchers at the University of Western Ontario, in collaboration with
the Board of Education for the City of London, Ontario. The goal of the project was
to examine the effects of the use of microcomputer networks in secondary schools,
across a broad range of subject areas and applications (see Goodson, Mangan and
Rhea, 1991a).

The project was structured to undertake separate investigations into the effects
of computer use in several distinct subject areas in the Ontario secondary curriculum; in particular: history and contemporary studies, geography, art, family studies,
electronics, and drafting. It also included studies of spreadsheet use across the
curriculum, and the effects of teachers' use of computers on their classroom administration. In each of these areas, the principal investigators[1] defined their own specific topics for scrutiny. Overarching these individual investigations was the more
general research goal of examining the effects of computer usage on the context of

classroom teaching and learning, and on the structure and presentation of curricular materials. In pursuing these goals, we sought to use a 'grounded theory' approach, which would allow prominent themes to 'emerge' from the data (see Glaser and Strauss, 1967; Strauss and Corbin, 1990).

Field research was conducted at two London-area high schools, which go by the pseudonyms of 'Brock' and 'Tecumseh' in our reports. Six teachers from Brock and five from Tecumseh (and their classes) were designated as the primary participants. Another nine teachers were trained in the use of the computers as a potential 'backup' team. These teachers have also been assigned pseudonyms for use in our reports. The Ontario Ministry of Education provided a networked ICON computer system for each school, as part of the project. At Brock, twenty terminals and a fileserver were installed in a single large 'laboratory'. At Tecumseh, the terminals were distributed through five classrooms and the library, in 'clusters' of three or four terminals each.

The project was intended from the beginning as primarily an intensive, qualitative study, and not a quasi-experimental effort. Nevertheless, by including two schools in very different neighbourhoods, with different computer network configurations, we hoped to avoid some of the gross biases that studying an even smaller cohort might introduce. Our approach also allowed some limited comparisons of the different schools and classrooms, and provided a wider range of data from a wider range of settings. The research team engaged in regular classroom observations over a two-year period. Data were generally recorded in qualitative case-record form, but a classroom-interaction analysis grid was also developed toward the end of the project. Use of this grid offered the possibility of combining our qualitative data with a modicum of quantitative measurement (Kyriacou and Chang, 1993, pp. 19–20). Some of the results of this mixed-method approach will be reported here.

Cultures of Subjects

Given that our focus in this research was on secondary schooling, a major variable in the take-up of computers was the subject being taught. To some extent each subject in the secondary school is a separate microcosm, a microworld with varying values and traditions. These traditions arise partly from the nature of the subject matters, but more particularly from the social and political processes which have formed them (Goodson, 1993; Franklin, 1986).

When we refer to 'subject area sub-cultures', then, we mean the general set of practices and expectations which has grown up around a particular school subject, and which shapes the definition of that subject as both a distinct area of study and as a social construct. The subject sub-culture exists previous to classroom realization (as well as in its expression within that realization), and previous to this project. Hence we refer to *antecedent subject sub-cultures*. For instance, art students may be expected to have a different set of priorities, a different set of classroom activities, and a different way of relating to both their class work and their teacher than students in a history class. At the same time, history students would expect their class to differ only slightly from their geography class, with similar teaching processes being used, and even some overlap in subject matter.

A number of studies have confirmed the central role which subject sub-cultures and subject specialisms play in the preparation of teachers. In 1970 McLeish's research on college students and lecturers found that: 'The most remarkable differences in attitude of any in the total sample appear to be between subject specialists' (quoted in Lacey, 1977, p. 64). Developing a more differentiated model of 'subject sub-cultures', Lacey noted that 'the subject sub-culture appears to be a pervasive phenomenon affecting a student-teacher's behaviour in school and university, as well as their choice of friends and their attitudes towards education'. This leads on to his arguing the case for 'considering the process of becoming a teacher as a multistranded process in which subject sub-cultures insulate the various strands from one another' (*ibid*).

We found evidence that teachers experience their subjects as separate sub-cultures (see Goodson, Mangan and Rhea, 1989, pp. 29–35; Mangan and Goodson, 1990, pp. 91–3). These subcultures now have long-standing histories, reinforced by generations of school practice. Despite their durability, however, we do not wish to reify these social constructs as monolithic or immutable; on the contrary, they are sites of continuous contestation, and ongoing processes of redefinition, even as they are reproduced (see Goodson, 1993). Individual teachers still find ample room within these sub-cultures for the expression of their own educational philosophies and pedagogical styles. For the purposes of this chapter, however, we feel that we should define the salient characteristics and practices of the subject sub-cultures we will be discussing. A rough descriptive outline of their features follows:

A   Social studies: history, geography, sociology
1   Content-oriented. Generally larger class sizes. Teacher talk domiates.
2   'Socratic' method is frequently cited by teachers. This is taken to mean:
   (a)   classroom lectures, often overlapping with reading assignments;
   (b)   frequent questioning of students during in-class reviews;
   (c)   repetition of material in several media, including examination questions.
3   A generally formal classroom format. Students usually sit in rows, face front, and work independently. Teachers tend to maintain an atmosphere of quiet, and group attention to a single task.

B   Art: commercial and visual arts
1   Less emphasis on content and lecture style, except in art history sections (note that this exception constitutes a blurring of boundaries; 'modern civilization' courses cover art history, in a style virtually identical to that in art courses).
2   A greater emphasis on individuality and creativity. Students are often urged to originate their own compositions. However, teachers will offer hints to students who are in difficulty. They are also capable of being didactic regarding issues of technique, colour blending, etc.

3 Higher frequency of individual coaching and demonstration.

4 As a corollary of the above, a generally less formal classroom atmosphere: more noise and movement, more casual conversation between teachers and students, greater tolerance for background noise (for example, music) and, in some cases, (with mature students) less strict monitoring of attendance.

C **Technological studies/family studies: drafting, electronics, foods, clothing**
These subjects offer a kind of middle ground between the arts and social studies: they are oriented towards the practical, but contain a fair amount of theoretical material.

1 Lectures and dictation of notes are fairly common, but usually only occupy the first quarter of a class period. The remainder of the period is usually taken up with a practical exercise.

2 In performing the practical assignment, there is a reduced emphasis on individuality or creativity. Instead, the emphasis is on the correct execution of prescribed instructions: measuring, drawing, sewing; cooking according to recipes.

3 Individual coaching is commonplace, but the relationship between teacher and student is still somewhat more formal, and classroom discipline is slightly stricter, than in most art classes.

All of these features can be seen to be linked to different production tasks within the subject sub-cultures. In social studies, students primarily produce written output or graphical displays; in art, drawings, paintings, and sculptures; in technological and family studies, a practical artifact. The nature of these tasks in shaping classroom cultures is also overlaid by other variables: the age level and difficulty grouping of the class, for instance. The atmosphere in one teacher's grade 9 class, for example, was quite different from that observed in her class for mature students.

Within our project, the established subject sub-cultures were confronted by a series of computer applications which were, for the most part, explicitly designed to conform with the subject guidelines issued by the Ontario Ministry of Education, and to emphasize individual, independent student interaction. Social studies applications included game-like simulations of historical situations and a geographical database system. The primary art software was an interactive drawing program which included advanced image-manipulation features, and was capable of producing full-colour printed output. 'Tool' software, including word-processors and spreadsheets, were available to all subject areas, but predominated in the technological studies areas. Technological studies classes also made occasional use of programs focused on nutrition and electronic circuit design.

Subject Sub-cultures and Classroom Interaction Patterns

One of the challenges for our project was to develop a methodology adequate to the assessment of the complex and multi-faceted nature of the issues we were concerned with, while also preserving a relationship to the participant teachers which did not become oppressive (see Goodson and Mangan, 1991, pp. 9–48). Our primary focus was on qualitative methods of classroom observation and personal interviews with teachers and students. We also felt, however, that sub-cultures would be reflected in observable, quantifiable classroom activities.

During the final semester of our classroom observations (September 1990–January 1991), we developed a system for tabulating observed classroom activity on two basic dimensions: *interpersonal interactions*, and *level of cognitive function* (see Goodson, Mangan and Rhea, 1991b, pp. 88–102). For the purposes of this analysis, we will refer only to the kinds of interpersonal interactions observed, which were recorded as proportions of total classroom teaching time. The definitions we adopted were derived from categories originally developed by Flanders (1970). A total of forty-four valid classroom observation sessions were recorded for analysis.

Classes were identified according to the teacher, subject, and time of day. We also identified each by classroom type. Classrooms were divided into:

(i)   regular classrooms — those without computer use;
(ii) computer classrooms, which featured an entire period of computer use in a cluster-equipped classroom;
(iii) mixed regular and computer classes, in which computers were used for part of the period;
(iv) sessions in the computer laboratory.

Before looking at the interview data regarding the interaction of computers with classroom cultures, it will help to review some of these observational data. This evidence generally reinforces the importance of the concept of subject sub-cultures to an understanding of the dynamics of implementing computers in the classroom.

Subject sub-cultures find expression through a variety of different expectations and practices, but most notably through different styles of teaching and classroom organization. The nature of these sub-cultures has already been described in more detail above. The application of this notion to our data implies a hypothesis about the character of classroom interaction: that, in general, art classrooms will be characterized by students involved in individual, creative work, with the teacher in a coaching and consulting role; whereas social studies classrooms will centre around more formal lectures and recitations, featuring a more teacher-centred pedagogy. We would expect family-studies and technological-studies classes to fall somewhere in between, reflecting their combination of fact-based and practical content.

In our analysis, we found several variables to be of interest to an evaluation of this hypothesis: the proportion of time spent in teacher-initiated activity; the proportions spent in 'recitations', i.e., question-and-answer activities (see Hoetker and Ahlbrand, 1969, pp. 145–67; Cuban, 1984; Hargreaves and Earl, 1990); and the proportions of large-group vs. small-group activity. Selected summary statistics from analyses of variance on these variables are presented and discussed below.

Table 5: *Mean proportion of instructional time devoted to teacher-initiated activity by teacher and discipline*

Subject Department	Mean Proportion of Period in Teacher-Initiated Activity	
	by Teacher	by Discipline
Art	.092	.153
	.233	
Family Studies	.101	
	.258	
		.249
Technological Studies	.298	
	.288	
	.400	
History	.356	
		.335
	.231	
Geography	.458	
	.282	
Overall	**.277**	
F Ratio	0.91	2.11
Df	10;33	2;41
Sig. F	.532	.135

Teacher-initiated Activities

Table 5 presents summary statistics for teacher-initiated activity, by teacher, and 'discipline', defined by collapsing classroom subjects as shown into art, family/ tech. studies, and social studies.

It is worth noting that the overall proportion of teacher-initiated activity in these classrooms was a good deal lower than the literature of classroom research might have led us to expect (for example, Cuban, 1984; Tye, 1985). This may indicate that, even before the introduction of computers, a more student-centred pedagogy had already begun to take hold in these schools. Such a pedagogy had been advocated in Ministry and Board documents for some time (see, for instance, Ontario Ministry of Education, 1988). Since we did not measure classroom inter-action in these classes prior to the start of our project, however, we cannot com-ment at any length about this. We are also unable to say whether the participating teachers were very different in their teaching styles from their colleagues in the same and nearby schools. For the purposes of our project, however, we wished to focus on the *differences* between subject groupings, and between the different forms of computer use. The generally high level of student participation observed, relative to conventional classrooms, must for the time being be treated as a back-ground constant.

Table 6: Mean proportion of instructional time devoted to teacher-questioning activity by teacher and discipline

Subject Department	Mean Proportion of Period in Teacher Questioning	
	by Teacher	by Discipline
Art	.011 .032	0.20
Family Studies	.006 .138	
		.051
Technological Studies	.064 .034	
History	.047 .169	
		.106
Geography	.056 .123 .154	
Overall	**.073**	
F Ratio	3.04	4.62
Df	10;33	2;41
Sig. F	.008	.016

Given the goals of our investigations, we noted that the differences among disciplines in proportions of teacher-led activity was in the predicted direction, but this difference was not found to be statistically significant. There is clearly a good deal of variance among the participating teachers. It was interesting to note the extreme cases: the art teacher at Brock was observed to initiate specific activities in less than 10 per cent of her class time, while one of the geography teachers at the same school devoted over 45 per cent of his class time to such activities.

Recitative Activities

Table 6 presents a summary of the mean proportions of time devoted to teacher questioning, by teacher and discipline, as before.

This table shows that the proportion of time devoted by teachers to questioning their students was generally low. However, three of the social studies teachers spent 12 per cent to 17 per cent of their class time in this activity, while the art teachers devoted 3 per cent or less to it. This contrast was statistically significant (at the .05 level) for teachers, and retained its significance when they were grouped into disciplines. We also measured time spent in student response activities; taken together, question and response activities accounted for a mean proportion of almost 20 per cent of social studies class time, but less than 5 per cent of art classes.

Table 7: *Mean proportion of instructional time devoted to small-group teaching activity by teacher and discipline*

Subject Department	Mean Proportion of Period in Small-Group Questioning	
	by Teacher	**by Discipline**
Art	911 .895	.904
Family Studies	.835 .644	.785
Technological Studies	.800 .797	
History	.437 .261	.464
Geography	.786 .353 .400	
Overall	**.644**	
F Ratio	2.55	8.13
Df	10;33	2;41
Sig. F	.021	.001

Small-group Teaching Activities

The amount of time devoted to large-group versus small-group or individual instruction was coded separately from the other activity types described above. Analysis of this variable indicates once again a statistically significant difference among teachers and disciplines, in the predicted direction, as shown in table 7.

The same art teacher who spent the least amount of time in teacher-initiated activity, for instance, spent the most on small-group/individual instruction. A clear pattern emerged across disciplines, with art classes devoting an average of 90 per cent of instructional time to small-group activities, while social studies classes were engaged in such activities for less than half the time, on average (but with a noticeable range of differences among teachers).

With this quantitative picture of sub-cultural differences in classroom interaction in mind, we can now turn back to the more ethnographic data to explore the meaning of these differences.

Teaching Styles and Teachers' Lives

In most cases, teachers perceive their pedagogical style as a limited arena of personal choice, in which they have the freedom and power to make minor variations in curriculum and pedagogy. These variations are constrained by both the funda-mental culture of teaching and the subject sub-culture.

In our project certain interesting juxtapositions of personal style and cultural factors emerged — for instance, in the use of educational technology and media. One of the geography teachers, Walter Harvey, liked 16-mm films, while the others relied more on models, maps, and blackboards. The history teachers all made exten-ive use of video cassettes. Diane Mirabella, one of the family studies teachers, regularly used overheads and filmstrips, but few other technological media.

Teachers varied the particular format of classroom discussions and Socratic questioning: relying on volunteers, or picking out individuals; having student-led discussions or teacher-directed quizzes. There were also observed differences in the degree of 'assigned cooperation': some teachers encourage more group work and student interaction than others. Similarly, some teachers were more inclined to rely on peer coaching and tutoring than others. Some have formal peer-evaluation pro-cedures; others had none.

More than one teacher said that teaching style was an expression of a teacher's personality. If this is true, the implication is that a change in style would require nothing less than a change in personality, as well as a change in culture (see Rossman *et al*, 1988). The difficulty of enforcing such a change should be obvious, and is sometimes acknowledged by the teachers themselves:

Elliot: I think that if I categorize my teaching style, it's been, like, fairly obvi-ously teacher-directed . . . But I think if I want to use the computers more, with three in the room, I've got to be more flexible in letting kids work at a different pace, work on different things at different times . . . So it means sitting down and doing some fairly, uh, drastic revisions of ways I've done things in the past, to tailor it more to individuals or to small groups.

In the life-history interviews which we conducted, teachers often expressed two basic themes regarding their teaching philosophies. First, that they cared deeply about their students, and were interested in opening up some form of novel learning experiences for them. Second, that their teaching styles derived directly from their concept of education and its intersection with their personal lifestyles. Diane Mirabella, for instance, said that she 'likes everything up front', and tries to teach the same way. Harry Thorne described himself as 'content oriented', and said he structured his classes accordingly.

Some of the more senior teachers, particularly from social studies, have indic-ated that they rely more on experience than on preparation to get them through their classes. Elliot Nance said:

. . . I find it fairly easy to come in some days unprepared, then fall back on my experience, or fall back on the fact that I know a certain page in the textbook has some information that's necessary, and to have the kids read it.

This may be taken as an indication of such teachers' complete immersion in and identification with their subject sub-culture. For them, teaching their subject comes naturally, and hardly requires conscious preparation.

Table 8: Mean proportion of instructional time devoted to various activities, by classroom type

Classroom Type	Type of Activity		
	Teacher-Initiated	**Teacher Questioning**	**Small Group**
Regular Classroom	.367	.095	.508
Regular & Computer Class	.153	.108	.754
Computer Classroom	.190	.033	.789
Computer Laboratory	.120	.019	.907
Overall	**.277**	**.073**	**.644**
F Ratio	4.627	3.080	4.233
Degrees of Freedom	3;41	3;41	3;41
Significance of F	.007	.038	.011

What are the implications for the introduction of computers of this close identification of teachers' lives with their professional practice? How does it influence their reaction to the challenges of classroom computing — challenges which not only confront their technical abilities and impose new demands on their time and energy, but which may demand significant changes in their teaching strategies and styles? Some of the answers to these questions may be found by returning to the classroom interaction data.

Teaching Subjects and the Introduction of Computers

As we have seen, the cultures of teaching are closely linked to the cultures of subjects in the so-called 'specialization years' of high school. These subject subcultures precede the introduction of the computer. They represent the terrain into which a new (alien) force, the computer, is being introduced. Given that these patterns of subject-based activity generally confirm our notions of subject subcultures, the relevant question for this project became: how does the introduction of computers into these classrooms affect the observed patterns? The answer, in brief, is that it has a profound effect, as revealed by table 8. This table presents the mean proportions of instructional time devoted to each of the kinds of activities identified previously, but broken down this time by classroom types rather than subjects.

When treated in aggregate (without regard to subjects), regular classrooms were observed to devote an average of about 50 per cent of their instructional time to small-group activities. Computer laboratory sessions, by contrast, saw an average of over 90 per cent small-group activity. Similarly, teacher-initiated activities were fewer whenever computers were in use. The computer, then, seems almost to impose a more individualized approach to teaching (even in classrooms that were already unusually student-centred). These findings are very consistent with those of Swan *et al* (1991). Part of the effect is probably due to the fact that the software is designed to be operated by an individual or a small group, and students

Table 9: *Summary of results from 2-way analyses of variance on proportion of instructional time by discipline and classroom type, for each of three activities*

Source of Variance		Type of Activity		
		Teacher-Initiated	**Teacher Questioning**	**Small Group**
Discipline	F Ratio	2.28	6.80	15.00
	Df	2;41	2;41	2;41
	Sig. F	.100	.003*	.000*
Classroom Type	F Ratio	4.62	4.60	8.65
	Df	3;40	3;40	3;40
	Sig. F	.009*	.009*	.000*
2-Way Interaction	F Ratio	0.55	0.29	1.52
	Df	6;40	6;40	6;40
	Sig. F	.770	.936	.205

* Significant at the .01 level

are free to work at their own, or their group's, pace. Field notes indicate that the large-group activity which did take place in the computer lab was almost entirely restricted to introductory instruction on the mechanics of running the programs.

As might be expected, where computers were located in classrooms and used as part of the lesson, the proportion of time devoted to small-group teaching fell between that of the computer lab and that of a non-computer class. The contrast among the types of classroom was significant at the .01 level.

The fact that significant effects were attributable both to the classroom arrangement and the subject area raises the final question as to whether these effects are independent of each other, or whether they are related or interact with each other. This was explored via a series of two-way analyses of variance, with discipline (grouped subjects) and class type as simultaneous independent variables. Table 9 presents a summary of results from the three separate analyses of variance, in which one of the dependent variables discussed earlier was assessed. For the sake of brevity, only summary statistics are shown in this table.

With one exception, significant effects for both discipline and classroom type were located on all three of the kinds of classroom activity discussed above — teacher-initiated, teacher questioning, and level of small-group interaction. However, *none* of these relationships showed any significant interaction effect. The two variables act entirely independently of one another.

What this implies is that, as we had suspected from earlier classroom observations, the forms of interaction favoured by the introduction of computers into secondary schools cut across the established pedagogical patterns of existing subject sub-cultures. Those patterns are clearly reflected in the differences between disciplines in conducting classroom activities. The introduction of computers creates completely separate patterns based on the type of installation.

The implications of this finding may be quite favourable, as they indicate that the technology pushes teaching styles toward a more individualized model. This is a trend favoured by many within the educational community, including officials of the provincial ministry. However, the impact upon teaching styles may also bode ill for the adoption of computers as a normal part of the teaching practice of secondary school teachers in some disciplines. To the extent that teachers identify strongly with the teaching styles associated with their traditional subject sub-cultures, they may be reluctant to adopt a technology which seems incompatible with those sub-cultures. The pattern of change observed during this research project may not persevere in areas where the change runs counter to the norms of the antecedent culture.

We are thus led from the detailed examination of classroom activity back to more global issue of the potential clash between the culture of computing and the traditions of high school teaching. This potential culture clash has arisen again and again as a central theme in our research (see Goodson, Mangan and Rhea, 1991a). It remains perhaps the central problem to be resolved if computers are to become truly productive tools for learning in high school classrooms.

The Potential for a Culture Clash

Teachers talked about their subject sub-cultures particularly with regard to patterns of classroom practice and classroom control, as can be seen in these excerpts from interviews with the art teachers.

> *Wendy:* People don't face the front in art rooms . . . they're facing each other in a circle around the room . . . And they get up and they move around all the time.

Although art requires freedom of movement and expression, this teacher was also concerned about classroom control, because her classroom environment was 'terribly unstable I'd say . . . most of my job is people control. It'd be nice if it was teaching art, just teaching art, but it isn't'. The insertion of computers into such an environment has the potential to either exacerbate or relieve problems of control. Independent in-class computer use was viewed by this art teacher as one way of keeping three students 'very busy, very happy, very absorbed in something productive. . . . That's always a big plus.'

Likewise, in family studies, the antecedent subject sub-culture favours a classroom where different students carry out different tasks. In short, an individualized classroom environment already exists, and the introduction of computers is fairly unproblematic in such an established classroom terrain:

> *Betty:* Well, in family studies we often have different groups doing different things.
>
> *Interviewer:* So that won't be a major adaptation for you, you'll be able to just . . .
>
> *Betty:* No. Especially the sewing project — I mean their rate of doing things is so varied in that some finish before the others have cut it out! So you have all these people at different stages, so I think it

will be handy for that. You can enrich the program for the faster ones . . . in a way that, you know, I think they would find interesting, rather than just another sewing assignment.

In other subjects, however, the pattern of 'whole class' teaching poses great problems for those wishing to introduce computers. We have found this particularly the case in some history and geography classrooms. Harry Thorne, when asked how computers fit into his social studies classroom, replied:

Harry: It's an extra right now, yes.
Interviewer: It's not in the fabric in your class planning really?
Harry: And I'm finding more and more it's difficult to actually think of ways to include it for an entire class. And I think one of the limitations is that there are only three of them in the room. I can't count on having the three here or the three in the geography room at any given time. And it's also a reflection that I haven't really sat down and tried to organize a class computer-related program.

Although the antecedent subject sub-culture provides an important variable in the take-up of computers in the classroom, there are commonalities as well as differences in the ways teachers introduce computers into their lessons. On the whole, we found *very few* examples of teachers fundamentally re-working their lesson plans and pedagogy. This was expressed in a continuing theme in the interviews that the computer was 'just another tool' — 'just another way of learning' (see Carlson, 1991). What this phrase probably summarizes is the belief that computers will *not* substantially change the way teachers conduct their lessons and their classroom learning. Commercial art teacher, Barb Cunningham stated that:

I would like seven to ten computers in here, because I know a lot of times we don't always have to be on the computer and, in the business, *the computer is just another tool. It's just another medium.* And if you go to a studio . . . now what they do — you know — they go to the drafting table, work something up, work up the graphics, go to the computer, do what has to be done by the computer . . . They bring it back if they have to paste something up or — you know — if they have to put in an illustration or whatever, they have to scan something, they scan it . . . so um, *basically it's just another tool.* (emphasis added)

Participating teachers generally conceived of the computer as being used for routine, *existing* practices is the theme of 'replacement'. Small bits of existing lesson plans are replaced by computerized bits but the basic objectives and structure remain much the same. Carl Higgins, a drafting teacher, described his approach this way:

Let's suppose that we have this *CAD Tutor* in place . . . It would be a very good thing when I've mastered it and I can sit down with three students and say 'I want you to do this exercise and this is how you basically go through doing it'.

Give them the demonstration, and then have them do it. And then rotate another three kids through. Uh . . . now I will eliminate something from the curriculum in order to insert that little piece, okay? So that gives me the time. So I'll kill something off that I don't think is as necessary as the *CAD Tutor*. And the same will apply to the electronics program. Uh . . . something that I think is more usefully done on the computer, I will eliminate the old method to make the space.

The computer is most enthusiastically taken up where it fits with existing practice and causes no substantial changes in content or pedagogy. In art, for instance:

Interviewer: So, do you feel that you've made any major or drastic changes to your lesson plans, or your teaching style, to accommodate these computers?

Wendy: I don't think so. I think it fits in quite nicely in the classroom.

Interviewer: Uh-huh.

Wendy: I don't think I've had to do too many things differently because of it . . .

Interviewer: So you feel they fit in all right in that way, as well?

Wendy: Oh, they especially fit in because of that set-up in the classroom. It's not mostly a teacher talking for half an hour, and students then doing their work. It's everybody working, and me helping them solve problems. And the computer is, is — just presents a new series of problems to be solved by the students, too, so . . .

This teacher, then, feels that the computers, as delivered, do not disrupt the culture of her classroom. By contrast, teachers in other subjects may feel they have to modify their use of computers to ensure that they do *not* disrupt the established sub-culture. Harry Thorne summarizes this pattern of the cooption of computers into the existing framework:

Interviewer: If we get geography software, is that going to solve the problem of your teaching style and your classroom management, or are there going to be new problems down the road even if there is geography software?

Harry: We're always going to have to adapt whatever they give us to our own teaching style, or our own content orientation, or whatever the case is. Because I dare say there will never be a program that fits me exactly, or what I want to accomplish. It may come close, but I don't think there will ever be one that I can say 'Hey, that's perfect for me, and let's go with it.' I may be wrong there, but what I've seen, I don't think so . . .

What seems to be at stake here are the traditional patterns of subject knowledge and subject learning. Subjects are well-established bodies of knowledge and social practices. They carry with them assumptions about 'worthwhile knowledge', 'good students', 'effective teaching', and 'excellent results'. Potentially the computer can enhance these established social procedures or disrupt them. Teachers can coopt the technology, but in some instances they can also 'surrender' to it. In extreme cases this can lead to the actual replacement of subject learning by technical learning — a replacement in short of the academic by the vocational. Not all teachers resist this. Ed Thompson, an enthusiastic innovator with computers, described the transition:

> Yes it has changed the way I teach geography. I've downplayed content and moved to teaching skills — in a way I see myself teaching computing first and geography second . . . and that's fair enough I suppose because knowing computing will get them jobs . . . whereas geography . . . well what can I say?

Of course this view expresses an extreme pendulum swing, directly away from subject teaching to technical training. In the process, Ed is actually led to denigrate the relevance of his own subject specialty. But the quote expresses the 'either/or' view that is prevalent among many. *Either* I can coopt the computer to broadly fit what I am already doing (and think I do well), *or* my existing subject and practice is *overthrown* and I become a technical trainer. Most of the teachers in our project were still ambivalent about this transition, but very few teachers articulated the view common in the rhetoric of guidelines and computer publicity: that computers will revolutionize classrooms and massively enhance the efficiency and scope of subject teaching and learning (see Levinson, 1990, pp. 121–6).

The co-option of computers by subject teachers is an example of a very common response to innovations, and to the lack of sensitivity toward teachers which often accompanies them. As one teacher pointed out: 'if you look at the history of computer use in secondary schools, it's like everything else, it's been brought on us from above'. Initiatives 'from above' are not always seen by teachers as well-informed or indeed well-intentioned. They are sometimes viewed as essentially political responses to powerful pressure groups in society. Hence by this view, it could be argued that it has been judged politically expedient to introduce computers to accommodate business and economic interests. Such an interpretation would certainly apply to the quote above, in which a teacher sees his customary practice being displaced by vocational demands.

Teachers often respond pragmatically to innovations 'from above'. In general they coopt the initiatives and continue broadly as before. In a previous study by Goodson (1980), a teacher summarized the general response to new guidelines in this way: 'The teacher searches out how to go on doing what has always been done in the new context.' The question in one teacher's words was:

> How can I do what I've always been doing in a new context . . . ? Though it would have been a new thing in terms of the syllabus (new guideline) . . . So it was a question of reshuffling his pack of cards, really. (p. 257)

With the introduction of computers we find evidence of reshuffling the pack of cards, but little evidence of anybody trying a new game. It is possible for the culture of computing to completely colonize some areas of the curriculum. In most areas, however, the antecedent subject sub-culture in effect colonizes the computer, and uses it to teach the existing subject in the existing way. In this established practice the computer becomes 'just another tool'.

Conclusions

We have provided evidence that subject sub-cultures are identifiable structures which are visibly expressed through classroom organization and pedagogical styles. A change such as the introduction of computers into secondary classrooms challenges these sub-cultures. It involves much more than the addition of a new technical armoury to existing classroom resources. The introduction of computers in fact sets off a range of *culture clashes* between antecedent subject cultures and the cultures of computing.

In this culture clash the teachers, who are at the centre of events, often see an 'either/or' choice: either I can coopt the computer to broadly fit what I am already doing (and think I do well), or I and my existing subject and practice are overthrown and I become more of a technical trainer. These views may represent only the early stages of the culture clash; perceptions may soften as cultural interplay and negotiation proceeds. On the other hand, after the special project reported here is over, teachers may return to the methods most compatible with their subject cultures and personal styles. We should not be in any doubt, however, that the teachers at the heart of this ongoing negotiation consider that there are major issues at stake.

Note

1 Principal investigators included Roger A Clark, Ivor Goodson, George Haché, Allan Pitman and John Rutledge. Research officers were Marshall Mangan and Valerie Rhea. Ivor Goodson was Project Coordinator.

References

BANGERT-DROWNS, R.L., KULIK, J.A. and KULIK, C.C. (1985) 'Effectiveness of computer-based education in secondary schools', *Journal of Computer-Based Instruction*, **12**.

CARLSON, E.U. (1991) 'Teaching with technology: "It's just a tool"', paper presented at the annual meeting of the American Educational Research Association, Chicago, April.

CUBAN, E.U. (1984) *How Teachers Taught*, New York: Longman.

FLANDERS, B.M. (1970) *Analyzing Teaching Behaviour*, Don Mills: Addison-Wesley.

FRANKLIN, B. (1986) *Building the American Community*, London: Falmer Press.

FULLAN, M. (1993) *Change Forces*, London: Falmer Press.

GLASER, B. and STRAUSS, A. (1967) *The Discovery of Grounded Theory: Strategies for Qualitative Research*, New York: Aldine.

GOODSON, I.F. (1980) 'Curricular conflict 1895–1975', PhD thesis, University of Sussex.

GOODSON, I.F. (1993) *School Subjects and Curriculum Change* (3rd ed), London: Falmer Press.

GOODSON, I.F. and MANGAN, J.M. (1991) 'An alternative paradigm for educational research', in GOODSON, I.F. and MANGAN, J.M. (eds) *Qualitative Educational Research Studies: Methodologies in Transition*, RUCCUS Occasional Papers, vol 1, London: University of Western Ontario.

GOODSON, I.F., MANGAN, J.M. and RHEA, V.A. (1989) 'Development of the research design', in GOODSON, I.F., MANGAN, J.M. and RHEA, V.A. (eds) *Emergent Themes in Classroom Computing: Interim Report #2 from the project 'Curriculum and Context in the Use of Computers for Classroom Learning'*, London: University of Western Ontario.

GOODSON, I.F., MANGAN, J.M. and RHEA, V.A. (eds) (1991a) *Curriculum and the Context in the Use of Computers for Classroom Learning*, Summative Report from the Project (3 vols) London: University of Western Ontario.

GOODSON, I.F., MANGAN, J.M. and RHEA, V.A. (eds) (1991b) Classroom interaction analysis', in GOODSON, I.F., MANGAN, J.M. and RHEA, V.A. (eds) *Closing the Circle: Conclusions and Recommendations: Volume 3 of the Summative Report from the Project 'Curriculum and Context in the Use of Computers for Classroom Learning'*, London: University of Western Ontario.

HARGREAVES, A. (1993) *Changing Teachers Changing Times*, London: Cassell.

HARGREAVES, A. and EARL, L. (1990) *Rights of Passage: A Review of Selected Research About Schooling in the Transition Years*, Toronto, Ontario Ministry of Education.

HOETKER, J. and AHLBRAND, W.P. JNR (1969) 'The persistence of the recitation', *American Educational Research Journal*.

KYRIACOU, C. and CHANG, I.W. (1993) 'Mixing different types of data and approaches in evaluating a curriculum package', *Research Intelligence* (BERA Newsletter), summer.

LACEY, C. (1977) *The Socialisation of Teachers*, London: Methuen.

LEVINSON, E. (1990) 'Will technology transform education or will the schools co-opt technology?', *Phi Delta Kappan*.

MANGAN, J.M. and GOODSON, I.F. (1990) 'History, geography and social studies', in GOODSON, I.F., MANGAN, J.M. and RHEA, V.A. (eds) *Illuminative Evaluation of Classroom Computing: Interim Report #3 from the project 'Curriculum and Context in the Use of Computers for Classroom Learning'*, London: University of Western Ontario.

ONTARIO MINISTRY OF EDUCATION (1988) *Student Retention and Transition: A Selection of Program Models*, Toronto: Ministry of Education.

ROSSMAN, G.B., CORBETT, H.D. and FIRESTONE, W.A. (1988) *Change and Effectiveness in Schools: A Cultural Perspective*, Albany, NY: SUNY Press.

STRAUSS, A. and CORBIN, J. (1990) *Basics of Qualitative Research: Grounded Theory Procedures and Techniques*, London: Sage.

SUTTON, R.E. (1991) 'Equity and computers in the schools: A decade of research', *Review of Educational Research*, **61**, 4.

SWAN, K., MITRANI, M., CHEUNG, M., GUERRERO, F. and SCHOENER, J. (1991) 'The changing nature of teaching and learning in computer-based classrooms', paper presented at the annual meeting of the American Educational Research Association, Chicago, April.

TYE, B.B. (1985) *The Junior High: Schools in Search of a Mission*, Lanham, MD: University Press of America.

9 Computer Studies as Symbolic and Ideological Action: The Genealogy of the ICON

(with J. Marshall Mangan)

The structure of schooling is always political and, because it is political, it is always contradictory. Complete social consensus on the purposes and justifications for public schooling has never been achieved, and probably never will be. Despite such ongoing tensions, however, state schooling has gone ahead, propelled by the interests of its various constituencies. As different groups push forward their agendas, and as professional research and practice impact upon the field, schooling has been modified and restructured (though its core remains remarkably stable and resilient). Compromises are struck periodically among the interests of business, parents, elected officials, professional educators, and school staffs. Often these compromises serve only to raise new conflicts, and to exacerbate the logical inconsistencies of the system. Logic usually takes a back seat to power, however, when political settlements are arranged.

Operating within this context, there are a number of functionaries in any education system whose roles encompass those of 'ideological workers'. Their job is to operate with the policy compromises which have been hammered out in the political arena, and to create a rhetoric of justification which will provide the appearance of a coherent philosophy to the socially constructed reality. Curriculum writers, ministerial staff, special commissions and school boards are all engaged periodically in this sort of ideological work, as are senior politicians.

If such a view of educational policy development seems excessively cynical, this is because we have intentionally presented it, initially, as unidimensional. We have emphasized the influence of politics upon symbology, in order to counter the impression that policy decisions flow from a carefully reasoned process of defining ends and means. In this form, the analysis is too linear and flat to capture the complex realities of the phenomenon. We do not mean to suggest seriously that ideologies are merely products of the process; they also feed back into it, to become new motivating forces. They are used to demand accountability from the system, and to spur further initiatives (which in turn require new forms of justification). And so the cycle proceeds: conflicts of power are reflected in, and condition, the confrontations of discourse. Symbolic action both precedes and follows educational innovation. Struggles are waged in public forums, in the pages of newspapers, in politicians' speeches and in research reports, while they also proceed in the board rooms, administrative offices, and backroom party caucuses of those in power.

It is important to recognize, however, that although we as critical observers can sometimes recognize the reciprocal influences of ideology and power, those connections are usually wilfully hidden from outsiders. An important function of the ideological apparatus is precisely to obscure its own operation. The appearance it tries to foster is not that of reciprocal influence, but of the one-way flow from logic to action. Ideological work always attempts to disguise its own function. To some extent, the work of sociological analysis is to uncover and recover what has been thus obscured, and to offer a new perspective on the rhetoric of power. By viewing symbolic action as a product of the need for a justificatory discourse, rather than solely as the statement of a motivating rationale, we draw attention back to the interdependence of politics and discourse. We highlight the ways in which the 'rationality' of educational innovation both contains and reveals the competing interests which it attempts to reconcile symbolically in its texts.

If we look at the dominant forms of justificatory discourse about schools, a number of different 'visions' or 'traditions' may be discerned but, of these, three have been historically predominant. First, the *liberal/academic* tradition defines a number of 'bodies of knowledge' representing the chosen academic legacies of the culture; this knowledge is to be learnt for its own sake, as well as for its mental value and as an introduction to the culture. Second, the *developmental/pedagogic* tradition chooses knowledge for its importance to the learner and the learner's ongoing cognitive and affective development. The primary criteria are the needs and interests of the learner. The final tradition, the *economic/vocational*, stresses the occupational destinations and needs of the learner. Knowledge is chosen for its value in providing a skilled workforce for the economy and to aid the learner in developing the knowledge and skills which will maximize his/her potential in future work.

By examining the introduction of computers into schools as symbolic action, we can see which of these traditions has been called upon and emphasized, and how the established rationales for schooling have interacted with other social and economic imperatives to create the present-day situation.

In this chapter, we will review some of the early history of educational computing in the province of Ontario, Canada — the years from 1980–1985, during which its justificatory rhetoric was largely developed — and follow this with some consideration of how computers are actually being used today. By applying Sendov's theory of technological innovation to the analysis of some recent research data, we will demonstrate that the rhetoric and the reality of educational computing have frequently reflected the conflicting priorities which normally condition state schooling, but that one tradition has dominated all others in the ideological construction of classroom computing.

The Genealogy of the ICON

The single largest and most important innovation of the last decade in Ontario schools — at least in terms of its impact on the budgets for education, and its effect on the entire range of grades and kinds of schooling — has been the introduction of classroom computers. Between 1980 and 1992, Ontario spent over $200 million of taxpayers' money on hardware and software acquisition alone (Goodson, Mangan and Rhea, 1991). It is reasonable to assume that local jurisdictions have spent as much as another $100 million. Since the bulk of in-service training and technical support has been left to the local boards, they have incurred another set of expenses in connection with these labour-intensive responsibilities.

If we use $400 million as a conservative estimate of the total cost of educational computing to Ontario's citizens to date, it is natural to ask what it is about this technological innovation which has made it seem so worthwhile. Why was it the preferred alternative to, say, hiring another 1000 teachers over the same period of time? Clearly, it must have had some powerful justifications, and some powerful people backing those justifications, to command such a large portion of the province's shrinking educational resources. The fact that the high priority of educational computing has survived the alternation of elected government among all three major provincial parties illustrates its extraordinary strength and durability.

We have sought the origins of this strength and durability in the genealogy of the ICON, the first of the 'Grant-Eligible Microcomputer Systems' (GEMS) approved and supported by the Ontario Ministry of Education. By looking closely at the formative years of the ICON, we can begin to trace the currents of social, economic and political pressure, as well as the development of a supportive ideology, which made this initiative both possible and necessary. Our search for genealogies of knowledge owes a good deal to Foucault's (1980) stated beliefs:

> The longer I continue, the more it seems to me that the formation of discourses and the genealogy of knowledge need to be analyzed, not in terms of types of consciousness, modes of perception and forms of ideology, but in terms of tactics and strategies of power. Tactics and strategies deployed through implantations, distributions, demarcations, control of territories and organizations of domains which could well make up a sort of geopolitics . . . (p. 65)

Ontario became involved in educational computing officially in the early 1980s, towards the end of an extraordinary political era. The Progressive Conservative party had enjoyed an unbroken period in power since the end of the Second World War, resulting in a form of one-party rule within the province. During this time, several major innovations had been introduced to the province's school systems, sustained by a long period of economic growth. The timeline shown in figure 1 highlights some of the landmarks in the introduction of computers to Ontario classrooms.

During this time, there was within the Conservative party and within the Ministry of Education, such a close identification of the interests of business with those of education and the population in general that it had the nature of an unquestioned, if not unconscious, axiom. When the project to develop a new educational computer was officially announced in 1981, it was at a seminar in Oshawa, Ontario (home of GM Canada). The seminar was sponsored by 'the Business and Industry Liaison Committee' of the local Board of Education, along with the Oshawa Chamber of Commerce. The Minister, Dr. Bette Stephenson, opened her remarks by stating that

Figure 1: Timeline of computer related activities*

1980 — 649 computers in Ontario schools

1981 — Establishment of Advisory Committee on Computers in Education
— Minister announces need for computer literacy for all students; plans for educational microcomputer
— 3239 computers in Ontario schools

1982 — Policy Memo 47, stating that computers were to be used creatively and for information retrieval; also announces grants for purchase of computers
— Call for software development to run on existing hardware
— 6000 computers in Ontario schools

1983 — Policy memos outline Ministry approach to implementing computers
— Specification of criteria for hardware in schools; as no existing units meet specs., they must be created
— Provincial assistance with purchase of computers (75 per cent paid); software to be developed by Ministry, field-tested extensively
— November: CEMCorp has ICON prototypes developed, meeting Ministry's specifications

1984 — Software developed, field-tested; six calls from Ministry for softward development proposals

1985 — Grants available to boards for hardware purchases; ICON only approved machine at this time
— CEMCorp joins with Burroughs
— Thirty products from initial software call have been converted from various systems to ICON
— 10,000 ICONS in Ontario schools

* Adapted from Goodson, Mangan & Rhea, 1991c, p. 19.

> The educational and training systems and the industrial sector must see themselves not as separate entities, but as partners in Ontario's future, with the well-being of each depending largely upon the effectiveness of the other. This is essential. (Stephenson, 1981, p. 2)

There could hardly be a stronger endorsement of the vocational model of education, but it was only the beginning of this extraordinary announcement. Dr. Stephenson went on to say that, of the educational computer applications current at that time, one of the most essential was a career-information database, which she described as 'a very important element in helping link the educational requirements of business and industry with the career planning of young people' (*ibid*, p. 5).

Perhaps it should only be expected that, in addressing a business-oriented audience, the Minister should emphasize business issues. The placement of corporate interests before those of other sectors was a fairly consistent feature of the Ministry's rhetoric throughout this period, however. Even so, there were other motivations mentioned. Stephenson's announcement alluded to some of the pedagogical changes that could be stimulated by introducing computers into schools, although she offered no research-based evidence of their efficacy. She also emphasized the need for leadership and coordination in a field that was likely to experience chaotic growth without it.

The essential point, from the perspective of the Ministry of Education, was that it perceived itself to be losing control of a major development in the province's curriculum. In general, the implementation of curriculum in Ontario is represented as the responsibility of the individual teacher. Centrally produced curriculum documents are always entitled 'Guidelines', in order to deemphasize their prescriptive nature. In practice, however, these guidelines have the force of policy.

Within this context, the helter-skelter introduction of computers into classrooms which began in the late 1970s caught the Ministry slightly unawares, and presented the spectre of subject material from other jurisdictions, especially the United States, entering school curricula through the back door of commercial software. Thus part of the motivation for introducing a centrally specified microcomputer system was the need to combat the perception that the government was losing or relinquishing control of the province's curriculum. The first step in response to this need was, not surprisingly, the establishment of a committee, announced at the same time as the computer development project:

> The Ministry in June 1981 established an Advisory Committee on Computers in Education with the central purpose of devising ways of establishing direction and control in the electronic communication field, similar to that exercised through Circular 14 (an approved list of textbooks). (*ibid*, p. 9)

Prior to this announcement, the Ministry had conducted a series of private meetings, whose composition was itself revealing. When the government decided to involve itself in educational computing, it turned (naturally, from its perspective) to its own experts, and to the Canadian Advanced Technology Association (CATA), an association of private microelectronics and software producers. The first meetings were held among CATA, the Ministry of Education, the Ministry of Industry and Trade, and the Ministry of Transportation and Communication (CATA, 1981, p. I. 1). These meetings resulted in a contract to CATA to produce a set of 'functional specifications' for a Canadian educational microcomputer. The authors who produced these specifications (six consultants from GTP Office Communications Corporation and IMATA Systems Corporation) list the people interviewed in conducting their study, and their employers. Of the fifty-nine names listed, twenty were from private computer-related companies, and twenty-six were from government agencies (including seventeen from the Ministry of Education). Only six were from post-secondary institutions (including three from the Ontario Institute for Studies in Education) and seven were from provincial boards of education.

These consultations were mostly internal, then precluding any chance of a broad-based public debate. Several of the companies involved would later form the consortium which committed itself to producing the hardware and software for the proposed system. Of the academic representatives present, half were from the OISE Department of Measurement, Evaluation, and Computer Applications. They also had a clear material interest in furthering the use of computers in schools, as their department would be the logical choice for development and evaluation activities. In fact, they were quickly appointed to do some of the major development and evaluation of the ICON, and in 1985 MECA became the host for the Software Development Assistance Centre, which carried with it a long-term budget of several million dollars and a full-time staff of three people.

There was a great deal of overlap between the people involved in these consultation sessions and those who had also formed the Educational Computing Organization of Ontario (ECOO) in 1980. By continuing the coordination among people from private business, schools, and universities who all had an interest in expanding the use of computers for education, ECOO provided for a more efficient prosecution of their common interests. Although it has presented itself as a kind of academic research association, organizing conferences and workshops and publishing regular newsletters, its actual functioning has more often been as a kind of lobby group for the expansion of educational computing in Ontario. Clearly, this group of experts had come to constitute a closed circle of discourse, addressing themselves largely to each other and reinforcing their own notions of speaking simultaneously for what they perceived as the common interests of the education community and the computer industry.

The Politics of Technical Specifications

The result of the working sessions organized by the various government departments and professional associations during 1981 was the production of a set of specifications for an educational microcomputer. The Ontario government contracted CATA to assemble these into a formal document. The specifications set high standards and high ideals for the use of computers in Ontario schools. Included were such things as high resolution colour graphics and sound synthesis capabilities, which were little more than possibilities at the time of writing, but which the authors felt might be important in the future. They also specified a local area network (LAN) type of architecture. Curiously, they did not specify either a large amount of internal memory (the first models had as little as 64K RAM), nor very high speed communications capabilities. This combination of features had the effect of making the specified computer unique — so unique that no existing machine could fill the bill — but also rather slow and limited in its operation. A nickname for this machine quickly emerged: the 'Bionic Beaver'.

The CATA 'functional specifications' document also reflected the policy imperatives under which it was developed, including the demand for centralized curriculum control documented earlier. As part of their introduction to the need for educational computers, they stated some of the 'emergent problems' which they saw arising from the era of educational liberalism of the 1970s. These included 'wide variation in: curriculums, standards and public expectations across the Province' (*ibid*, p. IV. 5). The production of province-wide standards for classroom computers was seen explicitly as addressing this 'problem'. Without such standards, the CATA consultants foresaw difficulties that would be 'similar to those of the early seventies and focus on the perceived lack of curriculum control' (*ibid*, p. IV. 8).

Within the space of less than a year, then, the Ontario Ministry of Education had moved to assemble a series of elite working groups who had, in turn, produced specifications for a state-of-the art educational computer. Guided by the policy imperatives of maintaining curriculum control and the rhetoric of high-technology business interests, the government of Ontario was poised for a major intervention which was clearly intended to convey a number of symbolic messages: that the government was on top of things, that it was in control, and that it was 'out in front' of this important development. The initiative was also surrounded by a justifying rhetoric couched in terms of international competitiveness, the needs of business, and only lastly, the possibility of enriching students' lives.

The process of mandating a standardized form of educational computer had to be carefully managed, in order to avoid the appearance that local boards were actually being ordered to do something. The approach that was taken, in the end, was not to enforce a particular computer configuration, but to make the selected system so economically attractive as to rule out most other alternatives on a cost basis alone.

The economic subsidization of the 'Bionic Beaver' was implemented through three different initiatives. First, a consortium of Canadian manufacturers which came to be called CEMCorp (the Canadian Educational Microprocessor Corporation) was given an order for $10 million worth of computers, provided they could be produced to the functional specifications written by CATA. The Ministry then moved to make CEMCorp's products attractive to school boards by subsidizing their purchase price by 75 per cent. Finally, in a more direct form of economic subsidy, the Ministry contracted for some $5 million worth of 'exemplary software'. The use of this term is itself interesting. 'Exemplary' in the technical sense used by the Ministry simply referred to the fact that the programs produced were supposed to *exemplify* the potential of the system; they were meant to be *examples* of what might be done. The fact that 'exemplary' is also used as a superlative, to connote excellence and exceptional quality, did not however hurt the image which the province was trying to create: that it was engaged in cutting-edge, state-of-the-art research and development. At various times, it was even stated that the hardware and software developed through these efforts might find markets outside of Ontario, thus creating an export business.

Whatever the motivation, however, there is little doubt that a major initiative was launched in 1980/81, aimed at designing an educational microcomputer which would become the standard in Ontario's schools. Over the next two years, which saw a major recession and record-high interest rates hit the province's economy, several participants in the initial consortium dropped out of the project. With additional incentives from the Ministry of Industry and Tourism, however, and the newly-formed Board of Industrial Leadership and Development (BILD), the project was pushed ahead. Finally, a working prototype was produced in 1983.

At a press conference announcing the completed prototype, Dr. Stephenson stepped forward again in her role as the head of both policy development and public relations for the project. She apparently felt the need to recap the justification for the expenditure of public monies on the 'Bionic Beaver', for she was quoted as describing the process this way:

When we started to look at this, we brought in the Canadian Advanced Technology Association plus teachers who had been involved in using a computer in the classroom, and worked out educational specifications which appeared to be appropriate for the kind of machine everyone wanted to see in classrooms. (quoted in Parr, 1984, p. 9)

This passage is very revealing of the kind of thinking behind the decision-making process which shaped this crucial initiative. It characterizes the group of industry representatives, government bureaucrats and closely-associated academics as defining what '*everyone* wanted to see in classrooms'.

The use of 'everyone' as a rhetorical means of creating instant consensus is, in fact, one of the most frequently occurring features of the discourse of computer advocates. At the same press conference, for instance, Robert Arn, President of Micro Design, stated that 'Everyone has accepted the necessity of letting students use the tools of contemporary society' (*ibid,* p. 7). This kind of statement not only makes a particular point of view appear to be common knowledge and common-sense, it also works to close off debate and to marginalize anyone who might have doubts about whether, in fact, students really do need these complicated, high-priced machines in their schools. For the most part, the public media cooperated in this project, supporting the modernity of the government's policies and depicting objectors as crusty and technophobic old fogies. As we argue later, such discursive strategies are important creators of a 'culture of inevitability'.

The Ideology of Educational Computing

What we have attempted to establish by this brief review of the early history of educational computing in Ontario is that, like many educational innovations, it was as much an ideological initiative as a technical one. In the process of introducing a new form of technology into classrooms, a certain version of the purposes of schooling was reinforced both through high level discourse and through the very real backing of government dollars. The vision of schooling which underlay the introduction of computers in schools was debated by only a very small coterie of insiders, who quickly took it upon themselves to speak for 'everyone'. The wider public debate which many people might have thought necessary, given the very high stakes of the enterprise, simply never took place.

By the mid-1980s, the ideology of educational computing in Ontario was fairly well-developed. For instance, the Assistant Deputy Minister of Education, Doug Penny, speaking in October 1984, said:

The new information technologies are rapidly becoming 'key technologies' whose utilization in all sectors of the economy is essential . . . all OECD nations acknowledge the need to take full advantage of the productivity improvements the use of the new information technology makes possible if they are to remain economically competitive. All recognize the critical role of the education and training systems in this process. This is seen to involve the dual functions of providing the attitudinal conditioning and computer literacy needed in the general population to permit the productive utilization of the new technologies. (p. 1)

The priorities of the educational computing initiative are clear. Education and training will be required for the dual function of providing the 'attitudinal conditioning and computer literacy needed in the general population'. Schools will then serve as sites for the development of requisite attitudes and skills for the economy. Once again, this is something that 'all recognize'.

However, schools are traditionally thought of and promoted as places where learning for its own sake might also go on. What have computers to offer here in return for their huge capital cost? On this point the Deputy Minister could only acknowledge the absence of clear evidence:

> The symbols and processes involved in the use of computers and the new information technology generally, will condition cognition and hence learning in ways we as yet know little about. (*ibid*, p. 2)

And he offered a rather desperate sounding final claim:

> If for no other reason, it would seem necessary to monitor 'the effects' on learning of the use of the new technology so that facilitating and/or compensatory steps can be taken in general education. (*ibid*, p. 3)

On balance, the arguments offered for computer-based education seem overwhelmingly strong as vocational training for the good of the private economy, and very weak, almost non-existent, as claims for enhancing general learning skills. In constructing the official justifications for classroom computing, competing visions of educational purpose were routinely ignored, allowing a one-dimensional logic of vocational training to predominate. Even that vision did not specify *whose* vocations were being advanced. Persell and Cookson (1987) have suggested that school computing is primarily a way of endowing future managers with 'cultural capital', rather than a real attempt to convey useful job skills to a clerical working class (pp. 123–34).

In closing, the Deputy Minister raised a further, apparently clinching, argument.

> Significant industrial development potential exists in the local procurement of the hardware and software needed for large-scale use in education. . . . These factors create a marketing niche which can be consciously exploited to assist the development of a domestic educational microcomputer design and manufacturing capacity . . .
>
> This is a happy instance when reasons of educational and cultural policy coincide exactly with industrial development objectives. (Penny, 1984, pp. 8–9)

It is far from clear that everyone interested in education agreed that this 'happy' coincidence was in fact at hand, but clearly the ideological work of this official was symbolically to efface any possibility of conflict between the priorities of business and the schools.

Computers as Symbolic Action

'For the key to social innovation is the technical innovation' (Williams, 1988).

The evidence offered above, though admittedly sketchy, raises issues of extraordinary importance for an assessment of the impact of computers in schools. It suggests that this innovation was as much a fundamental symbolic and ideological action, geared to mould the image of schools as functional components of the 'Information Age', as it was an attempt to improve pedagogy. In our review of the literature on the introduction of computers into schools in other countries, similar themes frequently surface. For instance, the *Journal of Curriculum Studies* carried a series of reports on 'Computer education and the curriculum' in the United Kingdom. There it was noted:

> There has been huge economic pressure behind the introduction of new information technology (IT) because IT is not just an education tool (as were, for example, the programmed learning machines of an earlier decade). IT is now pervasive in all economic sectors. The pressure has come from statements on the 'needs of industry', skill shortage, and on the 'growing demand for IT skills'. This latter pressure ('economic') has been particularly strong in the secondary sector where the *vocational significance* of IT has always been stressed strongly. (Wellington, 1990, p. 61)

Chris Bigum (1990) makes a similar point in reviewing the progress of IT in schools in Australia:

> The rise of the study of IT in the secondary school curriculum has been helped by a high demand by students, misleading advertising by the distributors of IT products, and a mass media whose only contribution to public debate has been fawning amazement. In the rush to put computer studies into the curriculum, the debate about whether such study belongs in schools did not take place. (p. 64)

These authors agree that it is economic pressures and the vocational tradition of schooling which have provided the 'engine' behind the introduction of computers in schools. From the point of view of the policy-makers, it is a process which can be understood as symbolic action, action which will illustrate and invigorate a policy commitment to particular values. It is meant to contribute to the restructuring of our consciousness of what schooling is about, of the social purposes of schooling. To understand this act of social and political reconstruction we must continue to focus on the discourses surrounding the new initiative.

As we have tried to show, the debate about the educational need or relevance of computers in schools never took place. Ontario government officials have been frank about the fact that there was little evidence about how computers impinged upon student learning and teacher activities, and in 1988 they were strongly criticized by the Auditor General for acting in the absence of such evidence.[1] But the fascination with IT seems to have an unusual power to sweep away deliberation. In the past, most school reforms have proved to be heavily contested and only spasmodically implemented, even when there *was* evidence of improvement for learners and teachers. Plainly, this time, other forces altogether were at work and this time with seemingly incontestable power.

By analyzing the introduction of computers as symbolic action, it is possible to see with considerable clarity which of the great traditions is favoured in the rationales constructed for the new initiatives. The new technologies are in fact so new that, somewhat unusually, it has been difficult for ideological workers to provide the usual rhetorical coverage of all the three main traditions. For once the economic/vocational priority is seen quite nakedly as *the* tradition being pursued. It is this tradition which stands to be primarily promoted by the introduction of computers in schools. Computers in schools as symbolic action may be seen as the latest phase in the recurrent attempts to vocationalize schooling, and to mould public consciousness to the view that education is predominantly about economic/vocational preparation.

Symbolic Action as Implemented

Since 1989, we have taken part in a detailed examination of the introduction of computers into Ontario's schools through our work at the Research Unit on Classroom Learning and Computer Use in Schools (RUCCUS) (see Goodson, Mangan and Rhea, 1991c). After several years of classroom observation, in-depth interviewing and general policy analysis, the symbolic importance of these initiatives in redrawing the map of state schooling has become more and more apparent. In general, the existing social purposes of schooling are little understood but greatly under siege.

At the level of immediate action and justification, computers have benefited from what we have come to call a 'culture of inevitability'. This is less our definition than the recurrent estimation of those we have interviewed about the introduction of computers in schools (see Mangan, 1992). Their arguments follow very similar lines, centring around two dominant themes:

> Computers are out there, they're everywhere, they've taken over society . . . clearly we have to have them in our classrooms . . . it's inevitable. (Teacher)

> Computers are now in every work place . . . obviously kids have to master them or else they'll never get jobs . . . So for our schools, their introduction is vital and inevitable. (School Board Official)

Students have echoed these themes in their interviews as well. These 'commonsensical' contemporary quotes can be traced back to many of the policy statements made at the time computers were being introduced into schools in Ontario, as reviewed earlier.

But what of the actual effects of the introduction of computers? Sendov (1981) has conceptualized the effect on schools as being made up of 'waves'. Economic and vocational pressures can be seen to launch the first wave, but subsequent waves collide more and more with the existing traditions, the everyday reality and the micropolitics of schooling.

The first wave ensures only that the computer is an *available* facility or resource. At this stage, then, the computer is clearly an appendage to the educational activities provided by the school. This may be seen as 'only' symbolic action, since the fundamental activities of the schools remain unchanged.

In the second wave, however, symbolic action moves towards educational and further ideological penetration. For instance, in the secondary schools the computer is not only available as an educational resource, but begins to be used actively in teaching the existing school subjects. Increasing numbers of specialist teachers begin to employ computers in their daily subject teaching. In using computers in this manner, they allow the computer to intrude upon the existing culture of the classroom. 'What is characteristic now for the second wave is the systematic reassessment of the aims and objectives of the individual school disciplines' (*ibid*, p. 16).

A number of participant teachers in the RUCCUS Project have commented on the manner in which the presence of computers begins to transform the way they present and view their subject. For instance, one teacher of geography, traditionally wedded to his subject as 'a very fact- and content-oriented body of knowledge' commented:

> Are we there to teach the kids geography, or are we there to educate them . . . in the use of computers, and every kid, I think, on this earth is going to be involved in the use of computers at some point, certainly in their working life . . . and maybe our job is to make them more computer literate (rather) than to teach them geography.

This is a massive shift for a traditional subject teacher to make. It is nothing less than an abandonment of the academic tradition and an embrace of vocationalism. This subject teacher's colleague confirmed the tendency, saying that what his colleague had said was 'no big deal'. 'If students learned less geography but more of other useful skills in my class I wouldn't be bothered'.

To quote Winner (1977) it would seem therefore fairly clear that 'artifacts have politics'. The installation of computers in a classroom is not a neutral technological act. It is an act which partakes of the symbolic to become an act of ideological penetration and conversion (see Bowers, 1988). The potential transformation of subject teaching means that the heartland of the 'academic tradition' is being subjected to important modifications. An artifact moved into the school for primarily economic purposes has begun to penetrate the existing academic practices of the school. The vocational tradition is beginning to increase substantially its territorial sway within the school. However, while it can be established that some subject teachers are embracing the computer, there are many instances of resistance to the computer among teachers. The battle between vocational and academic purposes is seriously joined when computers are introduced into the school — the second wave is, then, a period of vigorous contestation.

In the second wave the computer begins to affect the perceptions of subject teaching and, in some cases, to partially affect their practice. Here there is a good deal of contestation and some teachers retain their loyalty to a purist academic tradition and 'resist' computers in the classroom. There is at best only marginal change in practice, certainly nothing which resembles a transformation of practice and of learning styles which would justify the massive investment in IT (see Goodson, Mangan and Rhea, 1991c).

Let us now consider the possibility of a third wave, for it is here we begin to see the relationship to the 'academic' and 'pedagogic' traditions fully explored. The third wave, which is as yet largely hypothetical, will

> occur when IT influences the content and the aims of education itself as well as the method and the system of teaching . . . what would occur in a third wave is a reappraisal of the motive and aims of separate school disciplines in the context of powerful information technology systems and new infrastructures. (Wellington, 1990, p. 61)

The most interesting aspect of the 'three waves' model is the way that different traditions and rationales are given priority in each stage. In the preactive policy stage, and in the first wave of implementation, the introduction of computers as symbolic action is preeminent. Here, we have argued, computers serve a clear function in vocationalizing the discourse about schooling and opening up the classroom to computers, albeit as *additional* facilities for existing classroom activities. During the second wave, the reality of the challenge being presented to traditional structures begins to sink in.

The pay-off for the investments is largely wished onto the delayed and almost wholly hypothetical 'third wave'. Here education will be radically changed and classroom pedagogy transformed into an interactive and deeply-engaged set of learning activities. Here the computer and the pedagogic tradition, it is argued, will link up. Here those reluctant 'traditionalists' who have argued that computers will vocationalize schooling, erode existing academic values — and cost a fortune in the process — will finally have to accept that a new classroom world has been born.

Computer optimists largely point to this pedagogic utopia in defending the introduction of computers in the classroom. To date, however, there is negligible evidence of the third wave. As in the past, so with computers, the innovation has collided with the existing political economy of the subject-based curriculum and its associated interest groups, the school subjects. In part because of their own commitments to the academic traditions of education, some of these groups appear to be resisting, and confining the experiment to the 'second wave' level.

> The influence of a vertical subject-based national curriculum is a powerful force preventing the emergence of a 'third stage'. Information technology has not yet had any effect in changing the dominant view of the secondary curriculum based on forms of knowledge, separate subjects, and compartmentalized disciplines. In short, the effect of IT upon the content and structure of the curriculum has been negligible. (*ibid*, p. 62)

Hence, there is very little evidence of broad-based pedagogic change. In fact, the primary evidence of change that can be discerned is where some academic subject teachers embrace not new pedagogies but old vocationalities. The most tangible effect has been to vocationalize in some classrooms the teaching of academic subjects. In this sense the introduction of computers into classrooms begins to emerge both as preactive symbolic action and as interactive ideological action.

The political project underpinning the introduction of computers seems, then, to be emerging with some clarity. Unless there is increasing evidence of a third wave, many of the optimistic claims made for computers in education by theorists seem substantially unfulfilled. Instead, the vision of bureaucrats for whom 'educational and cultural policy coincide exactly with industrial development objectives' will reign supreme. Educators who remain committed to other visions of educational purpose need to challenge the culture of inevitability surrounding educational technology, and to reassert the value of their own traditions, if they hope to see those traditions survive the onslaught of symbolic action which has so far propelled the introduction of computers into schools.

Note

1   Ontario Auditor General (1988) *Annual Report*, Toronto, Ontario Auditor General's Office.

References

BIGUM, C. (1990) 'Computers and the curriculum: The Australian experience', *Journal of Curriculum Studies*, **22**.

BOWERS, C.A. (1988) *The Cultural Dimension of Educational Computing*, New York: Teachers College Press.

CANADIAN ADVANCED TECHNOLOGY ASSOCIATION (CATA) (1981) *Functional Specifications for an all-Canadian Educational Microcomputer*, Ottawa: CATA.

FOUCAULT, M. (1980) 'Questions on geography', in FOUCAULT, M. (ed.) *Power/Knowledge: Selected Interviews and Other Writings 1972–1977*, Brighton: Harvester Press.

GOODSON, I.F., MANGAN, J.M. and RHEA, V.A. (eds) (1991) *Closing the Circle: Conclusions and Recommendations: Volume 3 of the Summative Report from the Project 'Curriculum and Context in the Use of Computers for Classroom Learning'*, London: University of Western Ontario.

MANGAN, J.M. (1992) 'The ideology of computer literacy in schools', paper presented at the annual meeting of the American Education Research Association, San Francisco, April.

PARR, W.H. (1984) 'Bionic beaver', *Computers in Education*, 6–12 February.

PENNY, D.A. (1984) 'A provincial policy response to the high-tech impact of education', paper presented to the Carleton-Edinburgh Joint Seminar on High Tech Impacts on Education, Ottawa, October.

PERSELL, C.H. and COOKSON, P.W. JNR (1987) 'Microcomputers and elite boarding schools: Educational innovation and social reproduction', *Sociology of Education*, **60**.

SENDOV, B. (1981) 'The second wave: Problems of computer education', in ENNALS, R., GWYN, R. and ZDRAVCHEV (eds) *Information Technology and Education*, Chichester: Ellis Horwood.

STEPHENSON, B. (1981) speech to the seminar sponsored by the Business and Industry Liaison Committee for Oshawa of the Durham Board of Education, in collaboration with Durham College of Applied Arts and Technology and the Oshawa Chamber of Commerce, Toronto.

WELLINGTON, J.J. (1990) 'The impact of IT on the school curriculum: Downwards, sideways, backwards and forwards', *Journal of Curriculum Studies*, **22**.

WILLIAMS, R. (1988) *The Politics of Modernism: Against the New Conformists*, New York: Verso.

WINNER, L. (1977) *Autonomous Technology: Technics-out of Control as a Theme in Political Thought*, Cambridge, MA: MIT Press.

10 On Curriculum Form: Notes Toward a Theory of Curriculum

Sociologists of education who are interested in the school curriculum have long faced a paradox. The curriculum is avowedly and manifestly a social construction. Why, then, is this central social construct treated as a timeless given in so many studies of schooling? In particular, why have social scientists, who traditionally have been more attuned than most to the ideological and political struggles that underpin social life, largely accepted the 'givenness' of the school curriculum? As the curriculum wars rage in American higher education over the choice of 'canon', it seems to be a good time to begin again to theorize the school curriculum.

In many Western countries, the school 'curriculum' is back on the political agenda. In the United States, following the Holmes Group and the Carnegie Task Force and such publications as *Nations at Risk*, it is clearly in evidence; in Britain, the givenness of curriculum is being literally enshrined by parliamentary legislation in the form of a 'National Curriculum'; in Australia, the provinces are 'mapping' their curricula to discern commonalities, some scholars would argue, as a precursor to defining more 'national' curricular guidelines.

In these circumstances, it is important to review the state of sociological knowledge with regard to the curriculum, for our knowledge of the school curriculum remains severely undertheorized. Much of the work in this domain has been carried out by sociologists of knowledge, but pioneering work in this area remains partial and flawed if we are concerned with developing our theoretical understanding of curriculum. As Apple (1979) conceded, a good deal of the significant work in this field has been conducted in Europe: Emile Durkheim's and Karl Mannheim's early work remains important, as does that of the late Raymond Williams and, in the 1960s and 1970s, the work of Pierre Bourdieu and of Basil Bernstein. In the work of Williams, most of the theoretical focus was on the *content* of the curriculum.[1] Meanwhile, Bernstein (1971) pointed to underlying principles for the classification and framing of curriculum, but emphasized the relationship *between* subject content (pp. 47–69). It is interesting that the obsession with subject content is continued in Shulman's work on the knowledge base required for teaching. In Shulman's leading section on 'scholarship in content disciplines', one learns that 'the first source of the knowledge base is *content*' (Shulman, 1987, pp. 1–22).

The issue of relationships *within* subject matter has remained unexplored and untheorized. In this chapter, the question of the internal relations of curriculum—the *form* of curriculum—is analyzed: As Apple (1979) said, 'for methodological reasons one does not take for granted that curricular knowledge is neutral. Instead, one looks for social interests embodied in the knowledge form itself' (p. 17). The social conflict within the subject is central to understanding the subject itself (and hence relations among subjects). Because subject is not a monolithic entity, analyses that view subjects and relations among subjects in this manner mystify a central and ongoing social conflict. On this analysis an understanding of the internal relations of curriculum would be an important precursor to the kind of work that Bernstein has exemplified on the external relations and modalities of curriculum.

A less theoretical justification for analyses of curriculum form is the pervasiveness of what Connell (1985) called the 'competitive academic curriculum'. This form of curriculum sets the agenda and the discourse for schooling in many countries. The results are fairly generalizable:

> To say it is hegemonic is not to say it is the only curriculum in those schools. It is to say that this pattern has pride of place in those schools; it dominates most people's ideas of what real learning is about. Its logic has the most powerful influence on the organisation of the school and of the education system generally; and it is also to marginalise or subordinate the other curricula that are present: Above all 'the competitive academic curriculum makes the sorting and the hardening of hearts a central reality of contemporary school life'. (p. 87)

Yet the continuing dominance of the competitive academic curriculum is the result of a continuing contest within school subjects.

Conceptions of 'Mentalities'

By way of exemplifying a broader conception for studying school subjects, I will examine the emergence of certain conceptions of 'mentalities', since they provide antecedent assumptions for our contemporary social construction of school knowledge. In doing so, I am building on the work of others and am not following a consistent line of development. Therefore, I may be justifiably accused of raiding history, of dipping into periods without full knowledge or portrayal of the complexity of context. But my objective is not so much to provide a sustained historical explanation as to show how antecedent factors could be a factor in contemporary construction and consciousness. The aim is to show how we may pursue a longer time perspective on current events and how in doing so we may provide a reconceptualization of the mode of curriculum study that will allow us to connect specific acts of social construction to wider social impulses.

The notion of 'mentality' owes a good deal to the work of the Annales school of historians. Following them, I take the view that in studying historical periods, it is important to generate insights into the worldviews held by distinct cultural and sub-cultural groups. In this sense, mentality is related to the microconcept of 'habitus', as developed by Bourdieu and Passeron (1977) or 'resistance' as a distinctive view held by British working-class 'lads' in the work of Willis (1977).

In his work on Australian school reform, which derives from the Annales school, Pitman (1986) argued that 'with a given civilization, there are multiple cultures related to location, class, occupation, gender and any other relevant criterion':

> The dialectic relationships of the various groups with their material worlds and with each other permit the development of world views, or mentalities (mentalities) within these groups which are distinct from each other. For example, in the division of labor and the class exchange of labor to organizers of labor and owners of the means of production, then the participants in the asymmetrical exchanges interact differently with their material worlds, at least in relation to the nature of work. (p. 60)

Shapin and Barnes (1976) examined a selection of educational writings on pedagogy in Britain in the period 1770–1850. In examining the 'rhetoric' of pedagogy, they found 'remarkable agreement upon the mentality of the subjects of those programmes'. Different mentalities were ascribed, depending on whether the persons in question came from 'the higher orders' or 'the lower ranks' (p. 231).

Three Dichotomies

Three central dichotomies were discerned. The first places the *sensual* and *concrete* character of the thought of the lower orders against the *intellectual*, *verbal*, and *abstract* qualities of upper-class thoughts. The second places the *simplicity* of the lower-orders' thought against the *complexity* and *sophistication* of their betters'.

In *Wealth of Nations*, Adam Smith provided the crucial link between the division of labor and the division of mentalities (and, of course, curriculum). In patterns of exploitation and domination, this is the crucial rationalization to enshrine. Thus, Smith stated:

> In the progress of the division of labour the employment of the far greater part of those who live by labour, comes to be confined to a few very simple operations; frequently to one or two. But the understandings of the greater part of men are necessarily formed by their ordinary employments. The man whose whole life is spent in performing a few simple operations, of which the effects too are, perhaps, always the same or very nearly the same, has no occasion to exert his understanding or to exercise his invention . . . He naturally . . . becomes as stupid and ignorant as it is possible for a human creature to become. (quoted in *ibid*, p. 231)

For the elite, Smith was similarly strident: 'The employments, too, in which people of some rank or fortune spend their lives, are not, like those of the common people, simple or uniform. They are almost all of them extremely complicated, and such as exercise the head more than the hands' (quoted in *ibid*, p. 234).

The third central dichotomy concerns the *passive* response of the lower orders to experience and knowledge compared with the *active* response of the upper ranks. This spectrum of passivity to activity is perhaps the most crucial part of the conundrum of mentalities when related to the evolution of school knowledge. Hence

> the sensually-based, superficial and simple thoughts of the lower orders did not allow them to produce mediated responses to experience, or to make deep connections between different pieces of information, such as would permit them to be generalized for use as resources in a wide range of contexts. (Smith quoted in *ibid*, p. 234)

From these early stages, the link between the lower orders and specific, contextualized knowledge was forged. This need for immediate contextualized knowledge provided the diagnosis 'which justified the characterization of their learning process as passive and mechanical' (*ibid*). Knowledge was presented and accepted in such a way that connections were not made between specific and contextualized facts; the lower orders did not act upon knowledge or generalize from data. A devil's bargain emerged: The lower orders were taught specific, contextualized 'facts' mechanically, but the capacity to generalize across contexts was not provided or encouraged. Decontextualized knowledge was for others, then; for the lower orders, it became an alien and untouchable form of knowledge. In due course, it, too, ensured passivity.

In contrast, the upper orders could incorporate their perceptions, intuitions, information, and knowledge into coherent systems of thought and inference.

> By so doing, they could, on the one hand, extend their range of applicability, and, on the other, bring a range of abstract principles and symbolic operations to bear upon them. Thus, they could, unlike the lower orders, make *active use* of knowledge and experience. Whatever it was, it served to extend the possibilities of their thought. (Hence) in society, as in the body, the head was reflective, manipulative and controlling; the hand, unreflective, mechanical, determined by instructions. (quoted in *ibid*, p. 235)

Therefore, Shapin and Barnes judged that 'as one moved up into the higher ranks of society, one increasingly encountered more abstract, refined and complex modes of thought, and more extensive, finely structured and profound bodies of "knowledge"'. But alongside this definition of knowledge was the requirement that knowledge should be 'properly distributed', not 'improperly graded' or taught 'out of place'. Thus

> properly distributed, it could operate as a symbolic display of social standing, enabling the various orders better to recognize the hierarchy and sectors to which deference was due. And it might also serve as a medium enabling communication between the top and the base of society, a vehicle through which head could control hand. Incorrectly distributed, knowledge could stimulate the masses to aspire upwards and give them the resources to use in doing so. Although, perhaps, their natural inferiority would doom these aspirations to ultimate failure, the temporary turbulence would be troublesome and inconvenient. (*ibid*, p. 236)

The two distinct mentalities defined for the upper and lower orders were essentially cultural resources employed in a whole range of debates and discourses:

They are a tribute to man's skill and endless creativity in the construction of rationalizations and adaption of cultural resources to the exigencies of concrete situations. And it is as situated responses to particular polemical requirements and not necessarily as the coherent philosophies of individuals that we must treat these individuals. (*ibid*, p. 237)

In the process of favouring the 'head more than the hands', new patterns of differentiation and examination were emerging in English secondary schooling in the mid-nineteenth century. By the 1850s, schooling was developing links with universities through the founding of the first examination boards. Here was a structural response to the privileges of the higher orders and their allied abstract knowledge of the head. The universities, of course, were for 'fine minds' and developed curricula to 'train the mind'. They were unequivocally for the 'head more than the hands'; indeed, 'training the mind' was their exclusive preserve.

The links with the social order were then clear and were often explicitly stated as the university examination boards were constructed. For instance, the University of Cambridge Local Examination Syndicate was founded in 1858: 'The establishment of these examinations was the universities' response to petitions that they should help in the development of "schools for the middle classes"'.[1] Also at this time, the feature of curriculum mentioned earlier, the power to differentiate, was being institutionalized. The birth of secondary *examinations* and the institutionalization of curricular *differentiation* were then almost exactly contemporaneous. For instance, the Taunton Report in 1868 classified secondary schooling into three grades, depending on the time spent at school. The Report stated:

The difference in time assigned makes some difference in the very nature of education itself; if a boy cannot remain at school beyond the age of 14 it is useless to begin teaching him such subjects as required a longer time for their proper study; if he can continue till 18 or 19, it may be expedient to postpone some studies that would otherwise be commenced earlier.[2]

The Report noted that 'these instructions correspond roughly but by no means exactly to the gradations of society' (this statement could, as will be shown, be equally well applied to the Norwood Report nearly a century later). In 1868 schooling until age 18 or 19 was for the sons of men with considerable incomes independent of their own exertions, or professional men, and men in business whose profits put them on the same level. These students were taught a mainly classical curriculum. The second grade (up to age 16) was for the sons of the 'mercantile classes'. The curriculum for these students was less classical in orientation and had a certain practical orientation. The third grade (until age 14) was for the sons of 'the smaller tenant farmer, the small tradesmen (and) the superior artisans'. The curriculum of these students was based on the three Rs, but taught up to a fairly high level. These gradations cover secondary schooling. Meanwhile, most working-class students received only an elementary school education and were taught rudimentary skills in the three Rs.

In the post-Taunton period, as the university examination boards came into being, a hierarchy of social orders and associated curricula were, in effect, being established and linked to a system and structure of schooling. At the top, schools were for 'training the mind' and they developed links at the level of examinations, and at times future destinations, with the universities and with their classical curriculum. As one descended the levels of schooling, one found that the curriculum became progressively more rudimentary, was taught mechanically, and had a practical 'orientation'.

The Contest over Science

In the decades that followed, there were, of course, challenges to this 'political settlement' on levels of curriculum that corresponded so well to the gradations of society. Most notable was the battle over the inclusion of science. The perceived social danger of science, particularly applied science, was partly that education could be related to the cultural experience of the lower orders. There was knowledge that could be contextualized—not abstract, not classical, not quintessentially decontextualized but the opposite—knowledge whose relevance and interest might be secured for the lower orders. For the masses, a possible educational medium was at hand. Here, then, was a litmus test of the interestedness or disinterestness of school knowledge. In the early nineteenth century, opinions on science had been clear. Thus, a 'country gentleman' judged in 1825 that

> if the working classes are to be taught the sciences, what are the middle and higher classes to learn, to preserve the due proportion? The answer is obvious enough. There is nothing they can be taught by which they can maintain their superiority. (Shapin and Barnes, 1976, p. 239)

In his early work, Mannheim thought science to be 'disinterested knowledge', but science as school knowledge was plainly another matter, much more a case of 'interested knowledge'.

The problems raised by the 'country gentleman' grew in the period following 1825, for some successful experiments were under way to teach science to the working classes in the elementary schools. For instance, the Reverend Richard Dawes opened a National Society School in King's Somborne in England in 1842. Here he proceeded to teach science as applied to 'the understanding of common things'. In short, he taught contextualized science, but with a view toward developing the academic understanding of his pupils from the lower orders. Scientific knowledge, then, was contextualized within the culture and experience of the common people's children, but taught in a way that could open the door to understanding and the exercise of thought. This was schooling as education—and, what is more, for the laboring poor. But the curriculum was limited to elementary schools with predominantly working-class students. There is a clear evidence in contemporary governmental reports that the science of common things allowed considerable practical success in classrooms. One would be wrong, however, to assume therefore that the problem was solved and that the science of common things provided the basis for the definition of school science. Far from it. Other definitions of school science were being advocated by powerful interests. Lord Wrottesley chaired a Parliamentary Committee of the British Association for the Advancement of Science on the most appropriate type of science education for the upper classes. Hodson (1987) argued that the report

> reflected a growing awareness of a serious problem: that science education at the elementary level was proving highly successful, particularly as far as the development of thinking skills was concerned, and the social hierarchy was under threat because there was not corresponding development for the higher orders. (p. 166)

Wrottesley gave an example that confirmed his worst fears:

> a poor boy hobbled forth to give a reply; he was lame and humpbacked, and his wan emaciated face told only too clearly the tale of poverty and its consequences . . . but he gave forthwith so lucid and intelligent a reply to the question put to him that there arose a feeling of admiration for the child's talents combined with a sense of shame that more information should be found in some of the lowest of our lower classes on matters of general interest than in those far above them in the world by station.
>
> It would be an unwholesome and vicious state of society in which those who are comparatively unblessed with nature's gifts should be generally superior in intellectual attainments to those above them in station. (quoted in *ibid*, p. 167)

Soon after Wrottesley's comments in 1860, science was removed from the elementary curriculum. When it eventually reappeared in the curriculum of the elementary schools some twenty years later, it was in a different form from the science of common things. A watered-down version of pure laboratory science had become accepted as the *correct* view of science, a view that has persisted, largely unchallenged, to the present day. Science, as a school subject, was powerfully redefined to become similar in form to so much else in the secondary curriculum — pure, abstract, a body of knowledge enshrined in syllabuses and textbooks (see Goodson, 1988).

The fundamental insight is that even with a subject that is conceived of as a challenge to the traditional academic curriculum, incorporation can take place. Hence, science, which was thought of as practical and pedagogical, ended up as 'pure laboratory science'.

Continuities and Complexities

The early nineteenth-century pattern of differing 'mentalities' and differing curricula that Shapin and Barnes noted has had considerable durability. Of course, the continuities that can be discerned must be fully related to the complexity of each historical period. In this sense, I am only pointing to an agenda for future historical work.

The apparent continuities are sufficiently clear, however, as to warrant substantial further historical study. For instance, almost a century later, the Norwood Report advocated the notion of different mentalities and of different curricula and, indeed, of different schools to serve these mentalities. This Report led, in Britain, to the 1944 Education Act, which may be seen as institutionalizing a social and political order for schooling, built on a hierarchy of mentalities.

The Norwood Report argued that throughout Europe, 'the evolution of education' had 'thrown up certain groups, each of which can and must be treated in a way appropriate to itself'. In England three clear groups could be discerned. First,

> the pupil who is interested in learning for its own sake, who can grasp an argument or follow a piece of connected reasoning, who is interested in causes, whether on the level of human volition or in the material world, who cares to know how things came to be as well as how they are, who is sensitive to language as expression of thought, to a proof as a precise demonstration, to a series of experiments justifying a principle; he is interested in the relatedness of related things, in development, in structure, in a coherent body of knowledge. (Board of Education, 1943)

These pupils form the continuing clientele of the traditional subject-based curriculum, for as the Norwood Report stated, 'such pupils, educated by the curriculum commonly associated with the grammar school, have entered the learned professions or have taken up higher administrative or business posts' (*ibid*). Second, the needs of the intermediate category, the pupil whose interests and abilities lay markedly in the field of applied science or applied art, were to be fulfilled by the technical schools. Third, the report stated, with a partial view of educational history: 'There has of late years been recognition, expressed in the framing of curricula and otherwise of still another grouping of occupations'. This third group was to provide the clientele for the new secondary modern schools.

> The pupil in this group deals more easily with concrete things than with ideas. He may have much ability, but it will be in the realm of facts. He is interested in things as they are; he finds little attraction in the past or in the slow disentanglement of causes or movements. His mind must turn its knowledge or its curiosity to immediate test; and his test is essentially practical. (*ibid*, p. 4)

This curriculum, although ruling out certain occupational futures, certainly facilitated those who were destined for manual work. It 'would not be to prepare for a particular job or profession and its treatment would make a direct appeal to interests, which it would awaken by practical touch with affairs' (*ibid*).

The Norwood Report summarizes the patterns of curricular differentiation that had emerged through 'the evolution of education' over the past century or so. The close alliance between patterns of curricular differentiation and social structure was often conceded (as in the Taunton Report in 1868): Different curricula are explicitly linked to different occupational categories. The academic tradition was for the grammar school pupil, who was destined for the learned professions and higher administrative or business posts. The more utilitarian curriculum in the technical schools was for the pupil who was destined to work in 'applied science or applied art'. For the future manual worker in the secondary modern school, the emphasis was on utilitarian and pedagogical curricula; these studies were to 'make a direct appeal to interests which it would awaken by practical touch with affairs' (*ibid*). The close identity between different curricular traditions, occupational destinations (and social classes), and educational sectors was confirmed in the 1944 Education Act, which organized schools into grammar schools for the academic pupils, technical schools for the 'applied' pupils, and secondary modern schools for the 'practical' pupils.

The 1944 Act therefore produced an organizational pattern that was in close resonance with social configurations that were in the tradition established by the Taunton Report. However in 1945 the election of a socialist Labour government initiated a period in which the entrenched and explicit class-based educational organization came under substantial attack. In Britain the battle for the common school was fought late — a symptom of the entrenched class structure of the country. The comprehensive school was thus 'won' only in 1965. The 1965 Circular (DES, 1965) had sought to 'eliminate separatism in secondary education' (p. 1). But a close reading of the circular implies that the major concern, perhaps understandably at the time, was with eliminating separatism in the form of different types of schools and buildings.

Indeed, there were clear indications that far from expecting a new synthesis of curricula, the main concern in 1965 was to defend and extend the grammar school education that had been confined mainly to the professional and middle classes. The House of Commons motion that led to *Circular 10/65* was fairly specific:

> This House, conscious of the need to raise educational standards at all levels, and regretting that the realization of this objective is impeded by the separation of children into different types of secondary schools, notes with approval the efforts of local authorities to reorganize secondary education on comprehensive lines which will preserve all that is valuable in grammar school education for those children who now receive it and make it available to more children. (*ibid*)

What was unclear and unspoken was whether the logic of providing a comprehensive education for all in the common school would also extend to providing a common curriculum.

Yet if it seems that the comprehensive school had thereby been achieved, a more systematic historical analysis of internal curricular patterns tells another story. In a sense, the move to the common school represents a change only in the geometrical axis of differentiation. Thus, in table 10 differentiation from 1944 is vertical, being based on separate school sectors.

Table 10:   Tripartite schooling: Educational system after 1944 Act

Grammar School	Technical School	Secondary Modern
Academic: route to universities	Technical knowledge	Practical/manual

Figure 2: Curriculum form

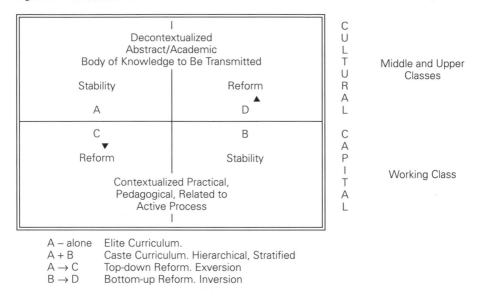

A – alone   Elite Curriculum.
A + B   Caste Curriculum. Hierarchical, Stratified
A → C   Top-down Reform. Exversion
B → D   Bottom-up Reform. Inversion

Comprehensive schooling limited all these separate types of schooling 'under one roof'. The class-based recruitment to the three types of school was thereby challenged by the fact that every child had the same 'equal' opportunity to attend the same, comprehensive school (notwithstanding those 'children of rich' parents who continued to go to private schools). But the results of this reform were less substantial when internal patterns were established, for *inside* the comprehensive school the old tripartite system was reestablished with a pattern of horizontal differentiation: that is, academic subjects, technical subjects, manual/practical subjects.

In many cases the last two categories effectively merged: the crucial distinction was between academic and non-academic subjects. Pupils were clearly categorized along these lines as 'academic' and 'non-academic'. Close studies of the reform of schooling from tripartite to comprehensive affords an opportunity for scholars of curricular history to reconceptualize curricular reform. Reform therefore provides a 'matrix of possibility' when the conflict over whether to redefine or simply renegotiate differentiation takes place (see figure 2).

In this matrix a range of possible combinations of curricula can be discerned. For instance, option A in figure 2 represents a situation that prevailed for a long time in Britain, in which the elite alone received schooling of an academic nature. Combining A with B provides recontextualized academic schooling for the higher orders and contextualized practical training for the lower orders—in effect, a hierarchical and stratified 'caste curriculum'.

Attempts to reform curricula can be top-down (A to C) or bottom-up (B to D). In the top-down model, academic decontextualized knowledge is distilled and made available to a wider audience (many of the curricular reforms in the 1960s were of this sort). In the bottom-up model, contextualized knowledge is used as a vehicle for more general theoretical education (as was the case with the Science of Common Things).

A Pattern of Structuration

The matrix of curricular forms illustrates a range of potential patterns for programming, developing, and reforming curricula. But behind the apparent flexibility lie established patterns of finances and resources. In Britain these patterns were established mostly in the period 1904–1917. Their establishment and continuance into the late twentieth century provide a historical instance of the social and political processes that underpin school subjects.

The 1904 *Secondary Regulations* list and prioritize the subjects that are suitable for education in the secondary grammar schools. The subjects were largely those that have come to be seen as 'academic' subjects, a view confirmed and consolidated by their enshrinement in the School Certificate examinations launched in 1917.

From 1917 onwards, examination subjects, the 'academic' subjects, inherited the preferential treatment in finance and resources that has been directed at the grammar schools. It should be noted that the examination system itself had been developed for a comparable clientele. The foundation of these examinations in 1858 'was the universities' response to petitions that they should help in the development of "schools for the middle classes"'.[3] (The genesis of examinations and their subsequent centrality in the structure of the educational systems are a particularly good example of the importance of historical factors for those who are developing theories about curriculum and schooling.)

The structure of resources linked to examinations has effectively survived the ensuing changes in the educational system (although new changes are currently underway). Byrne (1974), for instance, stated 'that more resources are given to able students and hence to academic subjects'; the two are still synonymous, 'since it has been assumed that they necessarily need more staff, more highly paid staff and more money for equipment and books' (p. 29).

The material interests of teachers — their pay, promotion, and conditions — are intimately interlinked with the fate of their specialist subjects. In schools, school subjects are organized in departments. The subject teacher's career is pursued within such a department and the department's status depends on the subject's status. The 'academic' subject is placed at the top of the hierarchy of subjects because the resources are allocated on the basis of assumptions that such subjects are best suited for the 'able' students (and vice versa, of course), who, it is further assumed, should receive favourable treatment.

Thus, in secondary schools, the material and self-interest of subject teachers is interlinked with the status of the subjects, judged in terms of their examination status. Academic subjects provide the teacher with a career structure that is characterized by better prospects for promotion and pay than are less academic subjects.

The pattern of finances and resources that emerged in the period 1904–1917 proved durable and has only recently been subject to substantial challenge. As a result, a common process of promoting and developing school subjects began to emerge in response to the 'rules of the game', defined in this manner for those who pursue financing, resources, and status (for a detailed analysis see Goodson, 1987 and 1988).

Conclusion

This chapter has noted that a polarized pattern of mentalities emerged in Britain in the period 1770–1850. For the 'higher order', mentalities were judged to be intellectual, abstract, and active, whereas for the 'lower orders', they were considered sensual, concrete, and passive. In time, these polarized mentalities were built into the deep structures of curriculum — they were, so to speak, internalized. In this way, the process of mentality 'production' was extended, for school subjects themselves became, in turn, the makers of subjectivities. A self-confirming circle was drawn around different social groupings. Given the resonance with patterns of cultural capital, this structuring of curriculum form was to prove a resilient settlement.

At the time that these constellations of mentalities, curriculum, and cultural capital began to form, a state schooling system was emerging. In time, therefore, these patterns were institutionalized — initially into a system of separate schools for distinct mentalities and curricula. Later, as common schooling was 'developed' (or 'conceded', depending on your location), the pattern of distinct mentalities and curricula remained a mechanism of differentiation *within* what was ostensibly unified and common. It is as if the mental/manual 'division of labour' is institutionalized in a 'division of curriculum'. Certainly with regard to the current policy associated with the new British 'National Curriculum', the emerging patterns of traditionalism, demarcated from new vocationalism, seem set to continue and strengthen this division (see Bates, 1989, pp. 215–31).

In the historical period considered here, the deliberate structuration of a state schooling in which the head rather than the hands was preferred can be clearly discerned. The academic form of curriculum was systematically favoured by the structure of resources and finances. Hence, a pattern of prioritizing certain social groups was replaced by an ostensibly neutral process of prioritizing certain forms of curricula. But though the name changed, the game was much the same. It is not surprising, therefore, that similar social groups continued to benefit and, likewise, that other social groups, as before, were disadvantaged. But the internalization of differentiation effectively masked this social process of preferment and privilege.

Thus, the focus on conflicts *within* the curriculum responds to this internalization of social differentiation. In short, to understand fully the process that is schooling, one must look *inside* the curriculum. Part of the complex conundrum of schooling is to be understood by capturing the internal process of stability and change in the curriculum.

Notes

1 University of Cambridge Local Examinations Syndicate (1958) *One Hundredth Annual Report to University*, Cambridge, Cambridge University Press.
2 *Report of the Royal Commission on School Inquiry* (The Taunton Report) (1968) London.
3 University of Cambridge Local Examinations Syndicate (1958) *One Hundredth Annual Report to University*, Cambridge, Cambridge University Press.

References

APPLE, M.W. (1979) *Ideology and Curriculum*, Boston, MA: Routledge & Kegan Paul.
BATES, I. (1989) 'Versions of vocationalism: An analysis of some social and political influences on curriculum policy and practice', *British Journal of Sociology of Education*, **10**.
BERNSTEIN, B. (1971) 'On the classification and framing of educational knowledge', in YOUNG, M.F.D. (ed.) *Knowledge and Control*, London: Collier-Macmillan.
BOARD OF EDUCATION (1943) *Curriculum and Examinations in Secondary Schools* (The Norwood Report), London: HMSO.
BOURDIEU, P. and PASSERON, J.C. (1977) *Reproduction in Education, Society and Culture*, London: Sage.
BYRNE, E.M. (1974) *Planning and Educational Inequality*, Slough: NFER.
CONNELL, R.W. (1985) *Teachers Work*, London: Allen & Unwin.
DEPARTMENT OF EDUCATION AND SCIENCE (DES) (1965) *Organisation of Secondary Education* (Circular 10/65), London: HMSO.
GOODSON, I.F. (1987) *Social Histories of the Secondary Curriculum*, London: Falmer Press.
GOODSON, I.F. (1988) *The Making of Curriculum*, London, Falmer Press.
HODSON, D. (1987) 'Science curriculum change in Victorian England: A case study of the science of common things', in GOODSON, I.F. (ed.) *International Perspectives in Curriculum History*, London, Croom Helm.
PITMAN, A.J. (1986) 'A study of school reform from the perspective of the annales school of French historiography: Restructuring Victorian schooling', unpublished doctoral dissertation, University of Wisconsin-Madison.
SHAPIN, S. and BARNES, S. (1976) 'Head and hand: Rhetorical resources in British pedagogical writing, 1770–1850', *Oxford Review of Education*.
SHULMAN, L. (1987) 'Knowledge and teaching foundations of the new reform', *Harvard Educational Review*, **57**, 1.
WILLIS, P. (1977) *Learning to Labour*, Westmead: Saxon House.

11 'Nations at Risk' and 'National Curriculum': Ideology and Identity

Whilst a good deal of our curriculum study should be conducted, as in the case of the London Technical and Commercial High School, at the school and local level other historical work is required to examine wider initiatives of a national and even global scope. In this chapter I focus on the phenomenon emergent in a number of countries of 'National Curriculum'. My primary evidence is of the emergence of the National Curriculum in the United Kingdom (UK)[1]: I focus on the antecedents to the National Curriculum and the arguments and groups through which it has been promoted, the structures, rhetorical, financial and political, which have been established to support it, and finally the content, form, and pedagogical assumptions embedded within it.

As in other countries, the National Curriculum debate in the UK has been precipitated by a widespread, and largely correct, perception that the nation is threatened by economic decline. Rhetorically then, the National Curriculum is presented as a part of the project of economic regeneration. Behind this broad objective, however, two other projects can be discerned. Firstly, the reconstitution of older class-based British traditional subjects[2], and secondly, a reassertion of the ideology and control of the nation-state.

A good deal of recent historical work has furthered our understanding of the origins of state schooling and curriculum. The common feature uniting the wide range of initiatives by states to fund and manage mass schooling was, these scholars argue, the endeavour of constructing a national polity; the power of the nation-state, it was judged, would be unified through the participation of the state's subjects in national projects. Central in this socialization into national identity was the project of mass state schooling. The sequence followed by those states promoting this national project of mass schooling were strikingly similar. Initially there was the promulgation of a national interest in mass education. Legislation to make schooling compulsory for all followed. To organize the system of mass schools, state departments or ministries of education were formed. State authority was then exercised over all schools — both those 'autonomous' schools already existing and newly proliferating schools specifically organized or opened by the state.

If the central project behind the initiation of state schooling and state-prescribed curriculum was nation-building, this may partly explain the response to certain moral panics which are currently evident. Above all is the new sense of panic over the *Nation at Risk*, the title chosen for the major US report on education in 1983. The perception of national crisis is common among Western nation-states.

Often the matter is presented as essentially economic: certain nations (for example, the USA) are falling behind certain other nations (for example, Japan) in terms of economic prosperity. But behind this specific economic rationale lie a range of further more fundamental issues which render 'nations at risk' and develop general legitimation crises. The globalization of economic life, and more particularly of communications, information and technology, all pose enormous challenges to the existing modes of control and operation of nation-states. In this sense the pursuance of new centralized National Curriculum might be seen as the response of the more economically-endangered species among nations. Britain provides an interesting case of this kind of response.

Behind the myths projected by the current UK government and echoed by some of the more sympathetic newspapers and media, the UK economy remains under-capitalized and in many instances, hopelessly uncompetitive. So much for the economic basis of the 'nation at risk'. But perhaps even more significant are the tendencies towards globalization of economic and social life. In the UK case this is rendered particularly acute by the impending full-scale integration into the European Community. Symbolically the Channel Tunnel will connect UK life with that in Europe. The 'island nation' will quite literally be opened up to subterranean entry. The fear of the nation being at risk no doubt explains the hysteria behind so much of the Thatcher government's response to European integration.[3] Pervasive in this response is the sense of a loss of control, a loss of national destiny and identity. The school curriculum provides one arena for reasserting control and for reestablishing national identity.

The move towards a National Curriculum in the UK can be traced back to the late 1970s. The key date in UK post-war educational history was Prime Minister James Callaghan's Ruskin College (Oxford) speech in 1976. Here economic decline and an accelerating sense of national demise (the UK had joined the EEC in 1973) were attached to the decline in educational standards which it was argued had been fostered in comprehensive schools by the use of more 'progressive' methods. Callaghan's speech called for a 'Great Debate' on the UK's educational policies. Following this initiative, in 1977, a Green Paper, *Education in Schools: A Consultative Document,* was issued. The arguments for a common 'core' or a 'protected' element emerged. The principal points of concern appear to be:

(i)   the curriculum has become overcrowded; the timetable is overloaded, and the essentials are at risk;

(ii)   variations in the approach to the curriculum in different schools can penalize a child simply because he/she has moved from one area to another;

(iii)   even if the child does not move, variations from school to school may give rise to inequality of opportunities;

(iv)   the curriculum in many schools is not sufficiently matched to life in a modern industrial society.

Not all these comments may be equally valid, but it is clear that the time has come to try to establish generally accepted principles for the composition of the secondary curriculum for all pupils. This does not presuppose uniform answers: schools, pupils, and their teachers are different, and the curriculum should be flexible enough to reflect these differences. But there is a need to investigate the part which might be played by a 'protected' or 'core' element of the curriculum common to all schools. There are various ways this may be defined. Properly worked out, it can offer reassurances to employers, parents, and the teachers themselves, as well as a very real equality of opportunity for pupils. (Fowler, 1988, p. 38)

The emerging 'consensus' that there should be a 'core' curriculum was further promoted in the period after the election of a Conservative government under Margaret Thatcher in 1979. The 1980 consultative paper, *A Framework for the School Curriculum*, argued that:

In the course of the public and professional debate about the school curriculum a good deal of support has been found for the idea of identifying a 'core' or essential part of the curriculum which should be followed by all pupils according to their ability. Such a core, it is hoped, would ensure that all pupils, whatever else they do, at least get a sufficient grounding in the knowledge and skills which by common consent should form part of the equipment of the educated adult.

Thus expressed, the idea may appear disarmingly simple; but as soon as it is critically examined a number of supplementary questions arise. For example, should the core be defined as narrowly as possible, or should it, for the period of compulsory schooling at least, cover a large part of the individual's curriculum? Should it be expressed in terms of the traditional school subjects, or in terms of educational objectives which may be attained through the medium of various subjects, appropriately taught? The difficulties and uncertainties attached to the application of the core concept do not mean, however, that it may not be a useful one in carrying forward the public debate about the curriculum to the point at which its results can be of practical benefit to the schools. (quoted in *ibid*, pp. 59–60)

These difficulties notwithstanding from this point on there was a fairly consistent drive to establish a core curriculum. Following the Conservative Party's third election success in 1987, this curriculum was established as a new 'National Curriculum', comprising the 'core subjects' of mathematics, English and science, and the 'foundation subjects' of history, geography, technology, music, art and physical education.

Alongside this specification of subject titles was a panoply of major new central powers over the school curriculum. The Secretary of State for Education and Science now has responsibility for specifying attainment targets, programmes of study, and assessment procedures for each specified subject area. It should be noted that these are powers for very detailed prescription indeed, these are not the powers of merely a general overview. Written into the parliamentary legislation is the obligation to assess pupils on the curriculum studied at the ages of 7, 11, 14, and 16. In addition, a National Curriculum Council and a School Examinations and Assessment Council[4] have been set up to advise on the research, development, and monitoring procedures required.

The styling of the new curriculum specifications as 'national', the composition of subjects included, and the wide ranging new power for governmental agencies suggest three levels of inquiry in coming to understand this new initiative. First there is the need for further inquiry of the theme with which we began: the relationship of these curriculum initiatives to national economic regeneration and national identity. Second the focus on a small number of traditional subjects raises the question of the social antecedents of this choice: we need to analyze the social and cultural, as well as political, choices which underpin the new National Curriculum. Third the initiative needs to be scrutinized in terms of the changing modalities of government control which are so clearly pronounced.

The National Curriculum and National Identity

The National Curriculum has been initiated with pronouncements casting national regeneration in terms of links to the economy, industry and commerce, in particular the so-called 'wealth creating' sector. Yet in practice the balance of subjects in the National Curriculum suggest that questions of national identity and control have been pre-eminent, rather than industrial or commercial requirements. For example, information technology has been largely omitted, whilst history has been embraced as a 'foundation subject', even though it is quite clearly a subject in decline within the schools.

The reasons for favouring history whilst omitting more commercially 'relevant' subjects are intriguing. On the face of it, this pattern of prioritizing might seem encouraging: sponsoring liberal education and humanist study over more narrow utilitarian concerns, favouring education over training. Regrettably this does not seem to be the case. History has, I believe, been chosen to revive and refocus national identity and ideology.

The recent National Curriculum History Group Interim Report provides information on the new curriculum proposals for school history. Firstly the Report confirms that prior to the revival initiated by the incorporation in the National Curriculum, history was a subject in decline: 'It now has a tenuous place in the primary curriculum and it is under threat in a growing number of secondary schools, both in terms of the number of pupils taking it, and as a coherent, rigorous and free-standing course of study' (DES, 1989, p. 4). One of the reasons for the progressive decline of history has been the growth of social studies and sociology. The latter subject is a very popular examination subject, but has been omitted in the National Curriculum in favour of reviving history. The questions therefore remain as to why has history been so favoured.

The Interim Report provides some evidence on this issue for the National Curriculum in history will have some distinctive features. At the core will be UK history which overall will take up 40 per cent of the timetable. 'This figure, however, is slightly misleading because children at key stage one infant level will study UK history almost exclusively, while pupils in the early years of the secondary school will study it as a core subject for just one-third of the time earmarked for history' (*ibid, Times Educational Supplement*). The focus of the National Curriculum on British history in the formative early years of schooling indicates a wish to inculcate at an early stage a sense of national identity. This desire for a major and increased UK dimension in history has plainly come from within the government. We are told for instance that:

> The issue which has hitherto aroused the most controversy is the Minister's insistence that the group should increase the proportion of British history for secondary pupils. At the moment, the group is planning to devote only one-third of the syllabus to British history as a compulsory subject for 11–14-year-olds. This figure rises slightly to two-fifths for 14–16-year-olds. Mr. MacGregor wants British history to be taught for at least 50 per cent of the time devoted to history in secondary schools. (*ibid*)

John MacGregor, appointed by Prime Minister Thatcher as the Secretary of State for Education and Science, was clear therefore where the government's priorities lay. Certainly the revival of UK history seems unrelated to any strong desires among history teachers themselves, where many disagreements have been voiced. These disagreements have even been voiced inside the select curriculum working group: 'At the heart of these disagreements on historical knowledge, British history and chronology, is the lingering fear among some numbers of the group particularly those who are teachers or educationists that the history curriculum will be dominated by rigid external testing and rote learning of famous dates in British history' (*ibid*).

National Curriculum and Social Prioritizing

The styling of the curriculum as 'national' begs a number of questions about which nation is being referred to, for the UK is a nation sharply divided by social class, by race, by gender, by region and by country. One of the shorthands for Conservative criticism of what the French Prime Minister has called the UK government's 'social cruelty' has been a reference to the danger of creating 'two nations'. This refers to the UK phenomenon of there being two recognizably different constituencies or nations inside the UK's borders: one nation which is richer and more secure and often resides in the so-called 'Home Counties' of Southern England, and the other nation which is less well-endowed, primarily working class, and lives in that 'other country' beyond Southern England. In truth, of course, the UK comprises a range of communities, segmented by class, race, gender, region and country; there are in fact far more than two nations.

Hence, in examining the National Curriculum as a social construction, it is important to establish whether the different groups which comprise 'the nation' are being treated equally, or whether processes of social prioritizing can be discerned. In this section, by way of exemplification, I focus mainly on the issue of social class but work urgently needs to be undertaken around issues of race, gender, region and country. In each of these cases the construction of particular priorities and the simultaneous silencing of multiple other claims need to be painstakingly examined.

The pattern of secondary schooling has a long history but a crucial watershed was the 1902 Education Act and the subsequent issue of the Secondary Regulations in 1904. At the turn of the century a number of alternative versions of secondary schooling were vying with each other. The well-established public schools and grammar schools carried the highest status and catered for the more elite social groups through a traditional classical curriculum, but increasingly the school boards administering local schools were providing education for secondary age pupils. In these schools a more vocational curriculum, covering commercial, technical and scientific subjects, were provided for a predominantly working class clientele.

The 1902 Education Act and the Secondary Regulations therefore arbitrated between these two traditions. Ryder and Silver (1970) have judged that the 1902 Act ensured that 'whatever developments in secondary education might occur, it should be within a single system in which the dominant values should resemble those of the traditional grammar school and its curriculum'. Likewise, Eaglesham (1967) judged that:

> These regulations were the work of a number of officials and inspectors of the Board. It may be argued that they gave a balanced curriculum. They certainly effectively checked any tendencies to technical or vocational bias in the secondary schools. They made them schools fit only for a selected few. Moreover they proclaimed for all to see the Board's interest in the literary and classical sides of secondary education. For the future the pattern of English culture must come not from Leeds and West Ham but from Eton and Winchester. (p. 59)

Whilst these two quotes present grammar and public curricula in too monolithic a manner the general point can be summarized in this way: 'Secondary education was in 1904 given so academic a curriculum that it suited only a few' (*ibid*, pp. 59–60). In this manner the settlement of 1902–4 chose the historical legacy and curriculum aimed at certain groups over that aimed at other groups and legislated that this model should constitute the secondary school curriculum. The 1904 Secondary Regulations outline clear guidelines; we see then curriculum as social prioritizing.

The division of post primary schooling between public schools, grammar schools and other schools preeminently for the working class, the elementary schools, and subsequently secondary modern schools, survived into the period following the Second World War. Opposition to the selective examination for deciding who went to grammar school, the so-called 11+, grew, and some experiments in comprehensive or multilateral schooling began in the 1940s. In 1964 a Labour government was returned, and began dismantling the existing divisive system and introducing comprehensive schools.

The implications of this change for the curriculum were substantial, and a range of curriculum reform projects were initiated through the Schools Council for Curriculum and Examinations founded in 1964. Whilst the comprehensive schools initially derived their main curriculum areas from the grammar schools, these reform projects sought to seriously apply the logic of comprehensive school reform to curriculum reform. For plainly without curriculum reform organizational reform was of severely limited significance.

Rubinstein and Simon (1973) summarize the climate of educational reform in 1972 following the raising of the school leaving age to 16, and the rapid growth of the comprehensive system:

> The content of the curriculum is now under much discussion, and comprehensive schools are participating actively in the many curriculum reform schemes launched by the Schools Council and Nuffield. The tendency is towards the development of the interdisciplinary curricula, together with the use of the resources approach to learning, involving the substitution of much group and individual work for the more traditional forms of class teaching. For these new forms of organising and stimulating learning mixed ability grouping often provides the most appropriate method; and partly for this reason the tendency is towards the reduction of streaming and class teaching. This movement in itself promotes new relations between teachers and pupils, particularly insofar as the teacher's role is changing from that of ultimate authority to that of motivating, facilitating and structuring the pupils' own discovery and search for knowledge. (p. 123)

The belief that rapid curriculum reform, with a range of associated political and pedagogical implications, was well under way was commonly held at this time. Kerr (1971) asserted in 1968 that 'at the practical and organizational levels, the new curricula promise to revolutionise English education' (pp. 178–200).

But at precisely the time Kerr was talking new forces were seeking to defend, and if possible reinvigorate, the old grammar school subjects. These were presented as the 'traditional' subjects. It is important to grasp that this reassertion of a subject-based curriculum is part of a broader strategy of reconstitution. Moreover, the reestablishment of traditional subjects is taking place at the expense of many of those new subject areas devised specifically to sponsor and promote learning across the full range of the comprehensive school: social studies, environmental studies, general science, urban studies, community studies and so on. These subjects had sought to develop new forms of connectedness to the interests and experiences of the pupils of the comprehensive school. The National Curriculum pronounces that the approach can now only take place at the margins and that the core curriculum will once again be those subjects 'traditionally' taught since their 'establishment' in 1904.

The comparison with the Secondary Regulations in 1904 shows the extent to which a patterning of schooling has been reconstituted in this new political settlement called the national curriculum.

1904	**1988**
English	English
Maths	Maths
Science	Science
History	History
Geography	Geography

Physical Exercise	Physical Education
Drawing	Art
Foreign Language	Modern Foreign Language
Manual Work	
Domestic Subjects	Technology
(Music added soon afterwards)	Music

The similarity between 1904 and 1988 questions the rhetoric of 'a major new initiative' employed by the government, and points to some historical continuities in social and political purpose and priorities. The 1904 Regulations embodied that curriculum historically offered to the grammar school clientele as opposed to the curriculum being developed in the board schools and aimed primarily at the working classes: one segment or vision of the nation was being favoured at the expense of another. In the intervening period more equalitarian impulses brought about the creation of comprehensive schools where children of all classes came together under one roof. This in turn led to a range of curriculum reforms which sought to redefine and challenge the hegemony of the grammar school curriculum.

Seeking in turn to challenge and redirect these reforms and intentions the political right has argued for the rehabilitation of the 'traditional' (i.e., grammar school) subjects. The National Curriculum can be seen as a political statement of the victory of the forces and intentions representing these political groups. A particular vision, a preferred segment of the nation has therefore been reinstated and prioritized, and legislated as 'national'.

The historical continuities evident in the National Curriculum have been commented on in a number of places. For instance, the *Times Educational Supplement* stated that 'the first thing to say about this whole exercise is that it unwinds eighty years of English (and Welsh) educational history. It is a case of go back to Go' (DES, 1989). In writing of the National Curriculum project, Moon and Mortimore (1989) commented:

> The legislation, and the much-criticized consultative document that preceded it, present the curriculum in needlessly rather restricted terms. Thus the primary curriculum was put forward as if it were no more than a pre-secondary preparation (like the worst sort of 'prep school'). All the positive aspects of British primary schooling so valued by HMI and the Select Committee of the House of Commons and so praised by many foreign commentators were ignored.
> The secondary curriculum, in turn, appears to be based on the curriculum of a typical 1960s grammar school. We would not take issue with the subjects included, but we believe that such a curriculum misses out a great deal. Information technology, electronics, statistics, personal, social and careers education have all been omitted. Yet, surely, these are just the areas that are likely to be of importance for the future lives of many pupils?. (p. 9)

The National Curriculum then can be seen as a response to a 'nation at risk' at two levels. Firstly there is the general sense of the nation-state being in economic decline and subject to globalization and to amalgamation in the wider European

Community. There the response is paradoxical. Nation-building curricula are often favoured over commercially 'relevant' curricula. The solution therefore may exacerbate the problem. Further economic 'decline' may follow leading to even more desperate attempts to reassert national identity.

Secondly, given that the UK is clearly a divided nation, investigation of the National Curriculum allows insights into precisely *which* nation is at risk. It would seem it is the elite and middle class groups which were perceived of as 'at risk'. For it is this group that have the greatest historical connections to the 'traditional subjects': these subjects have been revived and reinstated in the National Curriculum.

The perception of nations at risk and social groups at risk has further provided one source of support for developing the powers of central state over the school curriculum. This is the third level at which the National Curriculum is significant. In the central project of rebuilding the nation-state, the issue of reestablishing national identity and ideology has been dealt with but there remains the issue of rebuilding the power of the nation-state itself.

National Curriculum and National Power

In post-war Britain the national state's powers over education were increasingly devolved to local education authorities (LEAs). This made the schools more responsive to the local 'communities' than to 'the nation'. In addition the teachers' unions were able to assert a growing influence over issues of curriculum and assessment reform. As we have noted, this led some comprehensive schools to develop more comprehensive curricula which moved beyond the 1904-style academic curriculum 'suited to only a few'. The national state's loss of control, specifically loss of control over curriculum, therefore led to patterns of prioritizing which went a long way from the political settlement enshrined in the 1904 Regulations: the so-called traditional subjects. This loss of control therefore threatened those groups which had benefited from this political settlement. The social prioritization so well-established in the early twentieth century was plainly under attack. In short, the 'nation' as represented in these privileged groups was 'at risk'.

Of course reasserting the primacy of curriculum as a vehicle for the education of the elite and custodial classes entirely fits a version of nation-building. These leadership and professional groups are precisely those who will rule and administer the nation — it is consistent to remake the curriculum in their image and reconstruct schools as mechanisms for the selection of this national meritocracy.

But the form of this national reconstruction at the level of curriculum, of course, reflects the existing perception and situation of the 'nation'. Plainly at this point in its history the UK nation-state reflects the post-war period of precipitous decline. Since 1945 the large aspirations of the nation-state as a major imperial power, a major player on the world stage, have had to be severely redefined. A particularly problematic aspect of this imperial angst had been how to deal with the plurality of other cultures. This concern is often wished off into the field of 'multicultural studies' but is of course integral to notions of identity and democracy in general. Alongside ideological decline has been a savage experience of economic decline. In both of these aspects of decline the British establishment, the elite and the professions, have been implicated. As a result any campaign to reconstruct and revive the nation would have to respond to this experience of precipitous decline. The particular version of nation-building through curriculum is therefore likely to reflect this perception.

The definition of a central curriculum could in fact take a number of forms, but there are two major directions. One version would specify a common set of goals and objectives and certain amount of common content. In this version the teachers and students are allowed some flexibility and a degree of accommodation with local conditions and concerns is both expected and encouraged. This version of central curriculum would have resonated well with the experience of the UK educational system in the twentieth century.

A second version of central curriculum would prescribe in detail what is to be taught, learned and tested. There would be little allowance for choice on the part of teachers and students. One caricature of this version would be the mythical French Minister of Education who could look at his watch and say what every child in France was studying at any given time. This version of common curricula would go against the grain of twentieth-century UK experience.

That the 1988 UK National Curriculum in fact represents the second model of central curriculum says a good deal. It reflects the response of a political establishment that has experienced more than four decades of precipitous and accelerating political and economic decline. In such circumstances the replay of paranoid fears within the domain of the school curriculum seems an understandable, if indirect, response.

The unprecedented expansion of powers over the school curriculum has not gone unnoticed or unchallenged. The Cabinet's intention in the report on history has led the Historical Association, an august and conservative body representing history teachers, to question whether the government has any 'constitutional right' for such detailed intervention.

The major expansion of state power over the curriculum and over-assessment leads to a parallel diminution in the teachers' power and therefore has associated implications for pedagogy. At one level the new power over curriculum and the battery of tests represent a substantial push to make the details of teachers' work accountable to the state. The experience of the 1960s where teachers were judged to have superior expertise in assessing the educational needs of their pupils has been rapidly dismantled.

Much of the commentary on the new National Curriculum has been sympathetic and optimistic about the results of the expansion of state power. For instance, *The Times* carried an editorial on the passing of the 'True Education Bill', which argued 'most important, a national curriculum, accompanied by attainment targets and tests at key ages, will ensure that a large proportion of young people leave school literate, numerate, and more broadly educated than they are now'. Standards in short, will rise. That is because 'teachers will have a clearer idea of what is expected of them' (*The Times*, 22 October 1989). In short, greater accountability (and less power over definition) leads to clearer objectives and better work habits. This is a crude simplification employing an almost-Taylorist optimism about a strategy for tackling a most complex enterprise.

Lessons from previous historical episodes must be treated with considerable caution for we are not comparing like with like. Yet so clear have been the experiences of teachers and taught in the face of previous nineteenth-century government interventions in matters of curriculum and assessment that the pious simplifications behind *The Times's* viewpoint should be severely scrutinized. For it may not be the case that 'standards in short, will rise' rather 'morale, in short, will fall'.

A major experiment in state control of school curricula was conducted in the years 1862 to 1895. The teachers were made subject to a system of 'payment by results': the teachers' pay was linked to pupils' results in school examinations. E.G.A. Holmes (1928), a school inspector at the time, has left a detailed commentary on the results of this experiment. He notes that from 1862 to 1895 'a considerable part of the grant received by each school was paid on the results of a yearly examination held by HM (Her Majesty's) Inspector on an elaborate syllabus, formulated by the Department and binding on all schools alike'. The results of this mechanism were clear. 'On the official report which followed this examination depended the reputation and financial prosperity of the school, and the reputation and financial prosperity of the teacher' (p. 103). The Government therefore had established deliberate and detail control over curriculum and assessment and thereby over the teacher and student. Power was thus established, but what of the 'side-effects' on education? On this Holmes was adamant:

> The consequent pressure on the teacher to exert himself was well-nigh irresistible; and he had no choice but to transmit that pressure to his subordinates and his pupils. The result was that in those days the average school was a hive of industry.
>
> But it was also a hive of misdirected energy. The State, in prescribing a syllabus which was to be followed, in all the subjects of instruction, by all the schools in the country, without regard to local or personal considerations, was guilty of one capital offence. It did all his thinking for the teacher. It told him in precise detail what he was to do each year in each 'Standard', how he was to handle each subject, and how far he was to go in it; what width of ground he was to cover; what amount of knowledge, what degree of accuracy was required for a 'pass'. In other words, it provided him with his ideals, his general conceptions, his more immediate aims, his schemes of work; aud if it did not control his methods in all their details, it gave him (by implication) hints and suggestions with regard to these on which he was not slow to act; for it told him that the work done in each class and each subject would be tested at the end of each year by a careful examination of each individual child; and it was inevitable that in his endeavour to adapt his teaching to the type of question which his experience of the yearly examination led hmm to expect, he should gradually deliver himself, mind and soul, into the hands of the officials of the Department, the officials at Whitehall who framed the yearly syllabus, and the officials in the various districts who examined on it.
>
> What the Department did to the teacher, it compelled him to do to the child. The teacher who is the slave of another's will cannot carry out his instructions except by making his pupils the slaves of his own will. The teacher who has been

deprived by his superiors of freedom, initiative, and responsibility, cannot carry out his instructions except by depriving his pupils of the same vital qualities. The teacher who, in response to the deadly pressure of a cast-iron system, has become a creature of habit and routine, cannot carry out his instructions except by making his pupils as helpless and as puppet-like as himself.

But it is not only because mechanical obedience is fatal, in the long run, to mental and spiritual growth, that the regulation of elementary or any other grade of education by a uniform syllabus is to be deprecated. It is also because a uniform syllabus is, in the nature of things, a bad syllabus, and because the degree of its badness varies directly with the arc of the sphere of educational activity that comes under its control. (*ibid*, pp. 103–5)

Holmes provided more details of the working of a system of state prescription of syllabus and control of examinations:

It was preordained, then, that the syllabuses which the Department issued, year by year, in the days of payment by results should have few merits and many defects. Yet even if, by an unimaginable miracle, they had all been educationally sound, the mere fact that all the teachers in England had to work by them would have made them potent agencies for evil. To be in bondage to a syllabus is a misfortune for a teacher, and a misfortune for the school that he teaches. To be in bondage to a syllabus which is binding on all schools alike is of all misfortunes the gravest. Or if there is a graver, it is the fate that befell the teachers of England under the old regime — the fate of being in bondage to a syllabus which was bad both because it had to come down to the level of the least fortunate school and the least capable teacher, and also because it was the outcome of ignorance, inexperience, and bureaucratic self-satisfaction.

Of the evils that are inherent in the examination system as such of its tendency to arrest growth, to deaden life, to paralyse the higher faculties, to externalize what is inward, to materialize what is spiritual, to involve education in an atmosphere of unreality and self-deception I have already spoken at some length. In the days of payment by results various circumstances conspired to raise those evil tendencies to the highest imaginable 'power'. When inspectors ceased to examine (in the stricter sense of the word), they realised what infinite mischief the yearly examination had done. The children, the majority of whom were examined in reading and dictation out of their own reading-books (two or three in number, as the case might be), were drilled in the contents of those books until they knew them almost by heart. In arithmetic they worked abstract sums, in obedience to formal rules, day after day, and month after month; and they were put up to various tricks and dodges which would, it was hoped, enable them to know by what precise rules the various questions on the arithmetic cards were to be answered. They learned a few lines of poetry by heart and committed all the 'meanings and allusions' to memory, with the probable result — so sickening must the process have been — that they hated poetry for the rest of their lives. In geography, history, and grammar they were the victims of unintelligent oral cram, which they were compelled, under pains and penalties, to take in and retain till the examination day was over, their ability to disgorge it on occasion being periodically tested by the teacher. And so with the other subjects. Not a thought was given, except in a small minority of the schools, to the real training of the child, to the fostering of his mental (and other) growth.

> To get him through the yearly examination by hook or by crook was the one con-
> cern of the teacher. As profound distrust of the teacher was the basis of the policy
> of the Department, so profound distrust of the child was the basis of the policy
> of the teacher. To leave the child to find out anything for himself, to work out
> anything for himself, to think out anything for himself, would have been regarded
> as a proof of incapacity, not to say insanity, on the part of the teacher, and would
> have led to results which, from the 'percentage' point of view, would probably
> have been disastrous. (*ibid*, pp. 106–8)

In fact the experience of this episode of state intervention had long-lasting
effects. In 1944 when the government was drawing up the influential Education Act
of that year James Chuter Ede, parliamentary secretary to the Minister, said in a
speech to the House:

> ... there is not one curriculum for every child, but every child must be a separate
> problem for the teacher. The teacher is the servant of the State, and I hope that no
> one will say that the State should lay down the curriculum of the schools. Some
> of us were brought up under the old payment-by-results system, and were the time
> earlier, I could amuse the House with descriptions that some of my Hon. Friends
> know would be no caricature of the way in which State control of the curriculum
> prevented the development of a wise and sound system of education. (quoted in
> Chitty, 1988, pp. 321–34)

Holmes and Chuter Ede then warn us of some of the dangers that attended
a 'national curriculum and assessment' strategy. But the implications for teachers
and particularly pupils are of profound concern. The development of attitudes of
'mechanical obedience' strike at the very heart of the 'democratic' system of governance. This matter assumes great importance at a time when there is widespread
comment in the UK about the absence of constitutional rights and the consequent
possibility of substantial erosion of 'traditional' rights by more authoritarian government whether of the right (as at the moment) or of the left. The link between the
National Curriculum and mechanical obedience therefore highlights a major problem
with regard to the education of pupils with the capacity to be functioning citizens
in a democracy. I find the following statement about 'the erosion of British liberty'
particularly chilling in this light: 'Britons have been schooled to think of themselves
as subjects, not citizens; as people with freedoms granted by government, not with
rights guaranteed against government interference' (Broder, 1989, p. 7). The traditional school subject based National Curriculum plays a key role in constructing
the particular subjectivities of subjects in this sense (Corrigan, 1990).

Seen in this light the political project underpinning the National Curriculum
assumes a further dimension, for the hidden curriculum of the National Curriculum
is a reassertion of the power of the state in nation-building. This project is diamet-
rically opposed to the alternative project of educating pupils, from a plurality of
cultures, for active citizenship in a democracy. The history of mass mechanical
obedience as a bedrock for nation-building is well known, but it leads not to democracy but to totalitarianism.

Conclusion

The introduction of the National Curriculum in the UK has been linked to the problems of national economic decline and a belief that curriculum coordination will aid a project of national economic regeneration. Behind the rhetorical priority given to economic revival, two other agendas have been discerned.

First, the reconstitution of a traditional subjects-based curriculum. These traditional subjects evoke a past 'golden age' when schooling was selective and people 'knew their station'. A number of empirical studies have pointed up the links between traditional subjects and social class (see Goodson, 1988; and Goodson, 1993).[5] The obsessive presentism of many of the current government initiatives has successfully obscured this deeply-embedded connectedness which is of course relevant to the present and future of the UK as a class society.

In developing this commentary for a global audience, it is important to note the distinctiveness and strength of UK class politics. For instance, in the USA at the moment a debate is underway about defining a National Curriculum comprising traditional subjects. However, the intention, at least one important intention, is to provide rigorous academic subject-based courses of study covering curriculum content and form which will appeal to *all* children. Hence, the pattern of state and class-formation in the USA mean that a National Curriculum initiative will have sharply different resonances to those in a somewhat obsolescent class-based society like the UK. (This is not, of course, to say that an initiative in the USA will not have powerful implications for matters of class, race and gender.) Moreover, the patterns of civic culture, citizenship education and constitutional rights are sharply different in the UK from the USA: so that once again a National Curriculum will be likely to affect the two societies differently.

The second agenda in the UK is one of establishing new modalities of control over schooling on behalf of the nation-state. These new modalities will allow detailed control to be exercised over the school curriculum, both in terms of content, form and assessment. In the UK case this would seem a late and somewhat desperate attempt at nation-building, both in terms of nation-state governance and the partial propagation through curriculum of national ideologies, selective memories and images. It would seem possible that declining nations in their post-imperial phase have nowhere to go but to retreat into the bunker of the school curriculum. In this case, in particular, there may well be some lessons for the USA.

Notes

1 I have employed the term 'United Kingdom' as a statement of a particular governmental aspiration towards national identity. In many ways it links with a broader project of privileging a particular form of 'Englishness' (a form with which I personally have no empathy or sympathy). In the event as the National Curriculum proceeds it is leading to a fragmented response in the different 'kingdoms' — Scotland for instance has managed to modify the testing requirements for the 'National' Curriculum.

2 Subjects here might be read in both senses, as we shall see, the institutionalised school subject and the subjectivities that those institutionalised subjects seek to implant and patrol.
3 This section was written before the withdrawal of the UK pound from the European exchange rate mechanism and, of course, before the replacement of Thatcher by Major. Tory xenophobia has if anything increased since then.
4 Subsequently these bodies were merged.

References

BRODER, D.S. (1989) 'Mrs Thatcher and the erosion of British liberty', *Manchester Guardian Weekly*, **141**, 5.

CHITTY, C. (1988) 'Central control of the school curriculum, 1944–87', *History of Education*, **17**, 4.

CORRIGAN, P. (1990) *Social Forms of Human Capacities*, London: Routledge.

DEPARTMENT OF EDUCATION AND SCIENCE (DES) (1989) National Curriculum History Group Interim Report, quoted in the *Times Educational Supplement*, 18 August.

EAGLESHAM, E.J.R. (1967) *The Foundations of Twentieth-Century Education in England*, London: Routledge and Kegan Paul.

FOWLER, W.S. (1988) *Towards the National Curriculum*, London: Kogan Page Ltd.

GOODSON, I.F. (1988) *The Making of Curriculum*, London: Falmer Press.

GOODSON, I.F. (1993) *School Subjects and Curriculum Change* (3rd ed), London: Falmer Press.

HOLMES, E.G.A. (1928) *What Is and What Might Be*, London: Constable & Co Ltd.

KERR, J. (1971) 'The problem of curriculum reform', in HOOPER, R. (ed.) *The Curriculum Context, Design and Development*, Edinburgh: Oliver and Boyd.

MOON, B. and MORTIMORE, P. (1989) *The National Curriculum, Straitjacket or Safety Net?*, London: Colophon Press.

RUBINSTEIN, D. and SIMON, R. (1973) *The Evolution of the Comprehensive School 1926–1972*, London: Routledge and Kegan Paul.

RYDER, J. and SILVER, H. (1970) *Modern English Society, History and Structure 1850–1970*, London: Methuen.

Index of Names

Ahlbrand, W.P. 109
Anstead, C. 10, 51, 84
Apple, M.W. 9, 21, 137

Bangert-Drowns, R.L. 105
Barman, J. 84, 85
Barnes, S. 139, 140, 141, 142, 143
Barraclough, G. 2, 3
Bates, I. 148
Beal, H.B. 53–7, 59, 68, 72
Bennett, C.A. 84
Bernstein, B. 1, 7, 8, 20, 101, 137, 138
Bhaskar, R. 85
Bird, C. 25
Blumer, H. 2, 4
Bourdieu, P. 21, 68, 137, 138
Bowers, C.A. 133
Broder, D.S. 162
Bucher, R. 4
Burman, P. 101
Burston, W. 2
Butterfield, H. 3
Byrne, E.M. 34, 147

Callaghan, J. 151
Carlson, E.U. 117
Chang, I.W. 106
Chitty, C. 162
Chorley, R. 30, 32
Cohen, I.J. 56
Connell, R.W. 9, 100, 138
Cooke, R. 32
Cooper, B. 9, 85
Corrigan, P. 162
Cremin, L.A. 84
Cuban, E.U. 109, 110
Cunningham, P. 9

Dale, R. 6
Darby, Prof 32
David, T. 27
Davis, B. 1
de Certeau, M. 85
Deever, B. 68

Dowbiggin, I.R. 53, 56, 61, 72, 80, 84
Doyle, B. 73
Dunn, T.A. 80, 84

Eaglesham, E.J.R. 155
Earl, L. 109
Esland, G.M. 6, 7

Fallona, M. 76, 80
Fitzgerald, B.P. 33
Flanders, B.M. 109
Foucault, M. 124
Fowler, W.S. 151
Franklin, B. 9, 17, 18, 81, 106
Fullan, M. 105

Gaffield, C. 84
Gardner, N. 40, 41
Garnett, A. 25, 27, 28, 31, 34
Gaskell, J.S. 68, 70, 74, 77, 80, 82
Giddens, A. 85
Gilbert, E.E. 30
Ginsburg, N. 33
Giroux, H.A. 68
Glaser, B. 106
Goodson, I.F. 3, 7, 8, 9, 10, 14, 16, 42, 47, 51, 53, 56, 61, 72, 80, 84, 102, 105, 106, 107, 109, 116, 119, 124, 125, 132, 134, 143, 148, 163
Gowing, D. 29
Grubb, W.N. 84

Hadow 34
Haggett, P. 30, 32
Hamilton, D. 10, 14
Hammersley, M. 3
Hargreaves, A. 105, 109
Hirst, P.M. 15, 22, 32
Hodson, D. 143
Hoetker, J. 109
Holmes, E.G.A. 160, 161
Honeybone, R.C. 26, 28

Subject Index

academic legitimacy 21
academic traditions 3–5, 9
Advisory Industrial Committee (Canada) 54, 55, 60
America: education in 68
assembly 86, 87
assessment 8, 152, 162
Australia 9

Beal School 56–65, 73
British Sociological Association 40
Bryce Commission 25

CACE 40
Cambridge: St Catherine's College 27
Canada 9, 10
  cultural discourse 52
  high schools 60
  industry in 59
  schools 52, 59
  university matriculation 59
class size 86, 87
classroom
  culture 108
  divisions 39
  practice 3, 6, 10, 15, 54, 101
    reform of 15
    revolutionising 3, 13
cognitive contamination 7
Collegiate Institute (Ontario) 56, 69, 70
commercial education in USA 53, 81
commercial employment 74
commercial studies 54, 67–74, 76–82, 87, 91, 100
communication networks 6
community studies 1
comprehensive schools 1, 13, 29, 38–40, 145, 146, 151, 155
  academic knowledge and 146
  curriculum reform and 146
  subject groups and 146
computer applications 108, 125
computers in schools 125, 126
  business interests and 128, 129

policy making and 131, 135
social reconstruction 131
as symbolic action 123, 132, 133, 135
teacher resistance to 133, 134
as teaching tool 133
computers, classroom 10, 105, 106, 114, 115
computers
  art and 116
  classroom practice and 116, 117, 134
  cultural capital 130
  curriculum 120, 126, 128, 134
  in education
    ideology of 129, 133
    rhetoric of 123, 124
  education traditions and 132, 133, 134
  industrial development 130
  learning 119, 130, 131
  National Curriculum 153
  pedagogy 125, 135
  research in 106
  subjects 117, 118, 120, 126, 133, 134
  teachers 109, 120
  vocational education 119, 125, 130, 131, 132, 133, 135
continuity thesis 2
CSE 43, 45, 46, 47
cultural factors 3, 4, 7
culture: plurality of 158
curricular differentiation 144, 145, 148
curriculum
  academic subject-based 8, 16, 39
  change in 9, 10, 13, 18, 38, 46, 54, 56, 58, 60, 67
  'classical' 141, 142
  common core 151
  comprehensive schools 156, 158
  construction in America 68
  content 15, 17
  control by teachers 21
  control of 158, 160, 162, 163
  debates 1
  definitions of learning 138